ALSO BY JEFF HOBBS

The Short and Tragic Life of Robert Peace

The Tourists

Show Them You're Good

A Portrait of Boys in the City of Angels
the Year Before College

Jeff Hobbs

SCRIBNER
New York London Toronto Sydney New Delhi

Scribner
An Imprint of Simon & Schuster, Inc.
1230 Avenue of the Americas
New York, NY 10020

First Scribner hardcover edition August 2020

SCRIBNER and design are registered trademarks of The Gale Group, Inc.,
used under license by Simon & Schuster, Inc., the publisher of this work.

For information about special discounts for bulk purchases,
please contact Simon & Schuster Special Sales at 1-866-506-1949
or business@simonandschuster.com.

The Simon & Schuster Speakers Bureau can bring authors
to your live event. For more information or to book an event,
contact the Simon & Schuster Speakers Bureau at 1-866-248-3049
or visit our website at www.simonspeakers.com.

Interior design by Kyle Kabel

Manufactured in the United States of America

1   3   5   7   9   10   8   6   4   2

Library of Congress Cataloging-in-Publication Data has been applied for.

ISBN 978-1-9821-1633-0
ISBN 978-1-9821-1635-4 (ebook)

To Dad, Mom, Bryan, Lins, and Andy.
My own high school years were unremarkable
except for having you as their anchor.

You road I enter upon and look around, I believe you are not all that is here, I believe that much unseen is also here.

—Walt Whitman, *Leaves of Grass*

Author's Note

"Although my book is intended mainly for the entertainment of boys and girls, I hope it will not be shunned by men and women on that account, for part of my plan has been to try to pleasantly remind adults of what they once were themselves, and of how they felt and thought and talked, and what [strange] enterprises they sometimes engaged in."

So wrote Mark Twain in his preface to *The Adventures of Tom Sawyer*, and so was my own intention while spending many hundreds of hours with the young people—all high school seniors—described in these pages. I spent those hours in order to capture not just a vital, fleeting passage of life, but also a moment in our country—one whose significance very few foresaw in the late summer of 2016 when this work began.

I had previously been invited to speak at both Ánimo Pat Brown Charter High School and Beverly Hills High School, and so I was acquainted with administrators and teachers who graciously permitted me wide access during the 2016–17 school year and introduced me to the students whose stories comprise this book. During that year, I went to classes, dances, sports games, school board meetings, assemblies, plays, homecomings, proms, graduations. I visited homes and spent time with parents and grandparents and siblings. I willingly entered gridlock to intercept four separate points of the Los Angeles Marathon, in which one of the students ran. But for the most part, I just sat with these boys, typically over takeout from In-N-Out Burger, and talked frequently throughout the year—about their days, their futures, their hopes and doubts, their challenges both known and unknown, as well as the whimsical moments from which much of their lives was wrought. The stories within this book largely take place in schools, but this book is not necessarily about "school." This book is about people—mostly young people who are foolish and flawed and impulsive, of course, but who are also (I believe) among the best of us. They are certainly the future of us.

In my first remarks to these boys, I stated that I was not interested in having them try to represent a race, a neighborhood, a school, a socioeconomic condition. I asked that they try, as best they could, only to represent themselves.

I was physically present for many but not all of the events written. Those I was not present for were reported to me in detail by people who were there, including dialogue and other fine details.

The internal workings of individual minds were also reported to me in recorded interviews and written as closely to their descriptions as I am capable of—not quite in real time and stream of consciousness, but not far removed.

Data regarding neighborhoods and the various educational systems described were pulled entirely from publicly available documents.

A number of names have been left out of these pages, but only two names in the pages have been changed.

Ánimo Pat Brown
Charter High School

Florence-Graham, California

Tio
Carlos
Luis
Byron

Beverly Hills
High School

Beverly Hills, California

Owen
Jon
Bennett
Harrison
Jonah

PART I

Fall

Chapter 1

AUGUST 11, 2016

*It's school so it gets crowded, there's noise. But even when
it's loud, it's a healthy loud, people wanting to express their
opinions. It's a peaceful loud.*

—*Tio*

Tio

A young man wearing a navy blue collared shirt and khaki slacks
walked north along Juniper Street. A light backpack was strapped
tight to both shoulders, and he tucked a battered, much-decaled
skateboard between his forearm and hip. His hair was carefully
treated to form a slick vertical wave off his forehead, and he
walked with a slight limp gained from a skate park crash the
previous afternoon, his last of summer. He'd lost purchase on his
board during that weightless instant between upward momentum
and downward fall; he'd also heard a popping sound within his
knee upon contact with the asphalt but thought little of it. His
skin was bronzed by both his Mexican heritage and the myriad
afternoons spent skating over the past June and July, and his body
was lean and strong. At the corner of Juniper and 103rd Street,
he tossed his board to the sidewalk pavement and jumped on
in a fluid, propulsive motion. At seven thirty in the morning,

the sun already blasted down at a steep slant and he quickly sweat through his shirt. The summer's heat wave felt fixed and eternal. Gingerly, he pushed himself from his family's current bungalow, past the bowed stucco apartment complex they used to live in and the lot where at another point they'd occupied a trailer home for a time (Tio had spent his entire life on Juniper Street). He proceeded in a stairway pattern alternately left and right, west and north, along busy Compton thoroughfares and quiet residential streets, passing the elementary school at Ninety-Second and Grape Street, then the tall electric towers standing over dense weed entanglements on Fir Avenue, the Rio Grande Market on Eighty-Eighth, the Church of God in Christ on Milner. Cars made hard right-on-red turns in front of him despite the solid white walk signs giving him the right of way. Soon he met the massive concrete anchors of the blue Metro line connecting downtown Los Angeles with Long Beach along Graham Avenue, and he made his way due north, parallel to the tracks, toward school.

Thousands of young men and women were making their way around the South LA gridwork of streets. Many, like Tio upon his skateboard, wore muted colors beneath their backpacks: navy and khaki, maroon and khaki, white and khaki. They were headed to school as well, usually moving in small groups for reasons pertaining to both companionship and safety. Others on the street wore baggy shorts and sleeveless undershirts, brightly colored baseball caps tipped at odd angles, and multiple tattoos to signify allegiances or aesthetics or both. If those guys were out this early, it meant they'd probably been out all night—working—and were on their way home to sleep, too exhausted to bother anyone. Traveling alone and by skateboard put Tio in an inherently vulnerable position in this stretch bridging the neighborhoods of Compton (where Tio lived), Lynwood, Watts, South Gate, and

Florence-Graham (where Tio went to school). The in-between spaces made the dominant gang entities harder to ascertain. But he'd been getting to school this way since fifth grade, after he bought his first used board, much preferring the wobbly platform to the cramped, loud buses lumbering through Los Angeles traffic. Aside from witnessing a man take a fatal shot to the head from a car window when he was eleven (five steps away with a female friend, Tio had crouched and pushed her against the fence with his lanky fifth-grade body shielding her, relieved when the squeal of tires signaled the shooter's flight), he'd never had any trouble beyond the occasional empty taunt. Schoolboys were mostly left alone. Even the most menacing types tended to be respectful if not admiring of the aspiration required for young people—mostly poor, mostly black or brown—to trek to school early each morning. If any sketchy person approached, Tio just said, humbly, "I don't bang," and kept rolling. Police had halted him now and again, as skateboarders were generally associated with drugs and truancy. Usually they would just ask if he'd seen any suspicious activity or tell him to stay in school, stay away from drugs and bad sorts, stay off the street after a certain hour: all the tired commands he'd been hearing since toddlerhood. He figured that throughout the course of his youth, ninety-nine out of one hundred transits had been uneventful, so Tio always moved casually in the context of the ninety-nine while maintaining a modest alertness for the prospect of the one.

At the Firestone Boulevard Metro station, dozens of teenagers wearing the same navy/khaki binary streamed down the steps from the elevated train stop, past a colorful mosaic wall depicting a human body in prayer. Tio pivoted through and around them across the intersection, sometimes playfully tapping the head of someone he knew. He rolled past a long row of small furniture restoration and auto repair storefronts, really just one-car garages open onto the street, facing the tracks, replete with detritus. A right on Eighty-Third Street followed by a quick left on Beach Street brought him to the front gate of the one-story, modern building that was Ánimo Pat Brown Charter High School. Students who'd already arrived kicked soccer balls or loitered in the narrow, paved space between the fence and the school's glass door, or splayed themselves along the row of white picnic tables occupying the grassy side lot. The principal, an unflappable white man in his late thirties, gently ushered students inside with his kind, calm demeanor in advance of the shrill PA announcement indicating five minutes before first period.

Beach was a relatively quiet street, residential on the east side with single-story stucco bungalows on small plots sporting citrus trees, laundry lines, and the occasional fuselage of a decades-old car resting dormant. On the west side, where the school occupied the southern corner, stood a row of tall warehouses guarded by bent gates. A collarless Jack Russell wandered in and out of the driveways. The train tracks heading to and from downtown Los Angeles, four miles north, cut a graveled swath a few meters behind the school grounds.

Tio kicked up his board and limped inside. Ahead, he recognized a thicket of hair resembling an unmade bed atop a tall, wide, shambling frame. He yelled, "Yo, Luis, you got fleas in that thing, bro!"

Luis turned around, gave him the finger, and replied, "You know that because you can hear them talking?" This dig was in reference to Tio's large, protruding ears. He had heard variations of the same joke since elementary school, including from elementary school teachers, and found them uncreative. He didn't even bother with a rejoinder.

"Why you limping, bro?" Luis asked with more humor than concern.

"Ah, I fucked up my knee. Like maybe I severed some nerves or something? It's fine."

"People get surgery for that."

"Nah, nah, I'm good."

Carlos

"Shut the fuck up," Carlos whispered to Tio in AP Calculus class later that morning.

"I'm sorry, man. I just can't handle that it's August eleventh," Tio replied, exasperated. "They can't even say school starts in mid-August anymore. This is *early* August." He shook his head in unaffected grief, big ears rotating side to side. "I'm just not down with this."

Two hours into the year, they'd all gained a foreknowledge that the novelty of new classes and teachers would stale by the end of the week, and thirty-five more weeks would follow, and Tio could not help but express his dismay—his exhaustion with being seventeen—vocally. (Tio knew this wasn't a charming quality of his.)

"Just chill," Carlos said. He was slight in stature, five foot four with narrow shoulders. The growth spurts that had elevated Tio and Luis and so many others toward six feet and beyond since ninth grade had passed him over, and presumably wouldn't loop back around since he was already taller than his father. His voice was slight as well, though he deployed it with authority: "Pay attention."

"You're just as depressed as me, admit it."

Carlos paused before saying, a little mournfully, "Yeah, I am."

Tio kept muttering jokes under his breath, trying to make proximate kids laugh; Carlos knew that this was what Tio did when the material or something else caused him stress. He elbowed Tio gently and told him to shut up, again.

"But we're talking about rate of volume change in a can of soda—what does that have to do with anything in life?"

"That's a good point."

"Right?"

"But you still gotta quit fucking around."

"What would you do without me fucking around?" Tio asked. "You'd be so neglected and sad."

"And I would have finished this problem set fifteen minutes ago."

A week earlier, Carlos had been walking around the familiar streets of his Compton neighborhood with his older brother, Jose. They were wearing street clothes, eating fast food, in no rush to be anywhere or do anything, lamenting the end of summer while talking about girls and music, the school year ahead and the things each needed to organize in order to be semiprepared. His brother's company had always had a grounding effect on him, and so in their light talk he could harbor a sense of confident equanimity with the moment he inhabited, this quite lazy and aimless moment on the precipice of the most consequential stretch of school—and hence life—thus far. He had a premonition that elements would align over the course of the year, and high school would pass him over to a college that suited him in a very simple progression. In odd moments, usually alone, a small pressure lanced his chest as he wondered if all the potential he'd amassed during his first eleven years of school would prove illusory in the end for a kid who, from the perspective of any ignorant person driving past on Central Avenue, might well be dismissed as "just another Mexican without a real job."

Such a person wouldn't know, for instance, that he'd just spent three weeks at a Brown University academic camp taking college-level instruction, sleeping in his own room, meeting bright kids his age from all over the world. The time hadn't necessarily changed his life—it was just more school, far away—but it had proffered a glimpse into the human reach of the planet beyond South Los Angeles. He'd befriended a boy of Chinese descent who, having grown up in Alabama, spoke with the deepest of Southern drawls. He'd met white people who seemed genuinely interested in knowing him better, and were genuinely interesting once he came to know them better. He marveled at peers discussing immigration policy in lengthy detail who didn't seem to know who Cesar Chavez was. He'd turned in work to professors famous in their various, highly specific fields. He'd won a $30 bet that a preppy classmate would not only buy a bag of crushed kale posing as marijuana, but would smoke it and fail to notice the difference. And he had come home from Rhode Island with a long-distance girlfriend, his first.

Such a person also wouldn't know that his older brother walking beside him was about to begin his sophomore year at Yale.

Now his last high school summer had ended, and Jose had left again for New Haven, and Carlos finished his first, light homework assignments at the kitchen table in the compact backyard shack his family had been renting for ten years. Textbook notes for government, a sheet of equations for calculus, a chapter summary for English, reading about the structure of matter for chemistry, all of it basically interesting and conceptually simple for him, beginning-of-the-year stuff. Throughout, his phone dinged with Facebook direct messages and group chats, friends either asking for help on math or else transmitting inane, usually vulgar memes.

Then he opened a folder that contained form I-821D and its dense thicket of accompanying documents, which his school advisers had been helping him compile. In addition to a photocopy of his Washington State driver's license (Washington had a much more lenient ID process than California, so he and his brother had been licensed there: a sixteen-hour drive each way upon their respective sixteenth birthdays), most of the documents were school attendance records exhumed from the file cabinets of his elementary, middle, and high schools. He'd also gathered what records he could of doctor appointments, national exams, awards that he'd won, proof of extracurriculars like mock trial, Students Run LA, Minds Matter—essentially any official piece of paper bearing his name and a date in order to prove his continuous presence and schooling in the United States. Even though his parents had been as meticulous as they were capable of in keeping track of paper over the years, the gathering process had been arduous and basically a full-time job over the summer.

His sister, a seventh-grader, deferred her own homework by watching TV in the adjacent living room and fussing incessantly with her eyebrows—always her eyebrows, plucking, combing, lining. His father, having just gotten home from his job driving a delivery truck around the mammoth Chutes and Ladders board that was Los Angeles, tended to a pot of ravioli. His mother was working her three p.m.–to–eleven p.m. shift as a dispatcher for a different delivery company. Their home was somewhat removed from the street and its invasive noises. Even so, the firecrackers that blew up four or five times each night felt like they'd been set off right in their yard; Carlos had never understood the fondness Latino men maintained for their recreational explosives. All his life, they'd interrupted his homework on a nightly basis. Tonight was no different as he neared completion of his Deferred Action for Childhood Arrivals application, about the size and weight of a standard college packet. The stack of documents held such promises as the ability to work for wages and apply for federal college financial aid and to no longer endure the good-natured yet really-fucking-irritating jokes his friends made constantly about his status. Yet DACA also meant formally declaring his illegality while sharing with federal authorities the home address and places of employment of his parents. Deportation efforts were supposedly focused on the criminally inclined, but they'd been applied to people he knew: expulsion without warning, sometimes in the middle of the night, neighbors who had children in school and paid taxes, like his family.

His older brother had received his Dreamer status last year so that he could work at a data analytics company over the summer rather than manual-labor jobs in area warehouses as he'd always done before. Jose's application had been processed within two months, and no one dressed in black, bearing holstered firearms, had come to their door. So Carlos and his parents, after much recent dinner discussion, had decided that the potential benefits outweighed the risks. He'd communicated the decision to the school faculty, and they'd supported him through the technical process. Once submitted later this month, the mysterious standby period would settle in. All of his fellow seniors would spend much of this year waiting for colleges and universities to inform them as to their deemed worth or lack thereof. In Carlos's case, these universities would be among the most prestigious in the world. But because he'd been brought to the country a few months after he was born instead of a few months before, and thus was still here illegally seventeen years later, he would also be waiting for the United States government to inform him as to whether or not he could be called an American—well, not quite "American," but something adjacent, something temporarily legal. He hoped that this particular wait would not be a long one.

The windows were open and a nocturnal breeze had mercifully kicked up, but the residual heat from the day caused sweat to fall from his brow onto the papers that he filled out methodically, checking and rechecking each entry, as Carlos did in all things.

Owen

A tall, lanky, pale-skinned teenager lurked near the portal to the swimming pool, wearing a Speedo swimsuit and nothing else. A water polo game was in play, the first of the fall season. At a certain point, with the ball live on the far side of the twenty-five-meter pool, this kid crept across the beige deck tiles and then paused a moment on the pool's edge, the way comedians sometimes do before delivering a punch line. He jumped into the water sideways and upside down. He was capable of swimming skillfully, but he chose to doggie-paddle around in a circle. The spectators—fourteen or fifteen parents in the stands—didn't seem to notice as they alternately watched their children and intently tapped cell phones. He did some splashing for the benefit of the camera: a friend was filming this stunt. He spit water in a weak arc like a fountain statue. He back-floated. Then an intercepted pass led to a thrashing of swimmers in his direction. Now people began to see him and he felt their eyes. The time had come to exit the pool, and he did. His longish sandy-blond hair was matted down over his face, and his body shivered slightly as a coach stalked toward him.

"What are you doing?" the coach asked.

"I'm on the team," the boy replied.

"No you're not."

"I'm on the JV," he amended.

"I'm the JV coach!"

A moment passed while the coach simmered. Then this prankster, Owen, cocked his head slightly to the side and extended his forearms palms-upward in a sign of low-level contrition. "Okay, look, I played freshman year."

"But you're not on the team."

"I'm not."

"So . . . what were you doing in the pool *during a varsity game?*"

"I just had to do this."

"What?!"

"I'm sorry, I just had to."

The words didn't make sense to the adult, who maybe even half-smiled at the inexplicable nonsense of children. He jabbed a thumb toward the bleachers. "Just *get off the deck.*"

As he walked away, Owen received a thumbs-up from his friend, indicating that the video was saved and Instagrammable. Still wearing the Speedo and now a towel over his shoulders, Owen ascended into the bleachers and sat apart from the crowd, on a wet bench in a growing puddle of water. He parted his hair from over his eyes and put his glasses on and watched the coaches shout and point while the players splashed around seriously, and he remembered his own brief, unhappy water polo career, which had begun and ended during his freshman year three years ago—a lot of treading water interspersed with typically fruitless bursts of effort and the occasional fingernail gash across his shoulder or knee jab to the crotch. He didn't know why he'd ever played in the first place. Freshman year, he'd wanted to join a bunch of things before realizing that joining things for the sake of joining had little value when it came to passage through high school—though obviously much value when it came to college admissions. He was aware that today's shenanigans had no value at all to anything.

He'd entered his last year of high school with the goal of creating a "senioresque" experience. The goal was not couched in grandiose terms; he didn't want to become part of Beverly Hills High School lore by any stretch and didn't care if future seniors mentioned his name breathlessly two or three years from now: "Remember when Owen . . . ?" "Wasn't that Owen who . . . ?" He didn't even care about having vivid stories to tell at future reunions that he might or might not attend. He simply had realized that this was the final segment of a certain fleeting time of life, and he was compelled to create a few loony memories now—ones that might somehow stand out from the malaise of classes and the indistinguishable afternoons in basements with friends—rather than grow older retrospectively picking apart scenarios in which he *could have* created them, *could have* done something interesting or funny, but didn't. Doggie-paddling in the middle of a water polo game was not something he would have conceived of doing any other year. The exercise was pointless and a little bratty, self-consciously clownish, disrespectful to players and coaches. He might not remember it anyway. Then again, he might, during some odd moment in the life ahead, flash upon that minute spent in the pool, summon the video from a computer drive, and smile. The prospect of such a moment felt worth the effort and embarrassment.

"What are you doing?" Another incredibly assertive and gravelly male voice, clearly directed at him.

Owen turned around. He assumed the voice belonged to some parent irked by his violation of the game's sanctity, but behind him was the athletic director, wearing his usual reflective sunglasses and suit beneath crew-cut silver hair. "I'm watching the water polo game," Owen replied.

"You can't do that!"

"I have no other obligations right now." Though Owen didn't surf, he had a surf bum's cadence, with drawn-out vowels and accented syllables that meandered up and down in half octaves.

The AD crossed his thick forearms. "You're not wearing a shirt."

"No."

"Why's your shirt off?"

"It just is. I'm wet."

"You can't have your shirt off here."

"But this is a *pool*. We're watching a *water polo game*." He kept his voice, as best he could, earnestly observational, not overtly smug, as he gestured toward the team benches below, where twenty teenaged boys leaned forward on their knees with towels draped on shoulders, all of them shirtless and pale, just like Owen. And just like Owen, the AD seemed to have realized that this dialogue had drawn on far longer than its content merited.

"Just get a shirt on or get out," he said, and walked away.

Jon

Jon was still in school as dusk fell. Something about being at school hours after others had left was empowering to him. The hallways felt wider and taller, the classrooms with their bulletin boards of student work somehow more solemn. Even the posters on the walls advertising school spirit in ubiquitous, brightly colored phrases seemed to hold more power than they did during the crowded, frenetic days. Though Jon was familiar with all the various sectors of the school from having spent nearly six hundred days of his life there, the place still felt explorable when it was empty.

He wasn't the only one here, of course. Maintenance staff vacuumed and mopped, the security guard made slow periodic sweeps, teachers and administrators worked late, athletes remained out on the lit football field and inside the gymnasium. And the Beverly Hills High Academic Decathlon team secluded themselves on the second floor of the science center.

Aca Deca comprised nine teenagers from all four grades who had committed to staying after school every day throughout the year, sometimes for five or six hours, in order to study—not for standardized tests or AP exams, but to gain comprehensive knowledge of a randomly generated subject each year. Jon's freshman year, the subject had been World War I. Sophomore year it was new alternatives in energy. Junior year, India. This year they were immersing themselves in the art, literature, music, economics, and even mathematics of World War II. George Gershwin's "Rhapsody in Blue" played while the teammates quizzed one another on the nuclear physics that determined the war's Pacific front. To Jon, Aca Deca was a kind of celebration of nerddom, undertaken for no extra credit or tangible benefit except for a modest addition to one's college application. It was also an insulated venue in which to commune with like-minded peers, procrastinate, and be somewhere other than home. A great deal of giggling emanated from that room—high-pitched, staccato giggling, the kind most often heard from very young children caught up in some fresh delight, the kind that was easily ridiculed in a wider school setting but cherished here with this core group of outliers.

His father was waiting in his Hyundai outside at eight fifteen that evening; Jon usually rode the bus home but his father picked him up when he could. The sky above Moreno Drive was a deep, dark blue. The traffic lines on the nearby thoroughfares of Santa Monica Boulevard, Olympic Boulevard, and Century Park East sounded their many horns, fiercely protesting the basic reality of a city with too many cars and not enough lanes. But the plot of land occupied by the high school, with its curved sidewalks and clock tower and adjacent stadium lights, felt generally calm—incubated, somehow, from the surrounding madness of tens of thousands of people trying to get from one place to another at exactly the same time.

Jon and his father talked about baseball for most of the short ride home, using a residential street to evade the worst of the traffic, stopping and starting at the signs every block for a mile along with other in-the-know or Waze-influenced drivers. They crossed La Cienega Boulevard and passed La Cienega Park, composed of three baseball diamonds where, years ago, Jon's father had taught him to throw and catch. Naturally, the ball play had been accompanied by visions of accomplishing great feats of skill at the plate and in the field, leading future teams to many dominant victories. Now, in the last year of his playing career, he remained primarily on the JV team (technically, he was varsity, but his loaded afternoon schedule for the most part precluded practicing with them; he went to varsity games when he could) and lacked the size, speed, and fast-twitch muscle fibers to ever be better than a bit below average; baseball was yet another thing that Jon participated in, was okay at, and loved. And the game was an easy channel of conversation with his father—one of the few they seemed able to carry with constancy year by year. Baseball was one of the easiest subjects in the world to talk about, so it was mostly what they talked about together on this particular commute, and on any commute. They turned left on Gale Drive and parked in the lot beneath the wide, blockish condominium complex where Jon had grown up. The building stood on the very last, easternmost city block within the Beverly Hills school district, which was the reason Jon's parents had first placed a down payment on the compact two-bedroom on the third floor just before Jon started elementary school. Like thousands of local families, his had chosen to spend much of their income on a modest unit (that they were still paying off) within one of the most expensive zip codes in the country, giving up space and disposable cash for the guarantee of a good, free primary education. Jon was reminded of this sacrifice constantly and from all angles. Its resulting claustrophobia had in some ways defined his youth.

His mother was on the couch watching news on Chinese television while simultaneously texting with friends and relations in the motherland. An aromatic stir-fry dinner was still warm in the pan. Jon began unpacking books onto his desk in the corner of what was designed to be a small dining room but was used by his family as a multipurpose office and music room. While his father (a low-key, nonpracticing Jew) began watching YouTube clips of classic rock concerts, his mother detached from her phone in order to make Jon a plate and then, while he was a captive eater, intensively interview him.

In Chinese, she asked rapid-fire questions that, as ever, revolved around academics: math, physics, English, statistics. The year was too young for specific numbers to be raised, such as test scores and his GPA, but those would soon enough become the focus of her inquiry. For now, she desired to know precisely what he was learning and how well he was learning it. Jon was well aware that, like many Asian parents, she was highly concerned about his grades. He also knew that, beyond grades, she viewed school as the sole conduit through which she could relate to her son and show sincere interest in his life (she had only a minimal understanding of baseball and zero appreciation of rock music). Still, he had little stamina to rehash the day that had just unremarkably unfolded, and he gave mostly one-word answers until the dialogue naturally trailed off. The act of explaining—and justifying—his existence was a fundamental rhythm of life that most teenagers shared, he figured, but he also figured that few were obliged to do so with the acute constancy that he was. Caught in the complicated rubric of trying to ward off her interest without seeming to condescend, he simply wished that he were back in school.

Chapter 2

AUGUST 12—SEPTEMBER 1

Looking back, I think I realized maybe some of my complaints as a freshman, maybe some of them still hold true to some degree senior year. The key is not to give a shit about it to begin with.

—Owen

Ánimo Pat Brown Charter High School looked different from most structures in the surrounding environs; in a neighborhood that had seen minimal development investment for decades, the building looked new and cared for. The carapace was divided into colorful rectangles, and front classrooms faced the street through tall glass windows without wrought iron bars bolted over them (though bars surrounded the small campus plot, and multiple security cameras angled down from perches around the roof). The school had been established in 2006 by the Green Dot charter network, which had rolled out five other South LA middle and high schools over the previous seven years. This influx of institutions occurred in response to the poor and falling graduation statistics in the Los Angeles Unified School District (LAUSD), and it was made possible by the splintering-off of teachers from those same schools, the sometimes forcible transfer of space, the desperation of city and county politicians, and millions of dollars' worth of public and philanthropic investment—each one of those dollars controversial in the context of the vicious and ongoing public/charter conflict. APB had opened with 150 ninth-graders. Four years later, most of those students graduated while 450 more rose through the grades below, all there through either lottery or sibling preference. After two address changes brought the campus farther and farther south, away from downtown and toward the most impoverished districts in the county, the network procured and retrofitted the permanent campus on Beach Street in a decrepit building that had once been a mattress factory. The space was too small for its student body, precluding school growth, sports, and lockers along the walls. But it was permanent. The stability of a school carried a tremendous weight in any neighborhood. In the neighborhood of Florence-Graham and those surrounding it, where of the roughly ten thousand residents packed into each square mile, half were renters and a quarter lived below the federal poverty line, its significance was nearly cosmic, a signal of a promise that the nation had made many generations before and largely forgotten—or seemed to—in places such as South LA. For students and educators, the logistical challenges and basic discomfort of managing a cramped space were worth enduring in exchange for constancy.

Beverly Hills High School, by Los Angeles standards, was a historic structure. It had been christened in 1927 as part of the Los Angeles City High School District before Beverly Hills established its own district in 1936 (Beverly Hills itself was only first subdivided in 1907, following a failed stake for oil; before that, the land had been a lima bean farm). Over decades, wars, and social movements, the school adapted to changes both local and national, sometimes successfully, other times less so. The city of Beverly Hills was founded as a whites-only covenant, which was only overturned after extensive litigation following the arrival of black actors and businessmen in the 1940s. Diversity had always been a visible issue in the neighborhood and the school, with permits issued to applicants from a limited number of LAUSD middle schools beginning in the seventies—a program that ended in 2010 after years of contention from both local parents who feared the level of education would decline and permit-district parents who feared the phenomenon of brain drain from their schools. A citywide experimental busing program also initiated in the 1970s proved one of the causes of white flight from public schools, contributing to the proliferation of private schools in Los Angeles and a steep enrollment decline at Beverly (where an unusually large proportion of residents could afford private tuitions). The spaces were then filled by an influx of Persian Jews expelled from Iran in the seventies and eighties who made Beverly Hills the second-largest Persian Jewish community in America, altering the demographics of the neighborhood and the school. Enrollment again began to decline, falling from 2,400 students in 2008 (when Ánimo Pat Brown was a year away from graduating its first senior class) to 1,500 students in 2017. Rapid teacher and leadership turnover accompanied this exodus. Public school board meetings as often as not entailed a succession of parents yelling into the microphone about program funding, teacher tenure, whatever the issue of the day happened to be. Throughout such changes and agitas, the pale French Normandy façade of the high school peered down over the tiered lawn while teachers and teenagers filed in and out dutifully each day. The school had been built ninety years earlier to be a pleasing place to learn, with wide hallways, tall windows, durable wood, and finely wrought details. But like the streets surrounding it, the school had long ago been cast as a national symbol for wealth, disparity, and bad-to-mediocre TV and film—the aspirations and the psychosis of the American dream.

Within these two spaces, separated by much more than the twenty-two miles of city pavement between them, four boys began their senior years in 2016—four boys essentially anonymous among the nearly seven hundred thousand students in the country's second-largest school district, which also ranked fifth from last in per-pupil spending; four boys with over two thousand mostly unexceptional school days behind them and one hundred eighty highly determinative days remaining ahead; four boys residing in two neighborhoods, Compton and Beverly Hills, so alternately celebrated and maligned and caricatured that their names had long since come to signal more of a sociological condition than a geographical place; four boys passing through their daily lives beneath all the wonder and mundanity therein, with less than a year in which to shape the remainder of their time on earth, to resolve what their day-to-day existence would look and feel like five or ten or twenty or forty years from now; four boys born into the very outset of the twenty-first century and raised in a polarizing country in which technology had opened myriad channels between people while corrupting their ability to connect and to sustain independent thought; four boys existing, striving, questioning, experiencing. They spent large portions of their time, both consciously and unconsciously, measuring the value of their experiences, or wondering if they had any value at all—wondering if their lives would matter, if some piece of the world, however small, would be better for Tio's, or Carlos's, or Owen's, or Jon's having passed through it. They also spent large portions of their time on YouTube.

They were now in the final length of their passage through secondary school, what could be deemed the first consequential milestone in American life, bearing some of its first truly adult decisions. They were nearly, though not quite, men, and tasked with sorting out what manhood meant—this in a culture that still broadly marginalized the emotional lives of young males and clung to old tropes of machismo over vulnerability. They were about to enter the complex, biased, overwhelmingly confusing matrix that was contemporary college admissions, representing not just themselves but their schools and families. They struggled with the likelihood that friendships sustained in some cases for nearly two decades were about to be riven by the outcomes. Whether they were aware or not, the coming months, with all their inevitable hours of boredom and precious moments of connection and vital instances of hilarity, would embody the human condition that their lit teachers rhapsodized about so often and eruditely. Plus they had math to learn, and history, and chemistry, and English—and homework, reams of it.

Carlos

Carlos hadn't spoken English when he and Tio first encountered one another in second grade. When Carlos was five and about to enter kindergarten, his family had moved to South LA from northern Washington State, where they'd lived in a town called Brewster near the Canadian border, in a community of itinerant pear and apple pickers. At the time of their southward relocation in 2004, his older brother had been seven and entering second grade. His sister had been an infant. Neither Carlos nor his brother had ever really heard much English before, having lived exclusively among immigrant Latino laborers ever since they'd left Mexico. South LA had been changing demographically for years as Latino families were drawn to the area for its lowish rents and its promise of employment in factories, auto shops, food and cleaning services—jobs uneducated but industrious non-English-speaking people could perform. His parents found stable work in the delivery sector, his father as a truck driver and his mother as a dispatcher. Through family connections, they moved into a two-bedroom shack in a local couple's backyard, where Carlos shared a room with his siblings (their bunk bed had a sliding trundle beneath, such that the three could stack themselves while sleeping). Though the unit was unzoned and therefore illegal, compounding their stress as noncitizens, his parents could afford the rent and still have enough left over to sufficiently feed and clothe their children—as well as get them to school. Their extended family was already established in the area, so Carlos and his siblings had cousins and aunts and uncles. The landscape change from very rural to very urban was traumatic; he and his brother had once had freedom to traverse the wide fields often covered with snow alongside all the other young children of pickers, and now they had concrete and asphalt, all unobstructed sunlight and heat, a pervasive sameness in which they weren't permitted to go far or unsupervised because, on occasion, people killed other people in South LA.

Despite the growing availability of elementary ESL classes, his parents placed both him and his brother in regular classes at Florence Avenue Elementary School without any supplemental language aid. The decision was neither strategic nor ignorant, but simply based on the rationale that, since they were an American family, the children should experience school as Americans. Carlos spent kindergarten and first grade rarely understanding a word spoken or written by the teacher—though half his classmates spoke Spanish and so recess and lunch, at least, made sense. He imitated the motions of his classmates at any given time, pretending to write numbers or letters, producing gibberish. Because he was quiet and obedient, his teachers passed him along from grade to grade even though he was incapable of the work. By second grade he'd learned to read the basic sight words and equate them with speech, coming clumsily by English, which, with its unruly conjugations and phonetic variables, was a language far easier to abuse than to master. By third grade he was speaking more or less fluently, though tripping over sentence constructions often; placing adjectives before rather than after nouns was a particular frustration. He began journaling almost nightly, in English, as a way to exercise his language and composition skills and also mark the progression of his strange young life. Due to teacher shortages in the LAUSD, Carlos had the same two teachers from third grade through sixth, which was stifling for some students but a boon to him: he liked both of them, and the consistency of style and manner allowed him to ease into his second language to the point where he could *think* in English, the key threshold in the tremendous human feat of language learning. In fifth grade, he was placed in honors classes.

By this time, kids in school began viewing Carlos as simply a natural overachiever, one who could work half as hard for twice the grades. Some admired him. More resented him with an accompaniment of ridicule, that old side spur of jealousy—usually offered in Spanish because its insults sounded more penetrating.

"*Empollón.*"

"*Panocha.*"

"*Cobarde.*"

Carlos was easygoing and nearly impossible to anger, innate qualities he'd carried from youth. His grades, contrary to what classmates assumed, were not natural. He labored hard to earn them, hours each night in middle school, reading, writing, reviewing, retaining. He didn't advertise his efforts, because at age ten in the inner city, devoting time to school was not a source of pride. It was something he did at home under the watch of his family, behind walls and curtains.

At the outset of senior year, upon his unremarkable physical body, he carried the weight of remarkable expectations: he was the lone member of his class realistically capable of being admitted to a top-ranked university, possibly even an Ivy, and everyone in his orbit was aware of this—mainly because of his Yalie older brother, a living advertisement of Carlos's own potential. And so Carlos served as a kind of human metric of high achievement, and people tracked his every quiz score just as they looked to him to answer every question posited in class. This was exhausting, and what he truly wished to express—an ethos he'd spent much of his high school years forming without any platform from which to widely articulate it—was that these nearly six hundred kids in his school who looked up to him, the dozens he knew and the hundreds he didn't, had all grown up in the same place and were progressing through high school. They should all draw an intrinsic and powerful confidence from that stark reality, a pride not of place but of place within place. They could all navigate the city's labyrinthine bus system and buy groceries for their households and speak two languages and be responsible for young children and avoid the city's danger and metabolize the pain of watching their parents toil, often so that rich people didn't have to, while at the same time learning geometry and the canon of Romantic poets; they could all order these intellectual and emotional tasks, and that was an astonishing baseline from which they were all about to launch into the greater world.

But there was no national quantifying system for these aptitudes, no SAT section that measured how competent or resilient a person was, and so grades remained the sole means by which he and his peers could project themselves beyond their high school. And since Carlos had the best grades, as senior year began he was responsible for projecting not only his own potential but that of all of those kids who looked to him in class and whispered about him in the hallways. He was their emblem, if a sometimes reluctant one, and his task in the coming year was nothing less than to perforate the narrative in which he and everyone he knew had grown up, the one in which a high school diploma and blue-collar job signified a successful life.

Popular culture seemed quite absorbed with the differentiation of generations: baby boomers, X, Y, Z, millennials. X-ers behaved a certain way, millennials a different way, and so on. But since Carlos could remember, at community gatherings and holidays and quinceañera parties, all such talk and decision-making revolved solely around the *next* generation. So though this year's senior class somewhat straddled the border line between millennials (the last born in 1999) and Generation Z (the first born in 2000), he thought only in terms of "next." He and his friends, his older brother at Yale, and his younger sister with her eyebrow fixation, the kids on the trains and buses and sidewalks each morning, the hundreds of thousands of teenagers in high schools all over South LA: they were all members of the next.

Owen

Most afternoons upon returning to his home in Westwood (a neighborhood just west of Beverly Hills, similarly moneyed but free of the pop culture baggage), Owen climbed the narrow stairway behind the kitchen to sit at his mother's bedside. There, he described a few mundane details of the day, did what he could to mine them for humor, and tried to gauge her pain level without inquiring about it directly.

His mother had always been an incessantly active person as well as a creative parent. (On a flight with her when Owen and his brother were young and acting like obnoxious little jerks, she'd pulled an attendant aside and said, "I want you to come over and yell at my boys. Then I'm *really* going to yell at you. Then they'll be good. Okay?" The attendant had seemed dubious. "Trust me, it will work." When the attendant did as instructed, his mother had flashed a loud and maniacal outrage worthy of her soap star past—"How *dare* you speak to my sons that way!?"—prompting a mortified Owen to plead, "Mom, she's totally right, we were being terrible, we'll stop if you just *stop*.") At school, she was a fixture at school fund-raisers and performances; she was a staple in the lives of his friends, for whom she maintained an open-door policy at their home; she was constantly buying tickets for the family to random concerts and shows; and she was always writing and doing voice-over work for TV shows. Her stamina was awesome and seemed to expand with age, and she was also an electric wit whose offbeat humor penetrated even the cynical preteen in him.

Four years ago, when Owen was in eighth grade, she had fallen ill with flulike symptoms and steeled herself for a week of achy discomfort. But her symptoms didn't fade with rest and hydration and Tamiflu. When she did seem to recover after a few terrible weeks, she still needed help walking—at first just the modest support of a forearm, but soon Owen and his brother felt as if they were practically carrying her from room to room. She was exhausted and increasingly in pain. She only had the strength to be out of bed for eight hours a day, then six, then four. Then she could only rise for family dinners. Then she couldn't rise at all and they brought dinners to her room.

Her pain and immobility worsened, terrifying her husband and sons. Prescriptions didn't work. Doctors ran out of solutions. A succession of experts were confounded as their surefire remedies failed, and as Owen and his brother and father's erstwhile hopes ended in disappointment. The best diagnosis anyone came up with—this after months of agony and confusion—was that she had experienced the activation of a case of dormant Lyme disease picked up by a deer tick at some point in her childhood. The family latched on to this explanation, even if it seemed like a bit of a reach. In the meantime, she planned and executed Owen's Bar Mitzvah from her bed, attended his eighth-grade play in a wheelchair, talked him through middle school angst, and provided a consistent and wondrously uplifting presence amid all the downward emotional pulls of one's early teens. During these early teens, Owen also became inured to that aspect of life that many people his age were still sheltered from, or were able to consciously ignore, but was impossible to elude in the end: the awful randomness of chance and its countless forms and amorality and disregard for upturning the order of things. In his case, this randomness had manifested itself in the theory that a mite the size of a pinhead whose weeklong life span had played out two decades before he'd been born had injected his future mother with the bacterium *Borrelia burgdoferi*, and in its thrall he'd progressed through the confusion that was high school. His mother lived almost entirely in nightgowns and bathrobes.

She remained bedridden now, years later, while friends and work associates whirled through for meetings from the chair beside her while she sat propped up (Owen thought of her as a petite, blond, and hilarious incarnation of Brando's godfather).

Owen's older brother, now a senior at Tufts University just outside Boston, had preceded him at Beverly Hills High School with something like a classic high school experience: he'd been popular and athletic, he'd dated attractive girls and attended the best parties, he'd caused some trouble but had been hard to dislike—and he'd always been present for Owen, even from three thousand miles away, as a sounding board and wellspring regarding high school: safe, unjudging, and even tender. Being as they knew each other better than anyone else did, and that they shared the recent history of their mother's condition, Owen relied on his brother heavily once he first passed under the high school's tall, white, French Normandy façade at the outset of freshman year.

And so Owen could make little sense of the way he floundered through the first few months of freshman year, why he failed to immediately occupy the popular spaces of such realms as sports, parties, and girls, or why he was so jealous of those who did. From an awkward remove, he observed such self-designated peers with their cliques, their breezy, well-funded lifestyles, their general entitlement. Though Owen, the son of two highly successful TV creatives, could not refute his association with such privilege—couldn't deny that he lived in a big house or that his parents owned a second, beachfront home in Santa Barbara, that he was familiar with studio lots and acquainted with celebrities—he fairly quickly discerned that jealousy was a wasteful emotion and that his place lay elsewhere. The question became not just how to locate that place, but how to avoid the entire superficial act of positioning and simply exist as a human being with blood and hormones in his system, a body lengthening and a mind widening, a person with hopes and anxieties and judgments and an earnest desire to achieve originality and substance in his aspirations and to not be an asshole while doing so.

He did so—or at least tried—by spending most of his time in the basements of the same friends he'd had since elementary school, by committing to the school drama and media programs, by treating school culture as little more than a weird phenomenon to be observed, and by devoting so many of his evenings to sitting in the quietude with his mom, trying to make her laugh even as she, reclined among pillows and ever in the presence of pain, drew more laughs from him.

Tio

A shooting occurred outside Ánimo Pat Brown on a Thursday three weeks into the year, in the late afternoon. At the T formed by Beach Street and Eighty-Third Street, a few yards from the school entrance gate, two cars abutted and a member of one gang shot and injured a member of another gang, over either drugs, territory, initiation, or—statistically most likely—a girl. School had been let out two hours earlier, so only a few teachers and students were inside. The cars screeched off, and later the shooter's car was cornered by police a mile away. After a volley of gunfire, the man was dead. The following day, the administrative sector of the school, a clutter of desktops and printers visible from the front hallway through glass windows, was busy with police appropriating the school's security cameras to verify what had happened.

Students passed by and conjectured throughout the morning: either drugs in someone's backpack or some other code violation. Once the actual event was verified, no one seemed to give it much thought or want to talk about it. Since it didn't involve anyone in school, it didn't feel important.

"Just some shit that happened," Tio said with a shrug on the way into AP Language class.

Outwardly, as the first days and then weeks of the school year progressed and his knee pain gradually ebbed, Tio worked to project his defining aura of nonchalant joker, feigning apathy toward school and its consequences. He remained the guy with the skateboard, the guy with the combative wit, the guy with the confidence, the guy with the 4.0 who was cool with pretty much everyone—the guy whom anxious freshmen exploring these hallways for the first time could look at and aspire to emulate.

He didn't want a single one of them to know that, a few layers deep in his consciousness, he was scared: scared that the University of California school system he aspired to attend had set new application and tuition records each year; scared that admissions officers—the faceless administrators who would decide whether or not to open their portals for him alongside hundreds of thousands of other applicants—already harbored a fair idea regarding what South LA was and who came out of it and what a young man with the name *Tio* might be capable of; scared that he would fail to raise his self-proclaimed "garbage" SAT score of 1100 when he retook the test in October (the verbal section had crushed him; no matter how fluent a person was in speaking English, writing it was really damn hard when growing up in a Spanish-speaking home); and scared that the thousands of hours he'd invested in school might not amount to anything beyond the dictates of his birth: the flat sprawl of bungalow homes and apartment buildings, parking lots, mechanics, Spanish-language billboards, medium-sized palms, lawyers' offices, taquerias, liquor stores, McDonald's, check-cashing centers, churches, groups of men watching soccer games on small TVs in open garages, *mercados* advertising EBT acceptance, more mechanics, tens of thousands of people packed densely together, wary of strangers, working very hard for very little money, watering their flowers, waiting for their buses, hosting large extended family gatherings, coping with the difficult math of urban American life mirrored and refracted all around the sixteen square miles of South LA. Such math predetermined that boys like Tio would strive and strive and strive without the prospect of ever quite reaching.

He was familiar with anxiety from his freshman year at Ánimo Pat Brown, when he'd come to this charter school known for academic demands from his local public middle school not known for such, a self-proclaimed "dumb potato." Back then, the anxiety had spilled from typical freshman doubts regarding the workload and teachers and grades and friends and girls and, arching over all, his own uncertain capabilities. He and his freshman classmates who hailed from the same public middle school had been, for the most part, unprepared for grade-level work. They were not used to teachers making strict demands of them, both disciplinary and academic. They were unfamiliar with the concept of expectations. They were accustomed to being disregarded due to their skin color and countries of extraction, not exhorted to see themselves as exceptional, college-bound individuals. Freshman year had been a confusing one within this H-shaped alignment of three short hallways and twenty-nine classrooms.

Three years later, he'd gained much clarity. He could do the work. He got along with teachers. He had deep friendships and a girlfriend of three years. He would graduate high school and go to college. The 4.0 GPA he'd carried away from junior year spoke a great deal for these certainties. Yet it seemed that as his mind and worldview expanded and became more complex between freshman and senior years, so did the questions within it, the most resonant being: Was he worthy?

He heard his father's voice often. *"I don't know why you go to school . . . It doesn't mean shit . . . It's a worthless thing . . . A few grades don't make you better than anybody else around here . . . that high school's not gonna make you amount to something."* He'd heard the voice since he was a boy, resounding through the family's various small living spaces on Juniper Street. Even during entirely peaceful moments—baking Rice Krispies treats with his girlfriend, running along the Dockweiler State Beach waterfront in preparation for the LA Marathon, landing a new skateboard trick for the first time—that voice would be there, lodged firmly in his consciousness, affirming his unworthiness, intractable and imperious and acid in its surety. He knew that even if the following fall found him on some pristine college campus far from South LA, the voice would continue to sound and he would continue to resist being contaminated by it.

Jon

A Saturday in late August presented Jon with the rarity of a totally free afternoon. He slept in very late, close to noon—another habit that agonized his mother. Later, he locked a borrowed bike onto the rack on the front of a city bus and rode directly west for ten miles, to the edge of the bluffs where America ended. Soon he was pedaling along the palisades, sixty sheer feet above the beach and the Pacific Ocean. He made his way down the connector ramp to the Pacific Coast Highway and the bike path parallel to the shoreline, then headed north toward the Santa Monica Mountains and the fine oscillating groove their folds cut against the sky. The beach was wide and the people spread out, more so as he progressed away from the pier and beach clubs, past a series of unused volleyball courts, across a few jetties. He turned right on Temescal Canyon Road and had to ride standing up, pressing his full weight down into each rotation of the chain along the uphill passage. After a short ascent, he reached a small green space called Asilomar View Park. He left his bike on the bluffs and sat on a grassy outcrop peering down at the ocean surface, which, from this vantage, looked absolutely still, the ripples petrified. To his right, the mountains threaded along past Point Dume, a tall headland that cleaved the great bay. To his left, the famous Ferris wheel on the pier carried Angelenos and tourists around and around in the hazy marine layer. Jon took out his digital camera and began taking photos, a hobby of his. He'd also brought along his notebook, maybe to write a poem that no one would ever read. Here lay a brief interlude of total, self-conscious aloneness in a city of roughly ten million people, a patch of dry grass and rocks where the stillness countered his maniacally active days, a few moments during which absolutely no one knew where he was. A person could do this in Los Angeles: travel a few miles, enter a different realm, and disappear for a time. He looked around at the sublime and accomplished nothing.

The contrast between the way he spent these hours and the way his typical hours were spent was surreal. Jon's mother's approach to his school-related activities had always been rigorously concentrated, and Jon's earliest remembered feelings toward her involved a strange entanglement of love and exasperation. He'd always known that her attention flowed directly from her love for him, and that certain habits of his—particularly severe procrastination—caused her endless exasperation in turn. As a result, the two of them were parleying with each other always: for time and acknowledgment and respect and boundaries and affection that felt overly conditional. These negotiations were really a personalized version of the contrasts between the Western and Eastern worlds, and both Jon and his mother understood this to a certain degree even though the deep emotional aspects of, respectively, growing up and raising a son, seemed to nullify any kind of intellectual grasp of the root cause. He'd always dreamed of baseball glory; she made sure that piano lessons underpinned his childhood. He enjoyed creative approaches to learning; she believed in retention via drills. He was strategic about turning middling grades into high grades in the last weeks of a given term, and proud of being ranked fourth in his class; she did not comprehend why he would not aspire to perfect scores on every test and the top rank in his class. He'd grown up in a school-based culture of guilt; she hailed from a national culture of shame. He felt that the way he carried himself in the world and the achievements he came by represented himself; she believed they represented not just his family but their entire lineage (he knew that many of those hours she spent on the phone with relatives were spent boasting about his successes, down to decent scores on meaningless quizzes and unmemorable at-bats in JV baseball games). Jon was flustered by the fact that much of the friction in their relationship resided in well-established clichés characterizing the earth's two super-powers, all of which continued to be ubiquitously abused for easy comedy throughout popular culture. He wished that they might clash over more original content—or, better yet, not clash at all. But wishes were classified as such because they were unlikely to come to pass. When he was in middle school, a friend (who was not Chinese) had asked him if he'd read *Battle Hymn of the Tiger Mother* by Amy Chua, a celebrated memoir touting the merits of strict, Eastern parenting. He'd replied, "I don't have to read that book. I'm living it."

Meanwhile, the dialect from his mother's native region of China, which Jon had adopted himself and used at home, was very fast and built around heavily accented syllables; even casual, grounded discussions between them regarding these differences could sound to the American ear like frantic yelling. The volume in their apartment was loud.

Ultimately, Jon wanted what most teenagers wanted most of the time, that seemingly simple commodity that was deceptively confounding in the rhythms between parents and children: space. By virtue of the apartment layout, there was very little of it; he worked at the juncture where the kitchenette opened into the dining room, and she always cleaned both rooms in the evening, passing back and forth behind him every few moments, clocking his computer screen through the rapt lenses of her pretty eyes. His father, whose own desk was situated directly behind Jon's, usually listened to music through headphones or watched baseball on the TV mounted in front of their crammed work space.

During the first few weeks of school, since assignments were still light and left him feeling restless, he closed his books each night and played Debussy's "Suite Bergamasque" for a bit on the upright piano; his mother had been successful in propelling him not just to master the instrument but to find joy in its use. Afterward, he attempted to sleep in a twin bed opposite his mother's bed. She slept in his room because his father snored.

Chapter 3

SEPTEMBER 5—OCTOBER 3

I get very tired of people who all they want to do is hate on you, who want to make you weak until you show them you're good.

—*Tio*

Tio

"Damn the heat," Luis groaned upward toward the sun and to the universe at large.

"It's not that hot," Tio replied.

"It's almost a hundred degrees!"

"Fool, it's eighty-four and there's a mountain breeze!" Tio held up a weather app on his phone as proof. They were sitting on lawn chairs in the middle of the Labor Day carnival at a horse track in Arcadia, beneath the San Gabriel Mountains northeast of Los Angeles. Snowcaps could be seen on the tallest peaks, miles deep in the range.

"Well, maybe it's because I got more insulation than you." Luis motioned downward across his robust body.

"I'm glad you said it, because I was just about to."

"The point is, it's fucking hot."

"There's rarely any point to anything you say."

A third friend, Byron, laughed softly without looking up from whatever was on his phone screen. He opted not to join the squabble, which itself was an extension of the rootless running argument that Tio and Luis had been maintaining more or less since ninth grade.

They were at the carnival because they had the long weekend off school and could always make use of the thirty or forty dollars cash they earned running the game booths—water-dunk machines, bouncy houses, ring-toss games—which were owned by another friend's family. The work was boring, dirty, fly infested, and indeed quite hot: filling trash cans with strewn paper plates and plastic utensils and wasted food; policing the little kids, who tried to steal prizes constantly; observing all the parents, who appeared uniformly irritated, as if foretelling the inevitability of being generally harangued by life. But they were outside with stunning mountain views and access to free popcorn and funnel cakes, they sometimes met girls, and the wonder in a child's eyes upon winning a cheap stuffed animal somehow placed even the most jaded of them back in simpler times.

Tio had known Byron since those simpler times, in middle school. They'd gone to the same very rough public school that Carlos had attended (unlike Carlos, Tio and Byron hadn't been in honors classes). Then, Tio had been the outspoken arbiter of recess chaos and Byron the "emo" kid, always hovering alone on the periphery, a little dazed or depressed while he nodded to Green Day songs on his battered, outdated Nokia phone. Both had been smacked in the face by the demands and expectations of high school.

The dual purpose of ninth grade at Ánimo Pat Brown was to bring kids from underperforming public schools up to grade level academically while aligning them with the charter school's approach to classroom behavior, college prep, and discipline. Upon entry at age fourteen, Carlos was already on that level, as was Luis, who'd come from a charter middle school in the same network, with the same guidelines. Tio was decidedly not.

The chasm he'd needed to bridge was riven by the deep need for stimulation, both social and physical, that ruled him. Silence and stillness made him uncomfortable. In elementary and middle school, he'd known very little of either amid the overpopulated classrooms, the schoolyard hierarchy founded on confrontation, his own minute attention span. In an environment with close oversight, such as a private school classroom, he might have made for one of the many overprescribed ADD cases. In an inner-city public middle school, he was an irritant to be passed upward to the next teacher. Related to this quality in him was a mighty competitive spirit that, before high school, had no grounding tethers. In any debate, no matter how inane, he needed to plant the final barbed comment. In any skate park, he needed to land the last, most dangerous trick (or at least try to and fail). In any environment, he needed to be seen as the best—not the smartest but the most attention drawing. Through the first fourteen years of his life, much of his energy had derived from that pursuit. It had sustained him. It had also been a supreme academic obstacle.

From the outset, his freshman year at APB was difficult and sometimes humiliating. He'd never participated in a fulsome academic discussion before, in which motivated students led by invested teachers reasoned their way through poems, biological processes, and math concepts, in a controlled dialogue. In each period of each day, he fell behind within a few minutes, manically scribbling notes, losing the progression, then letting his mind wander to the more pleasing locale of what he'd do after school. The pattern repeated multiple times each day. He was not alone; this humbling puzzlement was actually part of the charter's intricate, four-year design of bringing students to college readiness. But he felt alone, particularly when sitting near Carlos, bewildered by the precision with which his middle school classmate could verbalize interlinked thoughts or logic out a geometric proof. APB had no sports teams, no fashion statements, and little in the way of extracurriculars. The only real means to stand out was in the classroom. Tio began sitting close to Carlos freshman year. Carlos established a Facebook group for designated smart kids to help one another on homework and keep Tio focused at night (they also swapped memes and YouTube videos and other time wasters). He began to feel less and less like an imposter even as he embraced a newfound humility. His grades rose gradually and then quickly. He could raise his hand in class with lessening fear of sounding stupid. Teachers began to notice him and offer the occasional word of encouragement—and even praise.

In the early spring of freshman year, Tio was writing an English essay (the craft of essay writing was one facet of the curriculum that continued to confound him) when his phone dinged. It was a direct message from Carlos, asking if Tio had had any success in calculating the volume of a difficult three-dimensional shape. *This whole problem set is kicking my ass*, Carlos wrote. Tio had completed the set an hour earlier, without much trouble. Carlos had overlooked the strategy of breaking the larger shape into smaller, simpler components and adding the numbers together. He related as much, and Carlos replied, *Duh. Thanks!* What was a minor stall in Carlos's night was a revelation to Tio, an influx of confidence so energizing that he could no longer sit still. One of his smart friends had asked him for help, which meant that he belonged among those friends.

Not long after that, his father started drinking again.

Jon

On Jon's first day of first grade at Horace Mann, one of four Beverly Hills elementary schools, a voice behind him declared, "That's my wallet."

Jon was rocking on the balls of his feet, peering ahead in line, anxious about the independent task of buying his first school lunch for $1.75, which his mother had tucked neatly within his Spider-Man wallet. He turned around. "No, this is my wallet."

The boy was bigger and taller, something Jon was beginning to understand might be a constant in his life. "No, it's mine. Give it."

Jon was confused more than afraid. The wallet had been in his backpack all morning. He'd seen his mother zip it in the back pocket. He'd just removed it from the same pocket a moment ago. He clutched it in both hands. "It's really not yours, though."

"It is mine." The boy spoke with such surety that Jon started to question his own ownership. He handed the wallet over and, now moneyless, stepped out of line and just stood by himself, watching others take their grilled cheeses.

A teacher's intervention revealed that the boy had an identical Spider-Man wallet in his backpack and he'd been confused upon seeing Jon's. Money and food were sorted. The two boys would become good friends in the following years. Yet moving forward, Jon still wondered if his entire school experience, first grade and beyond, would be defined by having bigger kids demand his lunch money and his giving it over without much objection.

It wasn't. He faced height jokes now and again, but those came mostly from good friends on the Little League teams that his father perennially coached, or from his mother. As he aged—and as his growth peaked at five foot four—Jon found that the timeless school trope of big kids picking on little kids lacked validity.

He had been born in the first month of the twenty-first century. The year 2000 was the year of the dragon on the Chinese zodiac. But since the Chinese New Year began at the end of January, Jon had technically been born in the final days of the year of the rabbit. The discrepancy went on to become a benign family joke, but as a boy Jon took its symbolism to heart—especially as his mother brought him to Chinese school every Saturday to learn her native language and complex heritage. The rabbit was supposed to be kind, compassionate, grounded, and creative. The dragon was lucky, enterprising, arrogant, and relentless. The duality of those traits—just like the duality of Aca Deca and baseball—seemed worth embracing. He didn't always agree with the cultural dictates that governed much of his life as well as his thorny maternal relationship, but they did ground him in the context of general teenaged disquiet.

In rare moments when a certain fragility impinged—a failed test, a snarky comment aimed his way, unrequited feelings toward a girl—he would think of his mother. She'd grown up in Nanchang, an industrial city in the northern Jiangxi province of China. Her father had been a local government official when the Cultural Revolution began, and as the country's zeitgeist had teetered back and forth over the decade before she'd been born, he'd alternated between wielding a relative amount of local power and sitting in prison in wretched conditions. Even as the country stabilized and his daughter grew up, he never came to trust the world they inhabited. The powerlessness of being ripped from home and thrust into a cage without recourse was itself caged within him. This unease in part inspired his daughter, once she finished college in the mid-1980s and then worked for a few years in Shenzhen, to travel to Los Angeles and earn an MBA. Like many cities, Los Angeles had its landmarked Chinatown district, but the true hub for Chinese culture lay in the San Gabriel Valley suburbs of Alhambra and Monterey Park, a few miles east of downtown. Here, one could drive for a dozen blocks along the thoroughfare of Atlantic Avenue without seeing English lettering on a storefront. The markets and food were excellent. The people were welcoming. The community was established and vibrant, the real estate and hence the economy owned by Chinese. Here, though 6,500 miles from home, she opened her own textile business focused on imports and exports, established an independent life, and felt well primed to live and work and prosper among a few hundred thousand people who looked like her and spoke her language and ascribed loyally to the culture she knew. Then a very odd development occurred: she married an American man, gave birth to a son and named him Jon, sold her business, and became a full-time mother in Beverly Hills.

While she challenged Jon in maddening ways almost all the time, he held tightly to her courage in not just weathering but embracing discomfort, in living as an outlier for the majority of her adult life—for him.

This outlook helped spare him the anxiety that plagued so many teenagers in Beverly Hills and beyond. The hallways were usually bright with talk and laughter during passing periods, and yet undercurrents of competition and insecurity and grief pulled beneath them. Jon preferred good grades to bad and aspired to acceptance to a competitive school, but in instances when he'd flubbed a final exam or knowingly turned in a lousy paper, he hadn't let disappointment or the prospect of failure seize him. He operated with a feeling that most errors were correctible. Not everyone around him could do the same.

During his high school tenure, through the human reach of the many groups with which he was involved, he'd known classmates who had overextended themselves to the point of exhaustion, who'd succumbed to the competitive pressures manufactured by the college admissions structure, or by their parents, or by their own internalized anxieties, or by all three operating in unison. He'd seen intelligent and talented and lively friends suddenly withdraw from the high-gravity chaos of feeling as though the outcome of high school would prove to be not just a crossroads but a reckoning, perhaps even a condemnation. He'd heard of self-harm.

His response to the trauma of those around him was always to text: *I can talk if you want to talk*. Not often but in certain indelible instances, these messages had led to hours-long conversations extending deep into the night, gentle back-and-forths exploring the invisibility of struggle. And he felt that he would return to such conversations often throughout his life, testaments to the simplest kind of help one person could give to another, which was to listen.

Owen

"Everyone's so kind of addicted to their drama," Owen said. "It's like this group of kids who don't have enough going on, so that they have to form this power group and try to get people fired arbitrarily, like for their own entertainment, or to pretend that they're movie stars." He was talking about a clique of classmates in the theater department who'd last year successfully engineered the replacement of a teacher, only because, Owen felt, they didn't personally like him. Owen had been appalled by the way a small, loud consortium of students and parents could wield undue influence in school decisions and a person's livelihood.

"You'll meet a lot of people like that in life, and they'll throw around a lot of drama," his father replied in his typical low and measured voice. "It doesn't mean they're bad people." The man chewed, considered what he'd just said, and added, "But sometimes, they are."

They sat opposite one another at a two-top in Petrossian, a small, austere restaurant on Robertson Boulevard well known for its caviar selection and over-the-counter gourmet fineries. Owen and his father ate here often for the standing Monday dinner date they'd kept since his brother left for college. The food was elegant, but they mainly came for the quietude and remove.

"What's maddening is that nothing I say—literally nothing—can change people like that. People who think that if what's happening doesn't fit exactly what they want to happen, then it's wrong and they have, like, a righteous mandate to correct it. If I try to be understanding and rational or whatever, it reinforces what they think. If I call them idiots, it reinforces it more."

His father thought for a moment; he never spoke off the cuff. He said, "We're all here because we're not all there." Owen had heard the expression a number of times before (the expression itself a fixture of show business as well as dive bar bathroom wall graffiti). His father tended to deploy it whenever his son's concern of the moment centered on the general frivolousness of the world and the people in it. He meant that everyone was a little bit unsound—and if that were not the case, then life itself would be fairly uninteresting and unfunny.

The friends who cycled constantly through their home called his father "Batman," because he was tall and imposing but didn't say much, and he always seemed to be lurking and watching from the shadowed corners of rooms. In truth, his father was just an introverted person whose humor and curiosity and very raw love came forth almost exclusively in the contained orbit of his family. Once, the question had brought Owen to weep openly onto his fancy dinner.

"So how is the whole Mom situation going for you?" his father asked. He always asked, even now, four years after her illness had become the crux of their lives, both testing and reinforcing the staidness of their family.

Now, Owen moved some braised leeks around his plate and replied with a variation of his usual answer: "You know, it still sucks."

Anyone aspiring to write half-hour television comedies for a living would probably be thrilled to follow the career path of Owen's father, who had served as a showrunner for the long-running and much-syndicated sitcom *Frasier* and proceeded to co-create *Modern Family*. His grandfather had written for multiple shows, including a famous episode of *The Mary Tyler Moore Show* entitled "Chuckles Bites the Dust," about the protagonist's processing of the death of a clown famous for the catchphrase "A little song, a little dance, a little seltzer in your pants." (Owen was ten years old when his grandfather passed away, and when his crushed father returned from the funeral he was waiting in the driveway with a bottle of seltzer tucked in his waistband as both an homage and a salve.) Before her illness, his mother acted, wrote comedy, performed voice-overs, and was the inspiration for the DC Comics villainess Harley Quinn. On any day of the week, Owen could turn on the television and likely locate something written by a family member—and in the case of *Modern Family*, often featuring sequences grafted from his own life, such as when he was rejected by a girl in middle school and when his mother accidentally shoplifted. What was never featured in these adaptations was his mother's being wheeled into cars en route to doctors while outfitted in pajamas and Ugg boots, or subjecting herself to therapy involving live beestings. As the comedic reach of his family extended far and was incredibly lucrative, it felt unfair to him that TV-watching Americans were privy to all the humor in his life and none of the sadness.

Yet he marveled at their sheer talent and the focus with which they applied it, especially his father and the way his intensive work habits were driven not by accolades and wealth, which he'd earned, but by the ancient challenge of constructing stories. By the nature of TV comedy sitcoms, these stories had to appear effortless, breezy, and organic. The task of building them was often the opposite: consuming, argumentative, obsessive. His father's creative focus was on family—particularly fathers and sons—and his work exemplified that baffling dichotomy by which the family unit was at once foundationally simple and cosmically complicated. His mastery over the comedic sphere of life and relationships and blood, as well as the methods by which he employed this hard-earned understanding as a parent, caused wonder in his son: the way he was able to articulate and interpret Owen's feelings with astonishing accuracy, genuine empathy, and—most of the time—a light touch. And in this way, too, Owen felt spoiled, a little undeserving, as if he'd been born to parents so intelligent and caring that they'd deprived him of the rite of stumbling clumsily and misunderstood through youth's travails, as most kids did, knocking into chairs and corners, gaining wisdom from poor choices.

He'd been raised to understand that he would always have everything he needed (a roof, food, good doctors, love) but not everything he wanted (cell phones, video games, the latest in vintage clothes, unconditional validation). He considered his parents' methods to be astute and healthy—a gift, even—and yet they didn't alter the truth that he'd been born into a situation in which very little that he ever achieved could feel to him—or be perceived by others—as earned. And so, in a macro sense, at age seventeen, he couldn't quite reconcile need and want and purpose and the currents between them when it came to the great scheme of living, let alone the standard expectation of college, which was why he was increasingly drawn toward the notion of fleeing that expectation and forgoing college entirely (in a recent conversation, a drama teacher he admired had mentioned acting conservatories, as opposed to college theater programs, as a useful entry point into the profession). The fact that such a notion was in itself a high privilege was not lost on him; he would never in his life be able to molt his privilege. But this half-considered path would at the very least be romantic and perhaps form a more expansive version of himself—even if it would confound and possibly anger everyone who cared about him, including the man finishing his dinner across the small table, nodding gravely at the fact that having a bedridden wife and mother really did suck.

Distilled to its simplest impetus, avoiding college also meant that Owen would not be the one to leave his parents in an empty nest.

Tio

It had happened before, when Tio was in preschool: his father's drinking. He vaguely remembered some shouting between his parents, some tense energy, and his father's spending a long stretch of time in the small pueblo in southern Mexico where both his parents had grown up before migrating. When his father returned to Los Angeles, the unpleasantness seemed to dissipate and their normal family rhythms resumed. At the time, Tio was spending his days at an apartment down the block where a lady provided neighborhood childcare, and also terrified him. From that time in his life, he remembered clearly hiding from her under stairways and blankets, but he'd retained only faint wisps of the psychic wounds his father carried.

Like many men in the neighborhood—like many men in America—his father enjoyed spending free afternoons with neighbors drinking beer and tequila, watching soccer games while arguing vehemently about wagers won and lost years ago. His father was a local handyman: neighbors would call him with a car problem, a refrigerator leak, a fritzy window-mounted air conditioner. He would go and fix it and negotiate for whatever they could pay. Accompanying him sometimes as a boy, Tio saw a kind of magic in the way the man could poke around a complicated assortment of wire within a metal box, diagnose the problem, and mend it with his hands and basic tools. Amid the heat and traffic and striving of South LA, his father had found a skill set that others depended on. The man had grown up in a rural pueblo with little in the way of machinery, come to Los Angeles, and taught himself a necessary craft; this was the narrative Tio had formed, admired, and desired to emulate.

As Tio progressed through his freshman year and his academic acumen improved along with his future college prospects, he began thinking that he could be an engineer. The aspiration was partly due to the school's robotics class, which he'd enjoyed, and the fact that he couldn't write well enough in English to consider a humanities-related pathway. But it was also entangled with his father.

"You fix things, you build things," he blurted one evening. "If I become an engineer, I'd be doing, like, the same thing, only bigger."

His father, for whatever reason, was not enthused. He seemed a bit insulted by Tio's emphasis on the comparative word *bigger*. The man seemed generally put off by all the clamor Tio had been making about his rising test scores, these other smart kids he knew at school, a four-year college. The state of being excited about school, novel to Tio, seemed to disappoint his father. For most any young man, a father's disappointment could be para- lyzing. For Tio, the way it stemmed from his own achievement and improving prospects was confounding. He seemed to have no recourse but to do what his father told him: be quiet and internalize this bizarre duality.

At this point, he was fifteen, a smart-ass, excited by his progress through freshman year and the vision of carrying it on into tenth grade. He'd initiated the beginnings of a romantic relationship with another freshman (he thought this girl had been "mad-dogging" him in math class with a cold stare until he realized this was just her resting facial expression). His muscles were filling out as his limbs elongated. He was surrounded by bright new friends. He felt as if he was banking potential daily, and then some valve ruptured in his father's soul.

He would sit alone at the kitchen table in the family's home on Juniper Street, draining a bottle or more of hard alcohol until his children came home from school. He'd always been critical or at least sardonic regarding his children's activities in a way they could interpret as rote: *Here's our dear old dad, grumbling about whatever again.* When amplified by liquor, his scorn was overpowering. Like Tio, his father was hyperactive, and when he wasn't working—which he wasn't while drunk—he spent much of his time incessantly cleaning their home. While he wiped counters and flipped pillows, he demeaned his children. Whatever he was angry about, whatever conception had formed in his mind during the preceding hours to be released in slurred Spanish, it seemed to have more to do with his reality than theirs. He told them they were lazy and they leeched all the family's resources, that they accomplished nothing each day, that they would never amount to anything and thus would always live at home, and so this rage within him would always exist and they would always be the cause of it.

Tio was aware that all of these insults were nonsensical, and that if a fellow skater at the park or even a teacher at school said any of it to him, he would be unaffected. He'd witnessed plenty of neighborhood drunkards stumbling around in the middle of the day railing against illusory slights. He and his friends would laugh and shake their heads—"Imagine being that guy." Now his father had become that guy, shuffling to and from the store for housecleaning supplies and booze. Tio had always figured that people drank in order to feel happy—the men in the garages, the women on the porches, the schoolkids at parties. Maybe it wasn't healthy or smart, and the vice often didn't look good or end well, but its purpose was ostensibly to infuse more pleasure into a given moment. His father seemed to drink specifically to pool all his unhappiness and regret together and project them outward in a futile exorcism. Tio's older sister, a junior at APB, began spending nights at friends' homes and seemed more content to remove herself from the situation than to engage in it. Through the eyes of his two younger sisters, nine and eleven, he saw the damage inflicted by a parent willfully becoming the worst version of himself. They grew quiet and restrained. Tio had friends who would have happily let him crash, but he stayed home. He did so not to protect his sisters, since their father's cruelty seemed relegated only to words, aimed mostly at Tio and his mother, but rather to distract them, play games, tell stories, lend their perceptions of their world at least an illusion of stability. In a silent understanding with his mother—who supported the family with a secretarial job and thus was funding the intoxication—this was his role, while hers was to deflect and endure and try to coax the man to sleep on the early side. His parents had been together since they were preteens. They were raising four children. This phase had happened before, and it had passed within a few months, and so it would again.

But it didn't, carrying on through the summer and into Tio's sophomore year, this drunkenness saturating their four-room living space as he rarely saw his older sister and grew weary of managing his younger sisters. Their home was spotless; their lives were miserable.

"It's not right, Ma, the things he says to you, things he says to me. He shouldn't be here."

"He's just being *machista* right now. He's had a difficult life. He's lost many people."

The two things that might have helped Tio find solace or simply focus on work were friendship and support resources at school, which were both abundant. But Tio mentioned nothing about home, neither to classmates nor counselors. He'd built a reputation for having overcome poor preparation to succeed at school, and for being easygoing, and funny, and a resolver of conflict. He'd become a rising leader at Ánimo Pat Brown. Confiding his home instability and his deteriorating facility to absorb it, in his estimation, would be admitting he was unequipped to handle something. The vulnerability required for such an admission was akin to a rescission of manhood.

In the meantime, Tio realized the fault in the admiring frame in which he'd always placed his father; he realized that the reason his father worked locally and off the books for dollars an hour was because he couldn't hold a steady job, because he was a drunk.

A full school year passed like this: coming home each evening and waiting for the yelling to expend itself and become snoring—gross, reverberant snoring—and then he would do what homework he could before, in the quiet moments lying in bed hours after his father had passed out, reviewing in his mind the words and gestures of that evening and all the others. In these moments, it would occur to him just how fucked up his reality had become; it would occur to him that, though these nightly patterns had become his normal, they were not in fact normal, which meant that he was not normal, which in turn meant that no matter how authentically he portrayed normality at school, he was just an imposter. This newly forming vision of himself was a distortion, but to him it was a truth. No matter how many tit-for-tat jokes he exchanged with Luis or how many gifts he gave his girlfriend or how many hours he devoted to assignments, that truth held fast inside him. And so those jokes, gifts, and hours deteriorated in value, and they gradually ceased. His father's accumulating incantations regarding the absence of promise in Tio's future, his spat words and squinted, grim eyes, were ten months of his life.

His grades fell and his friendships hollowed. He grew so accustomed to the put-downs and the rage, so distant from the person emitting them, that he could sit through each episode the way he could sit through a class: not listening, eyeing the clock, awaiting dismissal. B's appeared on transcripts, then C's, then a few D's. At first, during the fall of sophomore year, he was saddened to be feeling like a stupid-ass dummy again. As the year passed by, disappointment followed its natural course toward apathy, which was far more damaging. Maybe his father's hopelessness became a fixed part of him; maybe it was just very basic chemistry, a kind of osmosis of words into consciousness. In guidance class—a period of the day devoted to organizing and taking stock of what academic areas might merit more focus—the declining numbers manifested in gentle pep talks from teachers to bring the grades up, put in an extra few minutes of work each night, no big deal, small regressions were not uncommon. Tio would nod plaintively. "Yeah, I know, I gotta do that, I'll do the work."

The moments when he felt most authentically himself, most present within his own spirit, occurred at the skate parks of South Los Angeles. He wasn't a skilled skater at that time and for years had used his long penny board mainly for transportation. But he'd made an assortment of friends at the parks, and either with them or alone he spent any free hours working on aerial tricks, the dangerous variety in which the most risk drew the most respect. To master a skate trick, even a basic one, was to commit oneself to colliding with asphalt, from unnatural angles and from tall heights, repeatedly, dozens of times, while onlookers laughed. As Tio graduated from ollies to bench tricks to ramps to stairs, he bruised his bones, tore his skin, wrenched his joints, embarrassed himself. He did so with masochism and determination. And when he would limp home on weekend evenings to clean his wounds with dish soap, the burning sensation—if sufficiently excruciating—would override the man drinking in the next room, render him and his toxins irrelevant. Skating was above all contingent on the now, the precise instant in time and space. These instants were his young soul's only current nourishment. At new parks and outdoor stairways, Tio played a game where he would show up and start purposefully tripping on his ollies, the most basic jump. Guys nearby would jeer and curse him out and bully him away from the ramps. "You don't belong here, bro, you're taking up space." They sometimes sounded like his father. And then Tio would linger, threading his way around the obstacles, grinning, and then he'd casually hit a complicated trick, and another, board spinning beneath his feet, wheels landing in sync. The guys who moments before had been intent on physically injuring him for incompetence would laugh along with him, admiring the hustle, and tell him that he was good at this, that he belonged here. Somehow, the preplanned theatrics always made him feel like a man—like he could control how others perceived him.

On an unusually quiet evening in early April of sophomore year, his father stared out the street-side window through glassy eyes. Noise from outside entered the apartment, some argument between men, not uncommon. Tio had come home from the skate park shortly before and was thinking about going to his girlfriend's. He was texting with her when he heard his father's footsteps leaving the apartment and his mother pleading with him to come back. Tio watched through the window as his father approached the two men on the sidewalk up Juniper, walking with hands clenched. He told them to stop bothering the neighborhood and fuck off. These were men he did not know, so his maladroit attempt to quell the conflict exacerbated it, and the three men began fighting one another in a clumsy display of middle-aged pugnacity. Tio's mother called 911, figuring that whatever trouble this call might lead to was better than her husband's being injured or worse. A police cruiser rolled up with lights and sirens in a rare example of the term *quick response*. More cars and lights followed. Guns were drawn and threats were made, and then his father was on the ground, facedown, hands chained behind him. Tio went down to the street, and he heard something strange and penetrating: the sound of a grown man weeping. It was his father, bawling tears onto the asphalt, moaning to no one about how he was going to jail and he wouldn't see his family because his family would never visit him there. Beneath all the lights, the neighbors gathering to watch, the men proclaiming their innocence, the police conferring— the low-grade, semiorganized turmoil that had taken hold of the street—Tio's world was reduced to that sole image of his father's grief and regret. And Tio thought, *Shit, you're a stupid ass, crying when you directly caused all of this.* And he thought further, *We're going to have to separate the family because of you.* And he felt very much like a boy.

Over the rest of the summer, as the systematic component of the situation found closure with fines, his father remained in a state of contrition. Tio's aunt—his mother's sister—gave the family money for a plane ticket to send his father to their home in Mexico, where there would be people to watch him and help fix him. During the months he was away, the quietude that characterized their apartment became a vital resource that allowed him to reinstitute not just the habits but the pride he'd gained freshman year. The first semester of his junior year, he brought home three A's and two B's. His father returned sober. He resumed his below-board business fixing things locally. He continued to question the value of school, in a gentler way. He drank a lot of coffee.

Chapter 4

OCTOBER 4–OCTOBER 15

*If the recommendations are carried out and the Constitu-
tion amended as indicated, California's tripartite system of
public higher education, long admired by other states, will
be saved from destruction by unbridled competition. If these
actions now recommended are taken, California will again
pioneer in the field of higher education, its system a model
of co-operation for the whole nation.*

—*A Master Plan for Higher
Education in California*, Preface

Carlos, Tio, Luis, Byron

"I'm going to university anyway," Tio was saying defeatedly. "I got
all A's last year. I have A's now in AP Calc and AP Chem. Somewhere will accept me. There's no logical reason to keep working
my ass off."

"APs haven't gotten hard yet, though," Carlos warned. They
were in the backseat of Luis's car, driving aimlessly on surface
streets, Yeezy playing over the fuzzy speakers. Byron rode shotgun,
squinting out into the sun's glare through his wide-rimmed glasses.
They passed taquerias and markets and gated lots piled with used
tires. A packed city bus ahead kept stopping to unload and load

frowning people; LA city buses drew frowns across seemingly all cultures. They did this sometimes, just drove, gazing at their world, destinationless. The options by which to fill vacant hours in South LA were limited to one of two malls, mini golf, fast food, and video games. Tio was muttering about the upcoming SAT retakes. He needed to raise his scores from last year considerably if he was to think about top UC and private schools.

"My sister got a twelve hundred on her SATs. She got a bunch of C's. And she still got into UC Riverside. Fucking Riverside, that's a garbage school. Anyone who wants to go can go there. That'll be me." He was consoling himself, kind of.

"Why do you think I don't do shit?" Luis said from the driver's seat. "Why do you think I don't even go to school if I don't feel like it?" Luis enjoyed projecting an image of himself as a lazy underachiever. And while he might have been lazy, he was still taking four APs like Carlos. Over the course of their high school years, he'd refined the skill of turning C's into B's and even A's in the final weeks of any given semester.

Carlos said, "To do better than Riverside, particularly in engineering, man—you need not just the SATs but to keep all your other grades up. They still look at that shit."

"Engineering—you're going against all those Asians," Byron added. "Counselors won't say that, but it's true."

"Where the hell are we even going, Luis?" Tio asked. They were on a somewhat barren stretch of Firestone Boulevard east of school.

"We're going for some nuggets." He was referring to the McDonald's a mile or so ahead.

"Shit, I've got no money," Carlos said.

"Me, neither," Tio said.

"I'll spot you—my mom just gave me some yesterday. Where the hell is Victor when you need him? He always has money." Victor's parents owned the carnival business where they'd spent Labor Day.

"Why do you think he always has money?" Tio said. "He's fucking working." Then: "Is it even worth it to try to be an engineer? The Asians are good as fuck." He was joking, yet not.

"It depends," said Carlos. "Is it what you really want to do?"

"I guess so."

"Then it's worth it."

"Look at those cholos." Luis nodded toward three Latino guys in their twenties shuffling across the street in front of them. They had earrings and wore sleeveless shirts to bare elaborate tattoos across their arms and necks. "Say something to them, Byron," Luis prompted.

Byron was typically a quiet person who enjoyed being a part of this friend group without participating too much in the antics therein. But just like in middle school, where he would remain seemingly invisible for days until suddenly Tio and Carlos would see him in the center of a fistfight, Byron was disposed toward spontaneous, inexplicable outbursts of verbal hostility—as now, when he shouted out the window, "Fuck you!"

The men in the street looked up, more confused than upset, wondering who had said the words and to whom the words had been directed.

"What the fuck what the fuck?" Tio and Carlos hunched down, laughing.

"Why did you say that?" Luis yelled while rolling up all the windows and waiting anxiously for the light to turn green—also laughing.

"You told me to say something!" Byron said. He had a large head with thick hair on his tall, thin frame. When feeling indignant, his face looked like that of a boy on the body of a man.

The men glared through the windshield of the car at the four obnoxious kids in their navy blue collared shirts laughing and squirming. They shook their heads, saw that their WALK sign was flashing red, and hustled on to the corner of the intersection. Upon the green light, Luis accelerated. The others checked behind them and watched the men resume their days.

"Stupid shit!" Luis said. "You could have got us all lit up."

"Guess we're not going to McDonald's," was all Byron said.

"Hell no. Probably where the cholos are headed."

Though mystified by his friend, Tio was at least glad not to be talking of SATs and decisions and the general determination of his future. As Luis began to drop them off at their various homes, all they talked about was Byron's stupidity. The topic would no doubt comprise the bulk of conversation tomorrow, and the day after, and the day after that. As the story was retold, its components would morph and shift. The men would become taller and more muscular, and they would be carrying guns in their belts, and they'd rush the car with threats and obscenities and vows to hunt the boys down with their gang, and the boys would just narrowly escape with their lives. Crafting stories to be more interesting made the days more interesting.

The days sorely needed some interest. By this point, though the school year was still depressingly young, Ms. Reyes had begun visiting classrooms, her talk and commands holding grave stakes. Ms. Reyes was the school's lone college counselor, and her task in October was to begin laying out fall admissions deadlines. There were University of California requirements, Cal State requirements, community college requirements, and private school requirements. There were SATs and ACTs. There were common applications and early-action applications and early-decision applications. There were teacher recommendations and parent financial information and personal essay drafts. There were forms for federal financial aid, state financial aid, institutional financial aid, dozens of grants and scholarships, dozens more loan options, each applicable to different programs and choices of major. There were majors to choose.

There was the task of expressing who they were, in their cores, in six hundred words or less. And there was the quandary they all faced in some way: college admissions was the most important process of their respective lives thus far, and also the one they had the least control over. No level of elegance in a personal essay could change that C in biology junior year, or that freshman-year suspension for a meaningless fistfight, or that moment caught with a bud of weed in a backpack: certain marks had been locked in years earlier, when they'd truly been kids. In Tio's case, his sophomore year spent contending with his father had left a stark and irreparable crater on his transcripts.

Classmates soothed themselves by categorizing these demands as far-off abstractions or—worse—"busy work," that loathsome and ignorable bane of high school life. But the unignorable reality was that at Ánimo Pat Brown, 150 low-income high school students were vying to become 150 first- or second-generation college students. Ms. Reyes's annual task (she'd served in this capacity since the school's inception) was to package the national immigrant ethos, the titanic American dream, in the context of admissions forms that were as dry and endless as the high deserts northeast of the city.

The UC

Even with their massive thought and preparation, their engagement with the imminent college admissions process, the forms and essays and numbers and conversations—the sheer volume of brain space apportioned to college and all its layers of significance—there was no way to comprehend the vastness of the apparatus drawing them in: higher education in America. The students had their transcripts, their test scores, their essay ideas, their teacher recommendations. The college systems, both public and private, had generations of evolution and adaptation, budgets in which eleven-figure numbers were unremarkable entries, application pools that spanned continents, social and demographic and moral demands that were as complicated as history itself and ever changing, and a metaphorical assignation to represent nothing less than America's standing in the world as it was and as it would become. The relationship between applicants, with their individual experiences, and institutions, with their mighty mantles, was complex and nearly impenetrable, even as college in its essence was just a bridge, a simply conceived structure that existed to shepherd one over the obstacles separating two points: childhood and adulthood.

California was the most populous state in America, the most diverse, with the largest economy. Most of the country's technology was grown there, as well as most of its fruit and vegetables. The state was home to the largest number of very rich, and the largest number of homeless. In the mythos of literature and film, the place was bound—not always in a positive way—to the American dream. Open space, prosperity, progressive attitudes, pleasing climate: all were core to the land's promises, as were high taxes, bad air quality, tremendous disparity, and housing shortages. Or maybe tens of millions of people had just blithely wandered west until they'd struck the ocean. Regardless, for the state to function as an entity, a large portion of those people had to go to college, and that mandate was how, between 1860 and now, a single preparatory school in Berkeley had grown into 10 University of California campuses with almost 200,000 undergrads, 23 Cal State schools with almost 500,000 students, and 114 community colleges with 2.1 million students. This expansion was slow, messy, and contentious, as any such grand allotment of space, opportunity, and money was bound to be.

A crucial moment in this history occurred in 1960, when then governor Pat Brown—the namesake of Ánimo Pat Brown Charter

High School, whose significance in state history was barely thought of by students there—signed into law the progressive Master Plan for Higher Education, intended to give some stability of purpose and function to the increasingly sprawling enterprise by jointly reaffirming tuition-free college for all Californian students and by bringing the three systems under the same legislative governance while delineating specific roles for each. The term *tuition-free* was important in that it did not encompass "educational fees," which were relied upon for revenue, particularly after a 1978 proposition, passed during a moment of intense antitax, small-government sentiment, that greatly reduced real estate contributions to the public system (not until 2010 did the Board of Regents finally, officially begin applying the word *tuition* to these fees). Yet by any metric, the 1960 plan and the system as a whole fulfilled its mission to make some form of college education accessible to California high school students from all tiers of the broadening socioeconomic spectrum, from the wealthy and middle-class and poor, from white and black and Asian and Latino and Native American, from first-generation students and storied legacy families. Individuals benefited from increased prospects, the state benefited from a more educated tax base, the institutions benefited from expansion and renown in becoming what many statistics indicated and many people considered the leading public education system in the country. Over the latter half of the twentieth century, schools like Berkeley drew from an ever-increasing pool of high-performing students and professors and racked up Nobel Prizes to rival the Ivies while new campuses were added in underserved cities like Merced and Riverside. The story of the University of California was a positive one, but not without its murky areas and subsequent deep conflict. As ever, the primary driver of such conflict was money. As ever, money remained an emblem for disparities between race and class. The system was well funded, and so it became very strong. As it became strong, more people sought entry. As more sought entry, the system became very expensive. As it became very expensive, the powers that be grew more stringent regarding who had the right to go. Throughout, the population of California—particularly the lower-class population—grew rapidly.

Among families for whom paying roughly $20,000 per year for college was untenable, who tended to be lower-class and non-white, the calculations and sacrifices and quests for financial aid could be traumatic if not ruinous, while placement in more afford-able Cal State schools or free community colleges felt emotionally like second-tier status. At the same time, UC tuitions made the schools—particularly the top-tier schools like Berkeley—seem like an appealing, cost-saving alternative to the soaring inflation of private schools for families who could pay them; these families tended to be upper-middle-class and white. The universities themselves needed both groups, the former to fulfill its underly-ing progressive mission, the latter to afford it while also lending the coveted repute of being "selective." When limited to Califor-nians, the math and the ethics seemed to have a certain sustainable balance, if a clumsy one. Out-of-state and international applicants further complicated the admissions process with the fact that they paid significantly higher tuitions, creating much-needed windfalls for the system while, year by year, they took up significantly more space; they subsidized the placements of first-generation students while competing with them for admits in the system as a whole, in the individual schools, and in the majors within each school (a caveat held that a certain number of these students would become future taxpaying Californians contributing to the system's sustain-ability). Of UC undergrads in 2016, 18 percent hailed from outside the state, while just over 40 percent were first-generation. Latinos represented 39 percent of California's population and 54 percent of its public high school students, yet 31 percent of undergraduates at

UC Irvine, 24 percent at UC Santa Barbara, 21 percent at UCLA, and 13 percent at Berkeley. At UC Riverside and most Cal State campuses, Latinos represented around 40 percent of undergraduates, and they made for the overwhelming majority in the state's community colleges. All of these numbers seemed to reflect the complicated ethos and dichotomy of California, and of America.

No means existed for politicians, college administrators, student advocates, or students themselves to explain the true financial and demographic complexity of such a system, nor the roles that private universities filled within the apparatus, nor the moral obligations associated with all the many angles of discourse. High school seniors in the midst of applying would have to spend many long hours that they didn't have in order to gain any kind of perspective on its enormity and consequence. Having such a perspective probably would have frightened most of them and paralyzed some. More healthy to just talk about what they knew, with people they knew, focus on the tiresome minutiae, and remember always that their eventual acceptance or wait-listing or rejection from the schools they most desired to attend involved matters far beyond their own merits or means. Remembering such a cold reality was easy, and they were constantly reminded. Accepting reality, grappling with it, submitting to it, was much harder and, for some, corrosive.

Carlos

The UCLA campus was sprawling and green and bright. Charming brick classroom buildings stood beneath massive, modern science and research facilities. Carlos remained there after the school bus left for South LA. He'd spent the day at a conference for Minds Matter, a prestigious nonprofit college-readiness program for low-income students that had consumed his Saturdays for three years. Now he wandered around, observing the little pockets of college life. He found a tray of free sandwiches under a sorority recruitment tent and asked if he could have one, and the girls told him to take as many as he wanted. He pocketed three. Later, he passed a flyer advertising a reading by a poet whose name he recognized, and he found the lecture hall and sat in the back to listen. Afterward, in the evening, he took the city bus home, which required three changes and almost three hours, but he finished all his homework along the way.

Amid the emerging fretfulness of the college application process at APB, Carlos was further ahead and far apart from his peers because he was vying for a QuestBridge scholarship, the same program that had landed his brother at Yale two years earlier. QuestBridge offered low-income students full scholarships to one of forty universities in the country, Ivies and other schools of renown among them. The program was the most competitive contest he had ever entered. At APB, no matter how modest he was or how sheepishly he resisted being *that guy*, he lived on the pedestal fashioned for the elite. His grades and scores and leadership accolades placed him there. But he knew that poor kids with his scores and his achievements—as well as merits far surpassing his—were in schools all across America, crouched over desks, filling out applications to programs like QuestBridge, investing hours into the smallest details, the commas and periods and conjunctions that told their stories, that captured their promise. He was, sadly, pitted against them all.

The format of the program had applicants list their top college choices in ranked order. If Carlos were to be offered a scholarship—nothing close to a given—QuestBridge would match him with a school on his list, but not necessarily one among his top choices. Carlos had chosen MIT, Yale, and Princeton. He clicked these entries with the knowledge that tens of thousands of people his age in the world would be clicking the same with like determination. Less than one in ten of them would fulfill that determination. Of those, around 30 percent would be legacies.

The allure of the Ivy League (of which MIT was not a member, but inhabited its own rare echelon) had a fantastical nature even as modern research undermined the title's assurance of financial success and business connections and all the other accoutrements. Carlos was familiar with that research. In the hypothetical scenario that he might gain the opportunity to attend one of the eight Ivy schools, as his brother did, he would be traveling three thousand miles away from his parents and really anyone he'd ever known. He'd share a small room with one or more people whose experiences would likely be as foreign to him as his would be to them. Very few classmates would look like him. Administrators preaching diversity and acceptance would overlook or attempt to intellectualize daily instances of racism. Whether his DACA application was approved or not in the next year, he'd still be living in a country in which half the population firmly, loudly believed his "home" was Mexico—a place he'd never been allowed to visit. Success would make him something of a public figure locally, exposing his undocumented parents by association. He would be cast not only as his family's, school's, and neighborhood's success story but as society's as well: *See, this is what happens when you give a poor minority kid an opportunity.* It was a disingenuous narrative propelled mostly by the donor class, and one in which he had little interest in participating, but also little choice. As a scholarship student, he'd be expected to act grateful all the time, which was exhausting. A not negligible number of people sharing his financial background grew depressed and insecure in these places and, even if they graduated and proceeded onward to tremendous careers, were trailed by tattered strands of isolation.

Deeply aware of all these stressors, Carlos quietly persisted in the pursuit. He did so because the recognition paid dividends to his high school and teachers, because as a little brother he wanted to do what his big brother had done, because it would cast the middle finger to a lot of white people who hired brown people to clean their houses and watch their kids but weren't keen on their living in the same neighborhoods or attending the same schools. But above all, he did so because admission to an Ivy League school would further a chronicle that began seventeen years ago with a man and a woman in their early twenties crouched in a hot, dusty truck along with dozens of other strangers, not knowing much about the land that lay ahead, not even understanding its language, and yet certain that this land contained a greater opportunity for the two young boys they clutched in their arms than that which lay behind.

He had a 1400 on his SATs, good for the ninety-second percentile in the country but well below the average twenty-fifth percentile of current Ivy League students; he would take the test again in the early fall to try to raise the numbers into the high-1400s realm. He had a 4.6 GPA. He had a long résumé that included mock trial, student council, Minds Matter, Students Run LA, an internship at the Natural History Museum, and the Brown academic camp. He would have fawning recommendations from inside and outside the school. He had a brother at Yale. He had a moving personal story on which to center his essays and interviews. Though he had no citizenship, he figured that he had as good a chance as any, perhaps better than a few. Yet, he had a statistically high chance of failing at this. He'd never really failed at anything before.

People in Carlos's orbit, both peers and adults, often marveled at the high performance of him and his brother, two sons of undocumented, non-English-speaking delivery workers barely affording a backyard shack in South LA. The veneration they seemed to inspire made Carlos uncomfortable, sometimes outright annoyed. People wanted to know what the family secret was, as if they'd stumbled upon some potion that they were now withholding from others in order to stay ahead, akin to the way that wealthy families paid thousands of dollars for specialized test-prep courses and even personalized college consultants. In response, Carlos could have pointed to almost any parenting book or article regarding fundamental child psychology and habits. His parents read to them and encouraged them to read. They were present without being overbearing. They gave their children time for unstructured play. They emphasized good manners and gratitude. The house rules they instilled—clean rooms, home by nightfall, etc.—made rational sense rather than seeming arbitrarily authoritarian. They let them fail at things and sort through the aftermath independently. They made sure their sons felt comfortable asking for help. They challenged without competing. They set the expectation of good results without qualifying it with rewards and punishment. They never made their kids feel more special or deserving than anyone else they knew. They had family dinners together most every night. During these dinners, they tried to talk about ideas rather than gossip about people. They didn't complain about their money or circumstances. They didn't argue beyond marital bickering of the comic variety. They loved one another.

The only differentiating dynamic he could point to outright had to do with a pattern he observed in many low-income families around him, particularly in immigrant families, whereby achievements in school were pursued on behalf of, or in the name of, the parents; consciously or perhaps more often unconsciously, the hours spent reading and working through problem sets could feel devoted above all else to repaying the arduous jobs undertaken and financial sacrifices made by the elders: the next generation fulfilling the hopes of the last. Carlos's parents made it clear to their children—early, redundantly, sometimes exhaustively—that whatever they accomplished in school, they would accomplish it only for themselves. They'd never been allowed to apologize for a poor grade, but rather it was presumed they would improve out of disappointment in themselves. They'd never been permitted to gloat over a good grade, because they were expected to bring those home. When Carlos's brother had switched his college major from engineering to computer graphics—and had garnered some criticism from others for the perceived lesser prestige and prospects—their parents had remained encouraging. The children in this family owed their parents nothing except their own personal fulfillment. Otherwise, Carlos and Jose had been raised like normal American kids, even though they weren't considered American.

Owen, Bennett

The selection for Beverly's fall drama production, *Pericles, Prince of Tyre*, was certainly one of the Bard's lesser works—possibly not even written by him alone. In addition to its semi-low literary stature, a decision had been made, not by Owen, to set the play in outer space. The drama teacher was inordinately excited about the "high concept," overseeing rehearsals with her torso bent forward over her knees, mouthing lines to herself as they were spoken, taut. She was an older, tenured teacher, but this was her first year heading the department. The drama program had in many ways salvaged Owen's high school experience after his freshman-year struggles. The immersion of a production and the nervousness of performing, the earnest investment of a few dozen people into a single endeavor, had provided a reprieve from his tendency to overanalyze himself and overthink the antics of others. Now, after working his way up the hierarchy, through set work and minor roles, his penultimate theater production in high school was to be a mash-up of Shakespeare and *Star Trek*.

"Before thee stands this fair Hesperides, with golden fruit, but dangerous to be touch'd, for death-like dragons here affright thee hard." Owen had been cast as Antiochus, the murderous king engaged in a secret, incestuous relationship with his daughter that would incite the play's events. Owen's girlfriend—whom he'd been dating since the previous spring—was subsequently cast as Hesperides, the daughter, a decision meant to send some kind of cute wink toward the audience, which was in truth just awkward. "Her face, like heaven, enticeth thee to view her countless glory, which desert must gain—" He burst out laughing, not a situational kind of laugh but an autoresponse to thinking forward to opening night and how humiliating it would be to attempt these lines in front of the school, presumably with authority, while wearing a space suit. That he had worked very hard for years to land a central role, and that he would devote sixty or seventy hours of his time over the coming fall to this camp, alongside a girl he'd been thinking he might be in love with, elevated the ridiculousness.

"We're going to own this scene," he assured his girlfriend with wide glowing eyes facetiously imitating the teacher's enthusiasm. "Just possibly not our dignity."

He wondered if life would always seem to be so circumscribed by contradictions, or if it was just teenaged life, or if it was just his own life. He took theater so seriously that he typically vomited before performances of minor roles, but the role he had now was ludicrous. His mother's energy was bright and abundant, but she was bedridden. He loved his parents deeply but challenged them constantly. College was paramount in American life, but he didn't as yet see the point of it. He was thrilled to have a girlfriend he cared for, but in six months they'd presumably be leaving for different places. The structure of high school asked him to master five or six subjects of questionable utility, while those that truly interested him were on the fringes of the curriculum, if available at all. Los Angeles held thousands of potential adventures and hundreds of global cultures, but to leave his basement was a challenge. The most attractive girls always seemed drawn toward the biggest assholes. He wished he could play the piano, but he'd quit lessons in second grade because they were boring. He was factually a young man but in so many ways still treated as a child. He liked to believe that his ongoing ruminations regarding privilege and place were part of some larger, necessary American struggle with identity, but he was quite possibly just a basket case with too much idle time to think. The one steadying constant seemed to be that existence was absurd. And another contradiction lay in the degree to which Owen absolutely relished the absurd.

The previous summer, on a lark with his best and oldest friend, Bennett, he'd entered a citywide high school news broadcast competition using the satirical news program they produced and anchored for the Beverly Hills media channel. Essentially, they used their weekly hour to make lighthearted jokes about school. Because no other schools in Los Angeles made entries that year, the duo won by default and passed automatically on to the statewide contest in San Diego. Even still, only a few schools managed to send teams, and so, somehow, their little confection of a commentary show landed them in Louisville, Kentucky, for the national championship. For reasons they would never comprehend, the high school booked them hotel rooms at a casino an hour away from Louisville, a graceless hunk of a building planted in a rural area that seemed mostly populated by addicts of various stripes, prostitutes, and men who, if they weren't actual mobsters, certainly presented themselves as such. The assignment for the competition was to film and produce a two-minute segment related to the recent shooting massacre in Orlando that had killed fifty people at a gay nightclub. Since there existed no way to satirize such a ghastly American moment, and they'd never created earnest content before, they spent two days driving around the backwoods of Kentucky and ultimately chanced upon a small country town's pawnshop, where guns were sold, and spent three hours interviewing the incredibly interesting, loquacious, perhaps even profound shop owner about his strong passions for guns and other weaponry. They stayed up all night to cut together a two-minute news story and one-minute ad spot (featuring Owen standing within a soundproof audio booth that they'd happened upon, while an army general from a nearby recruitment stand, who'd been game to help them out, screamed at him from outside the glass). They lost the contest badly. And if the weekend hadn't fit the precise definition of absurd, the time had certainly been strange and unforgettable—as well as emblematic of the offbeat path they'd forged through school.

Most of their decade's worth of experiences together were not particularly memorable. He and Bennett had been friends—the very best of friends—since elementary school, at an LAUSD school down the street from Owen's home. Bennett was the lone child of a single mother who'd conceived him via an anonymous sperm bank donor. Daily and endlessly, wherever they were, they talked to one another in total comfort, most of the time volleying jokes and nonsense, now and again debating larger philosophical questions, and—rarely but indelibly—exploring the essence of their lives: Owen's mother's pain; Bennett's mode of fatherlessness; all of it. Often, when they hung up the phone after talking in the evening, they would exchange the words *I love you*, earnestly, platonically. (Junior year, Bennett was hanging out with a female friend when a female friend of hers came over and, right in front of him, began trying on shirts she'd just bought; when Bennett awkwardly, chivalrously began staring at the ground instead of at her topless chest, the girl noticed him squirming and exclaimed, "Wait, you're *not gay?*" Bennett replied, "No. Why would you think I was gay?" She said, "I assumed you and Owen have been fucking for years!" For some reason, she shoved him quite hard, and once he regained his balance he managed only to laugh uncomfortably.)

Before graduating from middle school and heading to Beverly, they'd been warned by older influences that high school had a way of fracturing even the deepest of friendships, that existing cliques would siphon off friends from groups, that people by nature outgrew one another. But Beverly had only strengthened the bond between Owen and Bennett, perhaps because their relationship was based on storytelling, and storytelling was rooted in observation, and Beverly Hills High School provided infinite material to observe. The running narrative between them—the narrative of their high school years—was constant and hilarious and perfectly balanced by Owen's tendency to overanalyze and Bennett's comedic command of the surface of things.

"I don't go to school to learn," Bennett was fond of saying. "I go to school to *turn stuff in*." His general philosophy pertaining to high school was cynical and kind of callous, and it was also a key element of the particular advantage he had when it came to remaining untouched by teenaged angst: unlike Owen, Bennett knew exactly what he wanted to do in his life. He wanted to go to New York University's Tisch School of the Arts, and he wanted to be a writer of films and television. His entire approach to high school revolved around that endpoint. He'd figured out precisely what grades he'd need in every class he would take over four years, and by and large he'd attained them. Even as he regretted that his goals were not more contrary to the culture he'd grown up in—his mother was an international news producer—Bennett was unwavering in his intentions and undistracted in his pursuit. Meanwhile, Owen wavered all the time; he was distracted all the time; he lacked a defined intention to pursue.

As his senior classmates prepared for the hypercompetitive morass of college admissions, and as the looming nature of the process began to coat much of what anyone talked about, Owen continued to suspect that he might be better off avoiding entirely what, for those of his circumstances, was more or less an American entitlement. He clung instead to small, swiftly passing moments such as the one he was in after the *Pericles* rehearsal, walking with

Bennett toward his apartment by Roxbury Park, kicking a tennis ball along the sidewalk, talking about the presidential election and Twitter in the media.

"The commentators keep calling tweets 'statements,' like it's something people think through," Bennett said. "A tweet isn't a thought. It's a hundred and forty fucking letters."

"A tweet is like a half thought—if that," Owen agreed. "It's like Larry King in that segment he used to do at the end of an episode saying stuff like, 'Marmalade is sweet.' And entire news cycles are based on them. And people actually pay attention and take Twitter seriously—that's what is, like, diabolical about it."

The walk, the conversation, and the atmosphere around them resembled pretty much every afternoon since fifth grade. But now these elements all felt ephemeral, moving forward too quickly for Owen's mind to process, let alone keep pace with. He was caught in a weird flux of missing moments—most of them void of much import but filled with old comfort—that hadn't even happened yet. He was missing them because he was fearful, sometimes terrified, of the blank space that spread beyond.

Chapter 5

If you want to get a scholarship thing you have to turn it in yesterday.

—*Luis*

Carlos, Tio, Luis, Byron

"You got all these scholarships for people like us, how come every Mexican in America isn't at Harvard?" Tio asked aloud.

"If Burger King and McDonald's both just gave me back all the money I've spent there, I'm good," Luis said.

They were referring to the multiple-page handout they'd been given listing scholarship opportunities and the fact that apparently every brand, corporation, foundation, bank, famous person, and rich person in America had a scholarship named after them intended for "underrepresented groups." Some were geared toward African Americans, Latinos, women, Asian Americans, or Jewish people. Some highlighted standout work in community service, social justice, poetry, science, leadership, robotics. Some were merit based, need based, competition based. Some were for $500, $1,000, $10,000, $50,000, $100,000. These were all separate from Sallie Mae, FAFSA (Free Application for Federal Student Aid) grants, Cal Grants, and financial aid from institutions, which could be labyrinthine themselves in the parameters by which they measured "merit" and "need." In the background spooled the horror stories of interest loans. Cumulatively, the information was dizzying.

Byron didn't participate in this conversation. Now that applications were starting in earnest, he'd become somewhat paralyzed by the process. Each day, he'd tell himself that tonight would be the night when he sat down and began composing lists. Each night, the information demanded from him was too overwhelming to attempt to organize. Being introverted, he had trouble asking for help, even from his friends. On weekends, he would sometimes ride his bike four miles north to the University of Southern California campus and coast along the brick footpaths between tall dorms and department buildings, past college students studying on blankets on the well-watered lawns; he would marvel at what college looked like even while procrastinating about doing the work required to gain access. That his father had just inexplicably brought home a full-grown Doberman, who hated Byron's own, beloved German shepherd, didn't help; he had to devote considerable energy to keeping the two animals separated inside and outside of their small bungalow home.

Carlos didn't say much, either. Being undocumented precluded him from a swath of aid options, so he had little to sort through. He was still waiting to hear from QuestBridge regarding the second-round results after he'd quickly cleared the first.

They were all in student council, a teacher-selected group of twenty-eight seniors tasked with organizing school events, community outreach, finances, and school spirit—a role that was an honor and also incredibly tiresome, as the various committees tended to alternate between general nonsense, infighting over ideas, and—once in a while—actually accomplishing things. Right now, they were debating ways to find a DJ for the fall dance skilled enough to maintain high energy and properly balance hip-hop with Mexican party music—but cheap enough to accommodate their $150 budget. And a contingent of girls was angling to redirect some of that money toward themed decorations, maybe aquatic.

"Are you thinking *Finding Nemo?*" Luis said.

"Or maybe *The Little Mermaid* is more badass?" Tio added. He and Luis could be formidable when forming a united front. At a certain point one of the girls threatened to strike Tio with a jump rope, the kind with a string threaded through cylindrical plastic beads. He grabbed a pair of scissors and threatened in turn to cut the rope. She hit him with it, and he cut it, and the beads scattered across the floor.

Tio scratched his head. "It didn't look like that many beads when I cut it."

The girl cursed him mightily in Spanish.

"At least now you'll never hit me with a jump rope again." Without being asked, he began picking up the beads one by one.

That evening, a few members of the student council remained at school in order to babysit children during an administrative presentation to parents. Compelling parents to become involved at this school was difficult, because most of them worked long hours, often far from the neighborhood, and many had younger children, hence the free childcare tonight. While parents sat in the gym listening to announcements in English and Spanish, Luis waded around a classroom filled with over a dozen kids ranging in age from three to nine. He and four others had a few miniature packs of potato chips and some juice boxes with which to divert them from destroying staplers, textbooks, laptops. They were supposed to be conducting some arts-and-crafts projects, but popsicle sticks and pipe cleaners predictably failed to engage the children at all. Instead, the tykes knocked over desks while Luis snatched dry-erase markers from clinging hands a little less quickly than the markers could be applied to the walls. Because of his size and breadth, his patchy beard, his never-brushed hair, he resembled an ogre under siege by small feral creatures. The parent meeting would last another forty minutes.

"I want to be a nuclear physicist," he said, "and this is what my life looks like."

That evening, after dropping off assorted friends, Luis came home to a scene that was roughly as farcical as the babysitting gig: his twenty-four-year-old brother stood pounding on the door of the bathroom in which his twenty-one-year-old sister had shuttered herself. They were screaming at each other through the wood. His brother's hair was slick with something viscous; two broken eggshells were scattered on the kitchen floor.

"Just open the door!"

"No way!"

"I have to go to the bathroom. I won't even touch you."

"I don't believe you at all!"

"I have to piss!"

Luis noticed that his brother had a box of Aunt Jemima pancake mix hidden behind his back. He smiled and joined the situation.

"I have to go, too. Really bad."

Their sister resisted.

"All right," Luis said, "I'm going to go on your bed."

She believed him because this was something he would actually do. As soon as she opened the door, there was a muted *poof* sound and her head was covered in pancake mix. The powder was in her hair, eyes, and mouth. Luis collapsed on the couch laughing while his siblings assaulted one another with various other pantry staples.

They hadn't always lived like this, the three of them at home together finding new ways to weave disorder. There'd been a substantial degree of oversight when their parents were still together and one or both of them would usually be home. After years of arguments, they'd separated between Luis's tenth- and eleventh-grade years. The kids had found it easiest to blame their father, since he was the one who'd physically left. He'd moved to Inglewood, a few miles west, and they'd barely seen him in the time since. In truth, they didn't really understand the nuances of marriage and parenting, and their mother had never tried to explain the why of it all; she didn't seem too keen to confront the why herself. In the meantime, Luis was occupied navigating school and getting into college, and his sister was pursuing a specialist degree at LA City College so that she could work as a therapist for autistic children. His brother mostly rode around on his motorcycle.

Their mother worked on a food truck, both day and night shifts, visiting TV sets and construction sites. When she was home during the week, she was severely tired. She had a new boyfriend with whom she spent her weekends, and so on Fridays she would leave money for her kids to spend on food, twenty or forty dollars. His sister was a wonderful cook, like their mother, and could summon magic from a few potatoes and a bag of shredded cheese.

Luis's role at school of comedic provocateur wasn't actually a role, but rather the emotional fulcrum by which he and his siblings steadied the imbalance of a recently broken home, opting for laughter over reckoning.

Jon

Jon had decided to apply early to Stanford University, about as competitive and expensive as a school choice could be. Even with his fourth-place class rank, it was probably a reach for him. As ever, he had no certainties, just a lot of pages to fill out on the web portal. But the uncertainties and the pages seemed worthwhile, even beckoning. Although Jon was not a stereotypical Beverly Hills kid, his life had unfolded almost entirely contained within a dome encompassing his apartment on the eastern rim and the school on the far west. During the summer, he'd worked as an intern at the *Beverly Hills Courier*, a small local paper. He used his student ID to see various speakers for free at the Saban Theatre, an art deco structure towering from the corner of his block. He caught Friday-afternoon movies by himself at the Westfield mall just beyond the school campus. He sometimes studied in the aisles of the Beverly Hills Public Library, collegiate in its inventory. He was very much in awe of his unlikely home, this gift his parents had worked hard to provide him. He was also beyond primed to flee its hold—and theirs.

He wanted to be well out of Los Angeles, in a place that would be a trek to visit or come home from, at a large university that was not just far away but that drew people from far away—and where the confines of his home, family, neighborhood, and age might open up onto some vast and unknown landscape. In his imaginings, Stanford—a six-hour drive without traffic—fit all such specifications.

Admission, were it to be granted him near the end of the fall term, would then segue into the question of tuition, always out there, not yet spoken of at home with his parents, just hovering shadowlike a few months in the future, after outcomes were known.

Between bouts with the application and its potential costs and consequences, he also performed the rather inconsequential duty of serving on student council, termed ASB at Beverly (Associated Student Body). There, representatives of all four grades were elected by classmates and responsible for a considerable budget through the year. Counter to the ample funding was the paramount challenge of trying to coerce the greater student body to care—about anything. School spirit was effectively nonexistent at Beverly Hills. Jon knew why this was and that the situation was neither complicated nor resolvable. The cessation of the permit program years ago meant there were fewer students who saw the school and its opportunities as a privilege rather than an obligation. The sports teams were perennially lousy. Class schedules allowed a large portion of students to leave school after lunch, and so of course they did. Teacher turnover was high, which had more to do with Los Angeles real estate than policy: home values were astronomical within a radius of many miles, and young teachers found the unsustainable commutes antithetical to a decent quality of life. The canvas of the city offered far more provocative things for students to do than, say, stay at school after hours to paint homecoming posters or cheer madly at a basketball game between Beverly Hills and rival Santa Monica High. For a large number of kids, leaving school as early as possible and maybe showing up at a dance for fifteen minutes in order to ridicule it was something they considered a rite of passage, a righteous rejection of the entire formulation of high school. For the small ASB group, spending many hours each week strategizing nifty, futile methods by which to cure this apathy was also a rite of passage.

Many parallels could be easily drawn between Beverly Hills High School—and high school culture as it was popularly perceived—and the nation's political and social climate in the fall of 2016: the hunger for contention as a form of amusement; the self-nurtured and oft celebrated unwillingness to listen rationally to conflicting ideas; the echo chambers of cliques and social media feeds; the self-propagating need to be "right" rather than informed. Jon felt that such parallels made for an insufficient and even disingenuous lens through which to interpret the way young people learned from one another. Though he observed peers say and do provocative things regularly, he was certain that everyone around him harbored the capacity for wonder in his or her heart. He could find something positive to say, and mean earnestly, about most every classmate he'd encountered. He was perhaps an outlier this way, but within his contained environment he held fast to an optimistic view of the wider world and its course.

Sophomore year, he'd taken AP European History with Mr. Van Rossum. In a new age of multimedia learning, of submitting videos in the place of papers, of iPads everywhere, Van Rossum was traditional. The desks in his classroom were arranged in equidistant rows, not a circle or clusters. A towering man of Dutch descent, he'd taught at Beverly for twenty-five years—and he'd taught by the exact same method, by standing in front of the class and lecturing. His was the best class Jon had ever taken, one in which he could just listen to the voice of a man far wiser than he disseminate knowledge with vigor, and he learned facts that were unexpected and interesting while building a greater understanding of the human condition—what education was supposed to be. Maybe the calmness of that class would prove to be an aberration, and maybe his gentle approach to the perspectives of others would haunt him with its naïveté, and maybe life in college and beyond would turn out to be (as the presidential election seemed to suggest) just a prolonged, incessant argument without prospect or possibility of a nourishing outcome. But Jon chose not to believe so.

Owen, Jonah, Bennett

The senior class of the 2016–17 school year had been born two years before 9/11. They'd been in preschool as the Iraq and Afghanistan wars entered their unending denouements. They'd been in third grade when their parents began contending with the Great Recession while America's first black president assumed office. They'd grown up in a world in which almost every person around them, at any time in any public or private space, was staring at a tiny electronic screen. They knew that their generation would be the one designated to face the consequences of the hundreds of billions of metric tons of carbon that humanity had projected into the atmosphere. The same generation had been characterized throughout their lifetimes as generally lazy and entitled and unequipped. The country they knew and read about and discussed in class and observed around them was irrevocably factionalized. The presidential election that unspooled during the first semester of their senior year seemed a surreal confluence of all the tumult and antagonism and disastrous choices—interspersed with small moments of progress—that had distinguished the country in which they'd been raised. For those with eighteenth birthdays before early November, thus able to vote for the first time, the election also signified their official participation in their country's future.

The details were a part of their academic and emotional lives. They discussed the candidates' policies, or lack thereof, exhaustively in class. They watched the debates for homework. They tracked the myriad controversies, both real and artificial, via bombastic headlines on any given website. They talked about what it all meant with their friends and families over meals. They wrote papers. Everyone seemed aware of the inevitable outcome regardless.

But what really captivated them was the way this election seemed to convert adults, particularly in the media, into their most moronic selves. They found some entertainment in watching gray-haired men on television jab their fingers to punctuate long strings of nonfacts (from the right), as well as the mournful monologues, complete with manufactured tears, expounding on the potential end of all things decent (from the left). And clearly entertainment— at least the profit that it generated—was the common denominator propelling all media. But it still seemed weird that certain people, regardless of political persuasion, were able to sustain lucrative careers making unsubstantiated arguments while they, as high schoolers, were graded in large part on their ability to articulate opinions and provide evidence. Their GPAs and their futures hinged on it. They were told that even if they didn't care much for history or English, this was the fundamental life skill to be drawn from those subjects: the capacity to analyze, to reason, to couch logic within arguments, to measure the veracity of what they heard and read. That this ability led to prosperity was implied to them all the time, resulting in the great frustration of thinking young people: being goaded to work very hard in order to gain a skill that adults rarely seemed to apply.

Maybe that was why Owen had problems with Jonah in government class. Owen could watch conservative commentators and scoff at what he deemed their nonsense. But Jonah, whenever he explained his Republican leanings, did so with measured tones and elaborate data. Jonah knew things that Owen didn't know about GDP percentages and global trade figures and employment sectors; he was a wonk. Owen was decidedly not, and he couldn't wield any numbers to backstop his refutation, only his own feelings—and he'd learned the hard way that feelings didn't play well in academic discourse. ("That's bullshit," he'd blurted earlier in the year, when someone was arguing that Obama had been a racist president, and even though he felt objectively correct, he'd still been bidden to make that clichéd walk to the principal's office.) In the time since, he'd learned to simply let Jonah and those who shared his views talk while he simmered within.

Owen wasn't a hyperliberal in the way that film industry sorts were portrayed to be or portrayed themselves as, often hypocritically. He wasn't even that interested in politics beyond talking through the state of the nation with his father during dinner. His views were moderately progressive and, in his own estimation, quite reasonable, probably shared by the majority of people in Los Angeles and well more than half of all Americans.

But Beverly Hills High School was a rare place in that conservative-minded people were overrepresented relative to the city as a whole. The stat was partly due to the concentration of wealth in the city, and partly due to the large population of Persian

Jews with strong Israeli sympathies. The school also drew people of different backgrounds with the quality and opportunity it represented. Jonah was a Beverly student because he, his mother, and his two siblings had spent almost the entirety of his life fleeing from his father in Orange County—an extremely wealthy man who'd had the means to render their lives legally and financially hellish since his parents separated when Jonah was in kindergarten. His childhood had been spent in various apartments and town houses, his mother scrounging for rent and legal reprieve while he contended with the materialism and anti-Semitism that manifested frequently among peers in those moneyed coastal enclaves south of Long Beach. He'd also regularly been forced to meet with social workers, lawyers, and other authority figures prominent in the custody battle; in those offices, he'd honed his quiet argumentative skills—always in defense of his mother. Just before his freshman year, they'd come to live in a small apartment on the eastern edge of Beverly Hills; he'd begged his mother to remove them from Orange County out of fear of a chance encounter with his father.

Jonah had always been aware that he went to school with a number of Republicans. His own views were gleaned from his maternal grandfather, a D-Day veteran and successful New York City contractor. Most of these peers didn't tend to be vocal about it day to day. But something about the 2016 election, the core nature of it and the edgy state of debate, paired with the fact that this was the first election they could truly engage with, unlocked a protesting instinct in Jonah—again reminiscent of all the dozens of hours he'd spent being manipulated by adults proclaiming to know what was best for him as a child and precisely how he should feel about it. He felt that certain teachers were claiming to be impartial independents while proselytizing a very one-sided interpretation of current events, and he found himself overcoming his general fear of conflict in order to contribute some semblance of intellectual balance. After three years of being known as a shy kid, the act of embracing his own voice in school was empowering— even if consciously annoying to others who knew nothing about his complicated origins, who saw only through the lens of their own influences.

Owen yammered about the topic of high school Republicans to Bennett on the evening following his principal visit, as he often did: these kids who, in his perception, didn't necessarily want their candidate in the White House by any stretch but used the prospect to be gleefully contrary.

"But don't you think it's kind of funny, though?" Bennett asked.

"I did in the beginning of the year, and now it makes me angry. And it's like, 'Why are you angry?' 'Why can't you just ignore them or laugh at them?' 'Why are you taking their views seriously at all?' It's because they're acting like assholes."

"But getting angry is exactly what they want. It's why they act like that. Your outrage and indignation are amusing to them."

"That may be so. I guess I'm happy to amuse them? Wait, no, I'm not. It's so confusing. It needs to end."

They were finishing up Bennett's short film for his NYU application, in which Owen's unnamed character was trying to log in to a website but forgot his password, that ubiquitous, time-sucking annoyance of modernity. The site prompted him with the security question *Who was your first girlfriend?* He typed, *Audrey.* The next question was *Where was your first date?* He replied, *Pier.* Then: *When did you break up?* Answer: *November.* This carried on. Typical security questions (*What is your favorite color?*) were interspersed with invasive ones probing the doomed fictional romance (*Who broke up with whom?*). The computer made that irritating little ding whenever he offered a disingenuous answer (*The breakup was, like, a mutual thing*). In the end, his character was finally induced to admit, in a now fretful state of self-sorrow, that "Audrey" was never really his girlfriend in the first place—he'd been deluding himself the whole time—at which point the computer granted him access to a porn site, and he pumped his fist.

Owen wasn't sure about the last flourish. "It's dicey for an application."

"It's a social commentary, or whatever."

"Whaa?"

"How people convince themselves to crave the maturity and exclusivity of a committed relationship, and engage with all the nonsense about feelings and guilt and whatnot, but really everyone's just driven by the fun stuff."

"So imagine if some crotchety old guy in NYU admissions ends up grading your movie."

"I think said crotchety old guy definitely watches porn and probably forgets his passwords."

"It's your movie, so . . . good luck, I guess?"

Owen considered a deeper element, perhaps subconsciously autobiographical, in Bennett's so-called commentary, which had to do with his friend's quest to find a real girlfriend by way of the Tinder app—a quest nearly as long held as that to go to NYU. Because of the app's ease of use, Bennett almost always had a casual girlfriend. He was well versed in the elusive art of text message banter; he couldn't conceive of going to high school in earlier eras, when trying to arrange a date meant actually calling someone on the phone. He also didn't have an older brother, as Owen did, to guide him through the confusing prompts and distorted chivalry of young romance, as Owen's had—extensively and with some wisdom.

In fact, Bennett did have an older brother, just not one who could pass on dating advice. His biological father had donated more than once to sperm banks during the time when Bennett was conceived. During his sophomore year, the far reaches of Google had enabled Bennett to locate a number of half siblings conceived via the same man, and then through Facebook he'd fostered relationships with them. One half brother was in the navy. A half sister was about to start high school in San Francisco. They'd begun gathering together sporadically the year before, and these connections proved bizarre and fascinating. None of them bore much resemblance to any of the others, but they shared odd mannerisms and even the same cadence of laughter. One afternoon they were scrolling through a Netflix queue and it came to light that all were huge fans of *Malcolm in the Middle*, a popular family sitcom from the early 2000s.

From these new acquaintances, he'd learned that their father was now raising his own family in the Bay Area. Though Bennett was not legally allowed to contact or see him until he turned eighteen, he scrolled through the man's Facebook feed constantly, even as doing so made him feel like a creepy voyeur to these happy-looking suburban strangers as they took hikes and sailed boats and blew out birthday candles. While he wouldn't have noticed a likeness if passing the man on the street, he didn't have to reach to find shared features in the hair, nose, eyes. And among the photos he noticed that his father's middle son was nearly his doppelgänger, and the image cast beams of wonder regarding origin and fate and the pull of blood. At times the sheer strangeness of the situation superseded girls and school and college and whatever Bennett had due on any given day. Midterm exams were nearing, as was the deadline for his NYU early application, but he spent valuable hours clicking on photos of a guy who'd masturbated into a cup for $50 almost twenty years ago.

Tio

The marine layer hanging over Dockweiler State Beach was probably a drag for some picnickers trudging with their chairs and coolers toward the water, but Tio appreciated the chill as he ran alongside roughly forty APB classmates. The ocean was a hazel color and large homes with wide windows looked down on it from the hills of the aptly named Vista del Mar. The closest thing APB had to a sport was a program called Students Run Los Angeles, a nonprofit endeavor by which a few dozen students trained a few days a week for the LA Marathon in February. Tio had already run it twice. In a typical weekday after-school training session, they jogged up and down the half-mile western edge of Washington Park, two blocks from school, repeatedly, for miles at a time. They were limited to this redundant stretch because the texture of the neighborhoods changed fast, and sometimes dangerously, such that venturing beyond carried too much uncertainty. Plus all the intersection stoplights made for frequent disruptions. Some Saturdays, like today, they would embark by bus for organized runs on the beach, intended no doubt to be cathartic and peaceful but in truth a little maddening; he'd rather have been hanging out on the sand at ease than dodging bikes and scooters on the footpath, in pain.

Later, sweaty, they disembarked from the bus in front of school. Tio couldn't help but say to the coach, "You didn't say thank you."

"Tio, what?"

"You didn't thank the bus driver."

After their last weekend run, the coach had harangued the group after they'd all left the bus, exhausted from the run, without acknowledging the driver.

"Tio, there are times when you need to just *not say* what you're thinking. This is one of those times."

Tio shrugged. "I'm just saying."

"That's what I just said to not do!"

Tio raised his palms and backed away, smiling. "It's cool. And *thank you*."

His runner's high made him feel happy and hilarious. The weekend still felt long, filled with promise. He intended to spend half of Sunday skateboarding, a quarter of it studying, and the remainder working on a draft of his college personal essay. He'd been grappling with his desire to write about his father's struggle with alcohol and the consequences Tio had weathered. He knew empirically that the anecdote would be compelling for an admissions reader, part of the gamesmanship of setting himself apart, but the thought of articulating that passage in his life in prose—and of sharing it with peers and teachers for review—was paralyzing.

He couldn't do any of it, at any rate, because he'd forgotten that they were going to visit his sister at UC Riverside, which meant a car ride in which the music on his headphones would fail to overcome the squealing of his little sisters while his father hunched forward with the wheel clutched in both hands, looking wholly defeated by this moment in his life. Riverside was an hour east of Los Angeles, a kind of gateway to the Inland Empire, that reptilian tail of medium-sized cities protruding into the dry, hot, brown expanse of Southern California desert.

The campus was vast, its 1,100 acres diluting the 23,000 students such that nowhere seemed crowded—the opposite of how Los Angeles felt. The architecture represented a very Californian clashing of early Mission Revival, fifties modern, seventies Brutalist, and more recent glassy façades. Tall hills covered with withered challo and saguaro plants filled the surrounding distance. Students passing in groups looked content enough; they were mostly Latino and Asian, some weighed down by stress and sagging backpacks but most appearing to enjoy the Saturday. His older sister certainly did. Though she suffered from homesickness—hence the family visit—she was thriving here.

Tio chased his little sisters across the grass as his parents unpacked the food they'd brought on a picnic table. He kept looking around at the hugeness of the place, the wide common sports fields and long walkways forming diamonds on the quads, the gigantic library, the space and freedom and peace that contrasted so sharply with his three-hallway school, his neighborhood dense with struggling people.

Many considered Riverside an "opportunity" school, a place for disadvantaged people to continue the long-odds pursuit of stability and success. This marker was signified by the relative sparsity of white people he observed walking around. For himself, Tio thought of Riverside as a benchmark of failure, a place where admission really meant rejection by higher-ranked schools. He knew this perspective was foolish, classist, perhaps racist in a way. And he was proud of his sister. But he was not alone in paying a tremendous amount of attention to rankings, prestige, the superficial scales that pervaded the American educational system—that pervaded America, really. The desire to stand out, to outperform others, comprised a large part of what drove him. It slanted his hours in the classroom, at the skate park, on SRLA runs, at mini golf. He easily acknowledged this quality in himself, loudly sometimes, even as he felt guilty about it. He didn't know if his competitive nature was an ingrained trait or whether it had bloomed during his younger years loosed unsupervised on Juniper Street or navigating the anarchy of public school recess. But it was his identity, and he complied with it, and so he regarded Riverside with near disdain even as they spent a tranquil afternoon talking idly over their mother's *sopes* and black beans and stuffed sweet peppers, laughing a bit, praising his sister's persistence with school.

Tio was uncharacteristically quiet most of the time. In his mind, he was visualizing himself here a year from now—here and not at UCLA or UC Santa Barbara or Cornell, here and trying to engage with school while convincing himself that Riverside offered just as much prestige and opportunity as those other schools, here and striving to be motivated from within rather than without—striving, in effect, to alter who he was as a person. The image was a projection, but it still both frightened and angered him. As they drove home at dusk, the steep hillsides along Highway 60 darkened until they looked like black waves swelling out of the midnight blue sky.

Chapter 6

*I like to think about what events have been important to me
over the past x amount of years, but I don't often actually
do it.*

—*Jon*

Carlos, Tio

Carlos had just learned that he was a finalist for a QuestBridge
scholarship, but in the current moment he was struggling to figure
out how to construct a maze out of cardboard in the school hallway,
the consequential and the inane braiding together as they always
seemed to do in this odd passage of life.

The first school dance in September had been "lit": the student
council had sold over 150 tickets at $3 apiece, the DJ had been skilled,
the dance floor full. As part of his student council committee job,
Tio had spent the evening encouraging kids to dance, which entailed
dancing himself as an exhortation. The optics of his gyrating amid
clusters of girls had not been appreciated by his girlfriend, prompting
an argument and breakup followed by the inevitable repair. Byron
had donned the school mascot costume, a gryphon, and led dances
with the gigantic felt head bobbing back and forth and his clothes
underneath sweat soaked. When the Yeezy song "FDT" came on,

everyone in the gym waved upraised arms from side to side while gleefully chanting, *"Fuck Donald Trump!"* until the supervising teachers put a quick end to the call-and-response. Toward the end of the dance, the Spanish version of Billy Ray Cyrus's 1990s song "Achy Breaky Heart"—"No Rompas Mi Corazón"—had begun blaring loud, the song a staple in Latino dance culture for reasons lost to time. Cheers erupted and almost two hundred teenagers lined up in a dozen rows and began line-dancing in unison. *"No rompas más, mi pobre corazón . . . estás pegando justo entiéndelo . . ."*

The Halloween dance a month later, for which Carlos labored to engineer the maze, was feeling grim in comparison. After ten straight weeks without a break, and with midterms approaching before the release of Thanksgiving, kids were generally unenthused about spending even an extra minute in the building. Student council was having trouble selling tickets; day of, they were only at ninety.

The problem with the maze was that this morning, the administration had decided that hallway lights needed to stay on for safety reasons.

"Could there possibly be a stupider concept than a Halloween maze all lit up by fluorescent lights?" Luis ranted.

Tio, as if to prove his engineering mettle, was determined to find a solution. He gained access to the maintenance closet and returned with a box of black garbage bags. Two hours followed of duct taping, bickering, and generally questioning why and how they'd come to be spending a Friday afternoon taping together what became a sad, drooping tunnel that would collapse with even slight lateral pressure. Inside they had a fog machine and sound effects of cackling laughter and ghoulish grumbling. A few student council members would take turns crouching in corners to grab the legs of passersby. The lights penetrated the plastic-bag roofing and infused the interior with an orange-ish haze that recalled a high-smog Los Angeles evening.

"No one's going to pay a dollar for this," Tio said, laughing and shaking his head.

"You'd be crazy to pay ten cents for this," Carlos replied. But he shrugged and, as the dance began, took his post in the front selling tickets. There wouldn't be much for him to do, as less than a hundred people came. The house parties organized that night in contest with the school event were well attended, judging by the constant social media stream of photos.

Tio wanted to be an engineer. Luis wanted to be a nuclear physicist. Byron wanted to work for NASA. Carlos wasn't quite sure, but his favorite subjects were calculus and physics, and he was also a formidable writer. Tonight, all those aspirations faded behind the task of making the Halloween dance somewhat less embarrassing than it promised to be. They were not successful.

Jon, Harrison

The following day was homecoming at Beverly Hills, which Jon and the rest of the ASB had decided to present as a community event. The idea had to do partly with outreach and partly with compensating for the prevailing lack of school spirit. In addition to the lopsided sports contests and thinly attended rallies, they organized a carnival with games and food geared toward children, hoping to draw local families to the campus. When floated in their meeting, the idea had seemed creative and doable enough. In practice, it entailed dealing with businesses: food vendors, table and chair rentals, game companies. Dealing with businesses meant dealing with adults, which was always demeaning and terrible.

Adults haggled in inventive and relentless ways. Because this was Beverly Hills High School, they presumed the coffers inexhaustible. Pricing schemes felt arbitrary and exploitative. Scouts casually missed scheduled appointments. Liability issues generated an endless back-and-forth, and then choices had to be vetted by the school administration—and all this for a homecoming event that half or more students not only wouldn't attend but would actively deride.

The day of, Jon worked in different game booths and was gratified to see a few hundred Los Angelenos come out with their kids. After the weeks of adult negotiations, he focused on the little children and their simple joy easily elicited by timeless games. He tried to recall what such joy had felt like when he was a dozen years younger and his parents took him to the Santa Monica Pier, the labyrinth of games and rides set upon the sea's edge seeming so boundless. Aside from the tent vendor showing up with crates of canvas yet no poles with which to raise it, and then somehow implying that the lapse was their fault, the carnival was very pleasant and even rewarding.

He and some friends caught the second half of the football game against Hawthorne School. The quality of play was poor, and the Beverly team was losing by thirty-two points, which was not an unusual result. The team had only four seniors out of a class of four hundred. One of them was named Harrison, and Jon enjoyed watching him play despite the score. Harrison was an avid filmmaker and had often helped Jon with homework videos in English class. He was tall and strong and effortlessly athletic, unlike Jon. But like Jon, he was a kind, quiet sort who always seemed more keen to listen than to talk. Familiar with his almost meek persona, Jon was always captivated when watching his friend determinedly collide his head and body with others even as the clock ticked toward certain defeat. The stands were half full, if that. A defunct oil derrick tower, the remnant of an ill-fated cash pursuit made by the school board in the 1990s and now a bizarre landmark on the campus, stood behind the field, and behind that rose the enormous glass high-rises of the Century City business district, those many towers of serious commerce peering down upon these teenagers tackling one another clumsily over a leather obloid. Fans laughed at the lopsided game; Hawthorne kids pointed and made jokes about dominance over the rich, soft Beverly team, because everyone liked to do that; Beverly football parents shouted doleful encouragement to their sons. Harrison continued to dive after wobbly errant passes with no chance of catching them, his helmet subsequently slamming into the turf while assorted large bodies landed on top of him. Jon physically winced a few times, his friend's willful punishment seemed like a metaphor for some idea or strand of reality that he could not, as of now, articulate.

Later in the evening, at the homecoming dance, Jon helped out at the food and drink stations. The gym was mostly empty for the first hour. A fair number of students began arriving later, not enough to fill the floor but still a respectable showing by Beverly standards. The dance peaked around seven thirty, and Jon watched a few dozen seniors moving in couples and clusters, some of them introverts who he knew wouldn't have been inclined to venture here if it weren't senior year, others more social types who also wouldn't typically have been at a school-sponsored and boozeless function were it not for some nostalgia in play. Everyone seemed more or less glad to be here together for a time. The feeling was fleeting; around eight, students began leaving in small and then larger groups, some for the after-parties hosted at student homes. Jon had never been to one, didn't desire to go now. He'd heard that it was common for the hosts to summon the police to their own parties so that they didn't have to contend with a wrecked house but could still make thousands of dollars in ticket sales (typically around forty dollars per person, more for underclassmen).

The gym all but emptied a half hour early. He spent the next ninety minutes carrying speakers and folding up tables and pulling down banners and picking up trash. In the yellow light amid the fallen napkins and paper cups and streamers, he felt a novel kind of melancholy that would become more familiar in the months to come: another moment past, generic as it might have been; another experience that would never be felt again; another increment of the ever-reliable marks of time falling behind while the ominous uncertainties of the next six months approached inexorably closer.

Carlos

The 2016 presidential election was a few days away, and school was hilarious. They watched late-night-talk-show and *Saturday Night Live* clips of both candidates being skewered. They did impressions. They circulated memes. In-class debates that had grown heated in October had softened the way fires do once fuel nears depletion.

At Ánimo Pat Brown, the students had endured almost a full semester of being asked to intellectualize, in some way, a Republican candidate whose entire platform was founded on a vehement charge that they were criminals who did not belong here. Throughout these months, their collective response had been laced with the humor of knowing this candidate would fail spectacularly.

With this knowledge, Carlos tried not to feel edgy about the election and the referendum it presented regarding not just his culture's place in America but his own individual DACA application and his parents' overarching legal defenselessness. They didn't discuss the prospect of the Republican platform other than to express incredulity, which was a salve used by his family and by most he knew; laughing indignation was easier to express and control than fear. But he observed the symptoms of his parents' stress. The dynamic of his family was odd in the context of traditional Latino culture, which placed a high value on masculinity. In his home, his father deferred to his mother in nearly all matters: discipline, finances, major decisions. When his mother had chosen to stop working for a few years to raise her children and instill good habits during that fraught passage through public middle school, she'd placed a high strain on his earnings. But he'd agreed with her, worked side jobs when he could, and as a result she was always present in the small shack as her three children came of age: to snap at them when they were being lazy or unhelpful, and to hold them when feelings had been injured at school. They all paid particular attention to her, and so Carlos was highly attuned, as the election neared, to her latent panic. She was anxious during the day about his father driving around city streets in a large, easy-to-target vehicle, and she was anxious at night about the news and viral rhetoric, and she strove, unsuccessfully, to keep all this anxiety invisible to her kids. The primary vent for her suppression seemed to lie in chastising them all constantly for nonexistent failings.

"Why aren't you cleaning?"

"I'm writing an English paper."

"But your room is a mess."

Carlos looked around the eight-by-ten-foot space he shared with his siblings. The only objects on the floor were his backpack and the stack of textbooks and notebooks that he'd pulled out of it. The beds were made except for the top bunk, which she'd been using to store boxes since Jose had gone to college. He'd also cleaned most of the house earlier. He looked at her. She grunted and marched elsewhere. His mother was barely five feet tall, but she could be scary sometimes. And now she was scared, evidenced by the Mexican news station his father was watching, the pundit exhorting Latino residents of America to be vigilant, warning of the possibility of World War II–like internment camps.

Carlos tried to focus on his paper, but his mother was moving pots and pans around the kitchen loudly and for no reason. He wanted to explain to her that he'd been studying stats and polls in school for over two months, and when they quantified the amount of racial disdain coming from the political right against the number of minorities living in America, the fears being stoked in their community were statistically unfounded. That his parents couldn't vote—that his family had no voice in this discourse, despite paying taxes—was only a symbolic disappointment, since California was the bluest of states. He wanted to explain all these things, but he couldn't. Her fear was born out of love, and in its hold she needed quiet empathy and patience from him, not an academic lecture.

The College Board

For seniors retaking the SAT or ACT or both, scores had been released over the prior weeks, and their concurrence with the national election seemed fitting. The opportunity for do-overs was gone. The numbers, those short pairings of digits that held such grand implications, were now fixed. The drudgery and anxiety that had led to them were past. The resentment of needing them at all was moot. Some students had managed to raise their scores from junior year and thus improve their lots, while others hadn't. This class had been the first to take a drastically revamped version of the SATs meant to leaven the innate, long-sustained prejudice of the test itself. The essay portion introduced in 2005 had been made optional. Obscure and infamous flash-card words had been replaced by entirely passage-based vocabulary. Evidence-based reading had replaced critical reading. Math included both calculator and no-calculator sections. A few more seconds on average were available per question. Penalties for wrong answers—and the strategic, time-consuming odds calculations required therein—had been dropped. The new version was purported by the College Board to be more predictive of success in college and beyond, and in essence the fairest one yet.

The ACT was very similar overall, though it had a section devoted to science and a heavier focus on geometry and other specific math areas. They both cost around $50, and $17 more if one took the optional essay sections (with fees, those fixtures of existence, for late registration, wait lists, etc.). Colleges accepted either one. The common wisdom was that students stronger in science were better off taking the ACT—though students who excelled in science also tended to do well in math, which was weighted at half the value on the ACT relative to the SAT. The SAT gave significantly more time per question, so students who didn't consider themselves to be stellar test-takers might fare better. At school and at home, much talk revolved around weighing one's strengths and weaknesses vis-à-vis the two tests. In truth—the universal truth when it came to admissions—everyone understood that more was always better, and nationwide students were increasingly opting for both, because studying for and taking a three-hour test once wasn't sufficient when those with whom you competed were doing it twice (or four or five times when accounting for retakes).

The SATs had originally been adapted, on a very small scale, from IQ tests given to soldiers during World War I, as an experimental means to quantify the intrinsic intelligence of college-bound people. Spurred by the proliferation of secondary education and economic forces and the competition inherent in the postwar American dream, the test became a central—for some *the* central—metric of attending college. The test had spawned an immeasurable volume of research, debate, and impassioned conflict over many decades—not to mention a test-prep industry with a market in the realm of hundreds of millions of dollars, possibly billions. This industry was considered by many to be unscrupulous, seen by more than a few as outright predatory and corrupt, and known universally to give people with money an advantage over people without it. The fabric of American life was woven from such advantages, just as the fabric of all life was woven from the desire of parents to help their children succeed by any means they had. Some had more means than others. Some had far, far more. Means had an awful lot to do with what the word *succeed* actually meant. In a partial acknowledgment, universities overall had professed to give less weight to test scores relative to the more personalized areas of student transcripts, and a small percentage had stopped accepting scores entirely. But students were still obliged to take them, so they mattered just the same and caused the same amount of stress.

The presidential election in many ways centered on disparity in America, more specifically on who was being left behind by whom, with divisions drawn along racial lines, income strata, sexuality, age, employment sectors—seemingly every group and subgroup had a claim to grievance (even outspoken members of the "1 percent" complained of classism). College admissions were rarely mentioned in a national forum, aside from broad progressive declarations that college should be free for every American and subsequent rebuttals invariably including the buzzword *socialism*. The role of tests in all this did not seem to arise—too tricky and mired in data, potentially alienating to voters. Easier to keep the message as broad as possible. But for those in high school, and for their parents, tests were a paramount symbol of inequality and access and racism, knotted with myriad interpretations of the question, what purpose did standardized tests serve?

On a basic level, these numbers were supposed to provide a baseline as to how one individual compared academically to all others in a given stack of applications. Tangential to that, they purported to indicate one's potential to thrive in various spheres of higher education. They might also in some way signal motivation in addition to aptitude, and the ability to operate under pressure, and time management, and reading comprehension. They surely provided a reprieve to a weary admissions officer late at night, after reading a few hundred individual essays, because after so many words that applied solely to the young person who had written them, here were numbers that in some way applied to all.

Arguments against the tests in each stage of their evolution were staples among educators, administrators, researchers, parents. As in most any arena, it was not hard to berate an existing structure, particularly one as cumbersome as the College Board and carrying as much history. Nor was it hard for supporters of the test to parry back. As in classrooms, as in families—as in all venues—the conflict between two entities both claiming to be not only right but righteous was a fierce and intractable one. A common criticism was that the SATs rewarded students with strong test-taking abilities often honed through rigorous private schools and expensive test prep; that test-taking was a crucial part of college and job-seeking was also a fact. The verbal section disadvantaged students who spoke English as a second language no matter how well they performed in school; this was clear and arguably racist. It was also difficult to equalize in an English-speaking country, and the counterargument was that such a student might well struggle academically and emotionally at a liberal arts college that didn't account for ESL in its curriculum the way many public universities did. Much research showed that dollars invested in outside test prep equated with measurable improvements—that points on the test could be purchased (this research was touted by test-prep companies even as it vilified them). Other research showed no correlation between monetary outlay and scores (this research was touted by the College Board, at least until the company launched its own, free online test-prep program through Khan Academy, at which point it stated that scores could in fact be improved through tutoring, but only their brand actually worked). In its core nature and volume, the debate aligned exactly with greater debates regarding opportunity in America—at once obvious and impenetrable.

"The test is bullshit" was a universal refrain among high school upperclassmen.

But the test was incredibly weighty bullshit, and more so for students of, say, a small and relatively new charter school serving a poor, Latino population, or an old, decently regarded but unlauded public school in a wealthy neighborhood—schools in which the direct competition among classmates was an unknown variable and a high GPA did not automatically imply a high aptitude when looked at from a remove. The students at these respective schools had very different experiences and very different school targets, and each target would give them room to describe their experiences. Each would also have an entry box for the figures gained from standardized tests, and in doing so would remind them that whatever they'd accomplished in the buildings they entered each day, alongside the kids they ate lunch with, would be measured against millions of others who entered different buildings, with different kids.

College was competition. Regardless of fairness, regardless of research or advancement, the tests embodied that competition with all its vastness and imperfection. With their scores as armaments or possibly hindrances, schoolkids were entering the competition now after endless months of lead-up, just as the endless months of lead-up to the presidential competition approached conclusion.

Owen

"What about inertia?" he asked his physics teacher.

"What, Owen?"

"What you just said. About the train? I'm pretty sure that's false."

His physics teacher had been explaining the theory of relativity using the classic train-car thought experiment, in which a burst of light occurs in the center of a moving train car at the precise moment that a train passenger, also in the center of the car, passes someone waiting on an adjacent, stationary train platform. To the moving passenger, the light will reach either side of the car at the same moment. To the stationary person on the platform, the light will reach the back of the car before it reaches the front. In trying to explain this quirk of light, the teacher had actually leaped into the air while pretending to be a train passenger, and suggested that if she'd been jumping on a moving platform, the platform would continue traveling beneath her while she was in the air.

"I don't think it's false, Owen."

"I'm pretty sure that when you jump on a moving train, you land in the same place. Like, inertia."

She replied that the physics of motion did not operate that way. Uselessly frustrated, Owen knew that he ought to let this moment pass on to the next—that he rationally should not invest himself in correcting his teacher—but he recalled being on the wrong side of this same debate at some point early in middle school, and some slightly neurotic part of him was compelled to make clear that, today, he was right. So he asserted that, according to her interpretation, if he were to toss a can of soda upward while on a moving airplane, the can would then become a lethal object flying toward the rear of the cabin at hundreds of miles per hour. She rebutted that the air pressure within the cabin prevented such danger. They spoke back and forth like this for a full minute. His classmates appeared engaged for the first time all period, though their entertainment was not his goal.

She finally sighed in his direction. "Owen, inertia is a completely different subject than the one we're talking about, which is relativity," she said, even though he was fairly sure that inertia and relativity were closely related. The teacher carried on. (The following day, she did find him to apologize for being confused.)

Inertia, relativity: both provided apt metaphors for life a third of the way through his senior year.

Pericles (in space) had happened. He'd spent five hours a day for two months rehearsing, they'd performed it, his costume had been ridiculous, he'd thrown up, a bunch of students had come, Owen had done the best he could with what he'd been given, and now it was over.

This was how Owen had come to experience the year unfolding: a bunch of stuff happening and ending, days passing with a distinct sameness that he strove, with full awareness of the long odds, to make memorable. Even his erstwhile ruminations on an alternative to the standard college path had concluded with his early application to Wesleyan University in Connecticut: a small liberal arts school attended mostly by people who looked and thought like him.

Nearly every motivational school speech he'd ever heard included some variation of the phrase *Find your passion.* He found it condescending of the adults to strike that point so reliably when so much about the arrangement of school seemed geared toward draining subjects of exactly that: passion. English and history reading homework was graded on how many notes they took in the margins; Owen could expound on a passage that moved him and receive a D, or he could highlight lines at random on each page for an A. Why he spent his time questioning the silliness of such contrarieties instead of just doing the page notes as directed was also troubling, and maybe emblematic of some greater, useless compulsion.

His problem came in the form of his ACT test score, which after much private tutoring and personal studying had been a stellar 34. His sudden placement in the ninety-ninth percentile nationally belied his B average at school. In addition, while going through the motions of his Wesleyan application, he'd been surprised by just how involved his high school career had in fact been: the drama program, the media program, varsity sports, school assemblies and tours, awards. He seemed overall to have become an expansive if unwitting ambassador of Beverly Hills High School. If the act of completing an application was fundamentally an act of storytelling, then his own story—as much as he was reluctant to admit it—was persuasive and seemed to render all his ruminations on purpose and paths and metaphors somewhat controvertible.

For a reprieve, he turned often to Instagram, not to scroll listlessly through the inanity that friends and acquaintances projected into the web, but to check on a particular user, a Texas-based man, whom Owen knew not at all. Over the previous summer, idling in a car with Bennett, and in a spontaneous waste of time inspired by time's wasting, he'd asked, "What do you think is the most valuable Instagram name that's still untaken—like what username could we claim that we would be shocked was still available?"

They had found their afternoon's activity: sitting in Bennett's car, listening to a Pandora stream, faces locked on their phones, testing name after name: @ChancetheRapper, @RussellWilson, @TheDixieChicks, @PaulRyan, @NewKidsontheBlock. All were taken. They foraged further into the realm of entities and inanimate objects: @TheStateofDelaware, @table, @chair, @umbrella . . .

"I was sure 'umbrella' would pull through!" Owen lamented.

"Who loves umbrellas enough to have it be their Instagram?"

As their determination waned, "What a Fool Believes" began playing through one of Owen's playlists, and he then tested out @thedoobiebrothers, which was unclaimed, and so a minute of thumbing keys made Owen and Bennett, these two guys in high school with nothing to do, the handle's proprietors.

Doobie Brothers fans around the country would reach out sporadically, at least those who didn't take a moment to realize that a private account with six followers and no posts most likely wasn't a legitimate Doobie Brothers resource. These enthusiasts tagged the account to pictures of albums they owned or concerts they'd attended, and Owen would always reply, "Rock on! #whatafoolbelieves." No one ever wrote back.

In September of their senior year, a person tagged @thedoobie brothers in a photo of a Doobies record, and Owen commented his usual. The fan replied, "YOU ARE MY FAVORITE MUSICIAN OF ALL TIME. Been singing your songs since 1974!" and followed with an alternating series of smiley-face and rock-guitar emoji. Inexplicably flattered—and also bored, the very state of being that had engendered this nonsense—Owen scanned the linked profile of a middle-aged male Texan (who referred to himself as "Tex") and found it littered with posts declaring President Obama a terrorist, Hillary Clinton a criminal who belonged in jail, immigrants the destroyers of America, and of course the one regarding the Doobie Brothers' enduring impact on his life. From his comfortable perch in Beverly Hills, Owen found it jarring, on a surprisingly genuine level, to have this direct if disingenuous channel with a true and ardent red-state human being.

He couldn't help but think hypothetically of what he would actually want to say—but would most likely be too afraid to say—were he and this person to be standing face-to-face. And then Owen realized that the man wouldn't care what some hipster-ish kid in Beverly Hills thought about his social media opinions; the man would probably laugh.

But there was an opinion that he did seem to care about. And Owen, as @thedoobiebrothers, commented on the original album post: "Hey tex, first let me say the doobies always appreciate a fan, but some of these photos are highly ignorant, offensive, and largely racist. The Doobie Brothers are respectful of all cultures and creeds, and these photos do not reflect the type of thinking we want our fans to have. It's time to stop judging people by the color of their skin. Come on, Tex."

The reply was swift and earnest: "I'm just excited y'all thought of me at all. I'll try to find the racist stuff on my site and delete it. I still love you guys." Momentarily, the hatred was in fact cleared from the feed, and Owen experienced a minor thrill that was loosely related to fame of some sort, or influence, or the simple surprise of having enough agency in the greater world to affect a stranger's thinking in a positive way—a feeling hardly ever experienced in the confines of high school or social media, and the precise kind that Owen sought in order to truly, profoundly value this time in life and its capacity for wonder amid the routine.

A few weeks later, when Bennett informed him that the Doobie Brothers did, in fact, have a very active Instagram account under the handle @DoobieBrothersOfficial, with hundreds of thousands of followers, Owen wasn't bothered. He was, in fact, grateful for this momentary and meaningless distraction from the ordinary path on which his ACT score placed him, and from current events in general.

Carlos, Tio, Luis

The day after the presidential election at Ánimo Pat Brown, a Wednesday, was subdued. The teachers began the day with a private faculty meeting in the gym, from which a few emerged in tears, including the principal, who later announced an early dismissal at 1:50. Positivity-laced videos were shown in many classes, along with more than a few references to the long arc of history's bending toward justice. Carlos quickly saw that the teachers as a whole were feeling overwhelmed by the need to figure out how to communicate with students, and to balance despair with resilience and hope. Their struggle signified how much they cared. During student government period, they spent the hour making inspirational posters. Some students wore signs around their necks reading, *Free Hugs*. There must have been over five thousand hugs exchanged among the students at Ánimo Pat Brown over the course of the day. Carlos's minimalist sign read, *Undocumented and Proud*.

For the most part, students and teachers just seemed spent from the energy required to process the previous night's results. They'd been led to believe by authoritative sources that one outcome was morally and mathematically certain, and the opposite had occurred. They slumped on desks and spoke very little in classroom discussions; teachers tried to initiate what would no doubt be a long and strenuous process of showing these kids that they didn't have to be scared. The most energetic moment occurred when the student council came together informally in the main foyer during lunch and began walking through the school with their signs. Carlos trailed behind to pick up stragglers while Luis led the procession, a borrowed bullhorn in hand, singing and chanting in Spanish. "If we stay positive and rely on our voices, they can't do anything to us!" They ended up outside in the small schoolyard under the basketball hoop, a few yards from the train tracks. Classmates were dancing and contributing chants of their own—none of them political rallying cries or profane tirades against the president-elect, but rather simple, full-throated proclamations, made to one another and no one else, that they were all here.

Residents of South LA were marching around various neighborhoods in mostly uncoordinated groups; videos were pouring out of social media streams; warnings came of potential riots. After early dismissal, everyone had to be wary getting home.

That evening, one of Carlos's mentors in the Minds Matter program, a film and television screenwriter, called.

"I don't understand what happened," he said.

"It's cool," Carlos replied, even though it definitely wasn't.

"I'm just so sorry that we did this." By *we*, Carlos deduced that he meant white men.

"It's not you. You've done as much as anyone to help."

"I don't know that I have."

Carlos told him to take it easy on himself, and that he'd see him in a few days on the USC campus for their regular mentorship session.

Then Thursday dawned, and the extra twenty-four hours' distance from the election seemed to release something primal, a fury, a desire for retribution of some kind. It coursed through the hallways in whispers and shouts and penetrated the classrooms. Even Carlos, preternaturally measured, felt it within his chest—compelled by the hours spent Thursday night lying in bed in an overstimulated state of picturing his father and mother working throughout that day, as they did every day, but now in a darkened climate beneath Southern California's abundant sun. Their jobs were relatively simple and necessary for local commerce. Now, by this reverberant national decree, their jobs were dangerous. And while Carlos would remain relatively sheltered in school, surrounded by adults whose life purpose was to nurture and protect him and his peers, his parents would be out there in the neighborhoods earning their living, their well-being a concern of essentially no one. His mother's recent anxiety had been well founded after all, despite the intellectual punctures he'd silently made in it, and he shared the anxiety now. He was also pissed.

Every generation in American history had experienced events that altered their beliefs in how the world aligned, or should align, or didn't align. Wars began and ended. Economies soared and collapsed. Politicians did wondrous and stupid things. New technology drastically shifted the rhythms of daily life. Innocent people died violently at the hands of the deranged. Business titans grew financial empires at the expense of the naïve and poor. The earth raged at random. Humankind used science to develop methods by which to destroy itself. Individuals reacted to these events in accordance with the amount of attention they paid, the degree to which they'd been personally affected, the beliefs instilled by time and place and parentage and culture and skin color. But collectively, such events—and the act of calibrating one's basic state of being in the face of the terribly uncontrollable—served to remind people how insignificant they were.

Carlos and Tio spent much of Thursday morning in the US history teacher's classroom. Male and female students drifted in and out of the class, sometimes just to shriek, "This fucking sucks!"and vanish back into the hallway. The room looked like most any room in the country in which US history was taught, with an American flag and a poster board featuring index cards where students had written, some time ago, what they most appreciated about their country. A few pages of the Constitution hung near the white-board, where an outline of the day's lesson was neatly written in bullet points.

A massive walkout of students from the area schools had been organized on Facebook and Snapchat. At a certain time, everyone was supposed to gather on the steps of Fremont High School and walk to Compton city hall. Carlos had no desire to join, as he felt intuitively that leaving school would cast the Latino population here, from the perspective of TV news choppers, as behaving exactly like the ingrates that the new president-elect had repeatedly described in order to stoke defensive outrage in the white working class.

Tio had a feeling that a lot of the kids being loud on social media about creating a movement would end up leaving school for home rather than walking in solidarity all the way to city hall. Luis confirmed this when he entered and said, "A lot of fools just planning to hit up McDonald's!"

"I could eat some nuggets right now," Tio replied.

A girl at the door said, "What's the point of marching in school or out of school or anywhere? What's the point of signs? What's the point of anything right now?"

She was distressed, yet the muscles in Tio's shoulders and upper back began quaking with anger. "What do you mean, what's the point?" he replied. "How can you ask what's the fucking point? The point was what you saw us do yesterday, to comfort people, to start using our fucking voices! You don't have to be a part of it, but don't hate on it." She scoffed, and he kept talking. "If we don't stay together and say what we know to be true about us, then when they deport you and your parents and your whole fucking family, you're going to look back and wonder why you weren't a part of it."

The girl was shocked, maybe a little scared of him. She murmured something and left.

In AP Calculus, they worked through complex triple-variable equations. In English they discussed whether Jay Gatsby was a hero or a villain. In AP Chemistry they carried out a lab experiment measuring the rates of opposing chemical processes in a reaction, trying to reach chemical equilibrium while contending with the tricky dynamics of enthalpy and entropy. At some point, word circulated that about sixty students were about to walk out and join the protest.

After class, Carlos and his usual group went to the classroom of Mr. Snyder, their government teacher. His room was the last in the horseshoe formation of the school, with tall windows looking out over Beach Street. The students intent on leaving had gathered at the school's front gate, where they faced the principal and a few other teachers and administrators. Inside, Carlos could faintly hear the principal's voice, ever calm, as he made a rational case for the students to finish the day in school. A small handful of them broke off and trudged back in the front door, heads downturned. Those remaining were resolute and their anger was visibly escalating with the sense of being contained. Acknowledging this, the principal stepped aside and the students filed out. He implored them to be smart and safe this afternoon. Two teachers followed the students into the neighborhood to help ensure the gentle commands.

"So fucking dumb," Tio said.

"Those are the people who probably don't give a shit about politics," Luis said. "They probably didn't even register voters when we were all out doing that. Not that it matters for shit." He was referring to a student council get-out-the-vote initiative during the fall.

Tio laughed. "Admittedly hard to register people around here where nobody's got ID. I think I got, like, four, and they were my aunt's friends."

The front lot emptied, and the students began disappearing around the corner of Beach Street and Eighty-Third, walking toward Fremont High—a place where on any normal day, an APB student would be harassed over the navy blue shirt.

Carlos stood by the window and stared at the now empty space in front of the school. The sky was gray and the air was cool and heavy and suddenly everything became quiet. A few food trucks had parked up the street in anticipation of dismissal. He and his friends lingered in the room even after the shrill bell dinged and a PA announcement directed students to resume their normal school day. Tio mentioned how his father was in Mexico right now, and after the election results had become official they'd spoken on the phone, and Tio had told him that he wouldn't be allowed to come home now. "I said to him, 'Guess I'll see you in, like, four years, maybe.'" He laughed. "But my dad's not as stupid as I sometimes think he is—he knew I was just fucking with him. He said, 'What's one fucking old orange man gonna do?'"

After a time, the classroom began filling with the next period's students, and the boys dispersed. Final exams were on the horizon and they had work to do. They always had work to do.

PART II

Winter

Chapter 7

It's this weird effort of prolonging this time in my life. As is the case with any time in your life, but especially high school is such a rich and odd experience, annoying in so many ways but also unique.

—*Owen*

Harrison

The coach relayed the final play to the field. The quarterback broke the huddle and jogged to the line. The cadence progressed emphatically to the snap. The ball was transferred to the running back, who had no lanes toward open space and was summarily wrestled to his knees. Beverly Hills lost their final game of the season, 63–8, to rival Culver City High School. That they'd scored a touchdown, their fourth of the season, was a minor but meaningful consolation.

Harrison wasn't on the field with his team. He stood on the sideline, to the left of the uniformed players, with his arm in a sling. He'd dislocated his shoulder while being wedged against the ground during a tackle two weeks earlier, tried to play through it even though he couldn't raise his arm from his side, then reluctantly admitted to the coach that he was finished. In four years of football—not just games and practices but summer workouts,

weight lifting, injuries, two-a-day preseason sessions with pads—
Harrison had won two games, once with the freshman team and
once his junior year. Then, he'd been self-described as "chubby"
and played offense and defense on the interior line. Over the summer before senior year, in a bid to play skill positions for a team
perennially lacking in skill, he'd lost forty pounds by exercising all
day while eating white-meat chicken and broccoli and little else.
This year, he'd led the team in touchdowns (with two), yards from
scrimmage, interceptions, and tackles. What he had to show for it
was the full separation of multiple shoulder ligaments that would
take months of painful rehab work to mend.

Harrison joined the line of teammates to shake hands with the
Culver City players. He stood tall and broad as he looked each
passing opponent in the eye earnestly and said, "Good game—
and good luck to you guys." He lingered on the field beneath the
lights for a time, embracing teammates and family, knowing that
the likelihood of his ever again feeling this particular measure of
closeness in his life was quite small.

His very favorite game experience had been a preseason scrimmage the year before, against Morningside High in South LA.
The bus had taken them from the pristine grass lawn in front of
Beverly Hills High to the patchy, trash-strewn field of the large
LAUSD school fifteen miles away. They'd filed beneath the rusted
bleachers, from which Morningside fans taunted them regarding
their clean white jerseys with orange trim, their predominantly
pale skin, their scared, apprehensive eyes. Harrison figured they
would be in for some punishment—and they were—but once the
game began and the first Beverly running back was driven down
by the first Morningside linebacker, Harrison witnessed something
he hadn't anticipated: the linebacker stood over the running back,
extended his hand to help him up, patted him on the lower back,
and said, "Nice run, man," even though it hadn't been much of

a run at all. A few plays later, the same running back lowered his shoulder to topple the same linebacker, and the entire Morningside crowd yelled, *"Ohhhhhh!"* in unison while players from both teams gawked in a certain shared glee regarding the unexpectedly violent collision. The scrimmage progressed in that way, hard-fought and respectful, and the Morningside fans even began applauding Beverly's one- and two-yard gains, perhaps in admiration of their losing efforts, more likely amused—but still energizing.

After the season's final game, Harrison returned home to the two-bedroom apartment he'd grown up in with his single mother. They lived about a mile east of the high school. The space was small but artfully decorated; his mother was a florist for weddings and events, and she applied her aesthetic talents at home. As a boy, he would sometimes be obliged to attend opulent weddings on multi-million-dollar estates—where he would sometimes also be obliged to witness his mother be admonished and belittled by obsessive clients—and she would always remind him that all the money manifested on these occasions had very little to do with happiness or well-being, and certainly had nothing to do with respect for others.

As they did most nights, they sat together on the couch eating dinner off trays (never microwaved, since she had a phobia for the appliance) while watching sitcoms on TV. The routine helped ease the devastating feeling of an ending: a camaraderie, a time of life, a pregame nervousness that was wonderful in its signaling how much he cared. She asked him what he was feeling, and he rubbed his shoulder and said, "It sucks." She was his best friend and understood that now was not the time to probe further.

Were it not for his size, Harrison might have passed through high school invisibly the way shy people sometimes do. He didn't drink or smoke and only visited parties when friends called him to pick them up as an emergency designated driver. He was artistically minded and unassuming around girls. He gave thoughtful gifts to his teachers, such as a sweater for a beloved dog, before winter break.

But like many high school football players, he'd entered his senior year thinking only of the games to play. Now no more games remained to be played, just an injury to nurse. He aspired to make the roster of a Division I college football program, but no coaches seemed drawn to the best player on a team that not only barely ever won but barely ever lost by less than thirty points. To play college football, he would have to walk on.

His mom had asked him how he felt, and he'd referenced the soreness in his shoulder. How he really felt was adrift. Very quickly, once the final horn had sounded earlier that evening, a reality began accreting that had been unimaginable seconds earlier. After devoting so much of his body and spirit to this game, after elevating it to the point where it was synonymous with life's underlying meaning, he suddenly learned that it didn't in fact mean much with regard to life. Games had a way of ending; life had a way of going on and on and on.

Owen

Sophomore year, Owen had served as equipment manager for the girls' volleyball team. He played on the boys' team and appreciated the game, and so the manager slot was a way to spend more time around it, see a bit more of Los Angeles during away trips, and satisfy his PE requirement. In a way that was earnest while acknowledging of the role's silliness, he embraced the job and gladly rooted for the team. At a game in Arcadia, a middle-class suburb in the San Gabriel Valley, he marveled at the sheer number of fans the home team drew. The gym was packed with bodies and loud. At Beverly, even home basketball games against Santa Monica High didn't rival this raucous and devoted energy. The people here apparently cared about their volleyball—a lot. Much of the considerable energy in the gym seemed to be directed at the Beverly girls, and in gross ways: teenaged boys, feeling safe in their numbers, yelling out crude, obnoxious, and foul comments, mostly revolving around the relative attractiveness of different players. Owen, among the very small cohort of Beverly fans and experiencing a surprisingly raw feeling of protectiveness for his female friends on the court, stood up at a certain point, arms outstretched, and said, "What an asshole." He didn't speak loud and didn't point the words to anyone in particular. He was really wondering why these students didn't have anything better to do on a Friday night than heckle volleyball players.

A few moments later, a voice rose above the din and—with a modicum of anxiety—he sensed that it was directed at him. He turned around. A middle-aged woman, someone's mom, was standing a few rows back, her finger thrust straight at him and her eyes like twin drill bits. "You better watch your mouth," she commanded. In a typical situation, he might have calmly explained the strangeness of her singling him out while, amid the tiers of bleachered humans around her, awful language resounded ceaselessly. But he understood how terrible an idea that was in the given circumstances, outnumbered and far from home in a context he couldn't quite grasp. That finger, those eyes. So he faced his palms toward her and said, "I apologize, ma'am. I shouldn't have said that." His contrition did not subdue the finger jabbing or the eyes or the rage.

"You better watch it!" she replied, to the glee of the boys around her. Owen tried to sit down, watch the game, be calm and dignified. But he felt a redirection of crowd energy, from the court toward him. After a time, he moved to the team bench on the other side of the gym. With the safety of the remove, he became calmer and joked about the interaction with the players. Coupled with the calm was the embarrassment of allowing this woman to intimidate him to such a degree. He began stewing, replaying the event in his mind

and discerning what he could have said or done to appear braver. When a Beverly player landed a spike, he spontaneously stood up, raised his arms, and widened his eyes toward the Arcadia side in a mild taunt. He felt slightly vindicated and resumed watching.

The game neared its end, and Owen contemplated the long bus ride followed by whatever the night would hold, which most likely was nothing that interesting. The person beside him tapped his shoulder and pointed across the court, where the woman was now exhibiting her sons: two brawny teenagers who looked as though they'd initiated, and won, a fight or two. The three of them just leered straight at Owen with knowing smirks. Then Arcadia scored a point, and the son on the left cupped his hands around his mouth and hollered, "Fuck you." Owen now was fully clueless as to what was happening, what boundaries lay between posturing and intent to harm. All he knew was that this didn't occur in Beverly Hills.

Owen had no choice, really, but to shrink into the bench, watching the game without seeing it. He located all the exits. He purposefully didn't turn around, but he kept hearing the mother laugh. He was terrified.

The game ended, and he stood. This was when he saw one of the brothers—the bigger one—lunging in his direction while the other made a performance out of holding him back. Their mother seemed to take pride in the theater. Though the trio remained in the far bleachers, the coach still positioned the Beverly players to form a phalanx around Owen. He left the gym this way, shuffling along in the middle of twelve teenaged girls tasked with protecting him. He spent the entire bus ride peering out the window, looking for cars that might be following. Not until he was safely home did he realize that all those volleyball fanatics had probably forgotten about him an hour ago.

His father was maddeningly unsympathetic after hearing Owen's rendering of the story.

"You shouldn't have called some kid an asshole," was his matter-of-fact takeaway. "You shouldn't have given the lady that look."

In his own defense, Owen cited the imbalance between action and reaction.

"Owen, you go to Beverly Hills High School. A lot of people in the world are looking for a reason to kick your ass." His father had gone to the school himself and had once been accosted at a bowling alley for wearing a Beverly Hills High T-shirt.

"Right. I guess it's a small price to pay, having a bunch of Arcadians want to kill me."

His father's rote advice—you shouldn't have said this or done that—was annoying, but it spoke to an element of being a person in the world that he was still coming to grasp. In high school and in his hometown, he pretty much knew how any given person would react in any given interaction. He knew how to calibrate and deescalate tension between people. He knew what his teachers' and peers' general experience was and how to weave humor without hurting anyone. Beyond this place and its patterns, he couldn't necessarily identify the margins of restraint. The cabalistic nature on display in Arcadia had truly unnerved him—though in later tellings, he would configure the story to be hilarious, and he drew much comic mileage from it.

Part of what shook him so much about the 2016 election, and the reason he walked the school hallways warily in the days and weeks following, was that the upset had overturned his confidence in others' behavior. Suddenly, mundane comments unrelated to politics were interpreted as viciously offensive. Actual viciously offensive comments seemed regularized. One teacher refused to provide instruction and served donuts instead. Another walked the hallways whistling "Ding-Dong! The Witch Is Dead." Boys wearing red *Make America Great Again* caps fist-bumped one another in passing while girls shuddered and wept. Maybe he was a bit of a snowflake, or whatever term Fox News was using right now, but witnessing at shoulder height the haughtiness of some and the fragility of others made him both angry and scared: angry because, in the span of one night, the sanctity of behavior he considered "normal" had been tilted; scared because he hadn't anticipated it, wasn't prepared for it, and didn't quite know how to situate himself within it. He was a noncombative guy, admittedly sheltered, and had little experience with someone else's rage—that of a mother in Arcadia or that of a hundred million Americans.

Carlos, Tio, Luis, Byron

At APB, Mr. Sandoval, who taught US history, preached a similar perception to his students. Fights of the actually violent variety didn't really happen here, and if any conflict did become physical, the disciplinary response was swift and sharp; one of the advantages of the small school space was that teachers could track physical movement and latent energy through the hallways and act preventatively to smother any forming tensions. But the primary deterrent was familiarity. Students here knew each other. They knew that Luis lacked a cap to his bluster. They knew that Tio would never relinquish the last word of a debate. They knew Byron was bigger than his quiet nature intimated.

Mr. Sandoval was in his late twenties and had grown up the son of school janitors in Pasadena before gaining admission to UCLA and majoring in Chicano studies, then earning his teaching degree. Tio had found in him a mentor and, maybe, a friend. He'd become interested in the nuances of Sandoval's journey—in how the teacher had not only fulfilled the first-generation-immigrant ideal of going to college but also located his purpose along the way: teaching American history to young people who, by virtue of race and class, had historically lived only in its margins. "Why come back to the ghetto to hang out with all us punks when you could have gone somewhere and made money?" Tio asked once with something like wonder. Mr. Sandoval replied in a low-key, straightforward fashion: "I love history, I'm good at teaching it, the money is decent, and yeah, you are a bunch of punks." He'd begun his career teaching at a large public high school in Watts, with a metal detector set inside the front door and gates bolted over the windows. He'd taught many bright, resilient, kind students there. But the disruptors who inevitably passed through his classroom were confrontational—both with him and among themselves—to a sometimes overpowering degree. The toll of constantly gauging the energy in the room was mentally exhausting, and it was professionally degrading. When a student approached and stated that if Mr. Sandoval didn't give him a passing grade, he would track the teacher down off campus and beat the shit out of him, Mr. Sandoval decided to transfer elsewhere. The decision was heartbreaking, as his entire reason for teaching high school—a reason shared by tens of thousands of educators countrywide—was to support young people facing challenges similar to those he'd faced not long ago. Specifically, his purpose was to teach US history to those most decimated by its long, often terrible currents—to abridge and fortify against the underlying racism of textbooks written by predominantly white academics.

At APB, he was able to do just that, for students who were for the most part receptive. But with the position came a new fear: that his students were too comfortable in turn.

"You can say stuff to people here, to me, you can say pretty much whatever you want, and no one's really going to do anything. Elsewhere, not even far away—like across the street in Washington Park—you say the same thing and it'll be really bad for you."

"But don't we all know that?" Tio replied. They were in a meeting for a student group that Tio and Mr. Sandoval had started in the fall, called Caballeros con Cultura, a kind of roundtable discussion regarding what exactly it meant to be a young Latino male in the world, how to maintain dignity and place in a society that seemed to feel most comfortable with their residing on the periphery. The group's purpose was somewhat vague, and Tio suspected that most of the two dozen present had joined because of how many girls he kept propagandizing would attend the C3 dance they were planning for the spring, but he strove to lead grounded discussions about manhood and what exactly it meant to be a man. "I mean, if I don't know you, I know what not to say to you."

"But I still watch you all developing habits here," Mr. Sandoval said. "Bad habits, of just blurting out stuff. Some really offensive stuff. Calling girls bitches, telling guys to shut the fuck up, making jokes about people being undocumented."

"We're all cool with each other, though. It doesn't hurt anyone."

"You sure about that?"

Tio laughed self-consciously. "Well, I'm a jackass. Everyone's aware of that, at least."

Mr. Sandoval spoke seriously: "I'm just saying, there're a lot of things you can get back. Like if you screw up one test, you study and do well on the next one. You waste money on some stupid shoes, you work and earn it back. Get evicted, find another place. But *words*, once they leave your mouth"—he eyed Tio again—"you can never get those back. And shit happens. Guys, girls, brown, black, old, young—it happens all the time around here."

Later in the day in AP Calc, as if to manifest purposefully Mr. Sandoval's meditation on behavior, Tio watched as Luis ripped a girl's shoe from her foot. She grabbed for it, cursing him. Luis was much taller and easily kept the sneaker out of reach.

"What the hell are you doing with her shoe?" Tio asked.

"She was bothering me."

Tio said, "She's bothering you and your response is to take her *shoe*?"

"Fuck it," Luis replied, which didn't make sense. He put the sole to his ear and pretended it was a phone, imitating the one-shoed girl. *"Heyyy, do you believe what she was, like, wearing today? . . . I mean what was she thinking . . . it's like oh my God!"*

"You're the reason I turned out rotten," Tio reflected. "Having to sit with you for four years."

Unable to get a hand near her shoe, the girl chose the more accessible route of biting Luis on the arm.

"Shit! Now I've got rabies!" They'd all been reading *Their Eyes Were Watching God* in English and were somewhat transfixed by the climactic hurricane, during which a primary character contracted rabies from a stranded dog. There'd been an overuse of the word *rabies* lately, but no student had actually bitten another until now. Luis then shot the footwear like a basketball toward the trash can halfway across the room, but he missed badly.

"We've been in school just too damn long." This was Tio's take-away from the nonsense.

Thanksgiving vacation and its nine days sans school began the next week. The days were not just a rest but a psychological release: from pop quizzes, college essays, waking up at seven and being told what to do for the next eight hours. For most everyone in school, the first two days of vacation were about sleep and phones and video games. Then a certain restlessness set in and group outings were arranged, either by train or by Luis's car. Tuesday night of the break found Carlos, Byron, Luis, and a few girl friends from student council in Koreatown, a large, dense district just west of downtown, for their first authentic Korean barbecue experience. (Tio was generally unavailable during holidays, because he spent the whole time skateboarding.) They parked and wandered around beneath tall apartment towers and shopping malls advertising karaoke in Korean characters backlit in bright neon. Dozens of restaurants lined Sixth Street, and they couldn't read the signs, so they picked one that seemed to have the most actual Korean people inside, portending authenticity. When they entered, all the employees looked toward the door. Carlos expected them to eye this young group of brown people warily, because that's what people did. Instead, everyone called out in unison an enthusiastic Korean greeting through wide smiles. They sat around the grill that formed a crater in the middle of the table. As the waiter lit the charcoal, they marveled at the young Korean children in the restaurant, toddlers composing artful bites of meat and kimchi on their forks and feeding themselves: no screaming, no running around the space wildly, no parents bribing them to eat one more bite, which was how they'd experienced childhood.

"How the hell is not one person in here arguing?" Luis asked.

"You know someone is," Byron said. "They just argue differently."

"Yeah, there's no way a six-person family makes it through a meal without getting pissed off at each other, I don't care if you're Korean."

The *banchan* plates came, confusing everyone. Kimchi, *bokkeum, jorim, danmuji, gyeran-mari*: they had no idea what anything was and so shrugged and dug in, wincing at the pickled-ness. After the small dishes were consumed—except for the pickled radishes, which they found inedible—the meat arrived, at which point Carlos looked at other tables and realized the meat was intended to be combined with what they'd already eaten. Later, the bill came—$22 per person—and the table experienced that wide-eyed, universal amazement and regret that often concluded group restaurant splurges.

"What did you think of the food?" one of the girls asked.

"I guess I have to think it was amazing now, don't I?" Luis replied, holding up the bill.

On Thanksgiving, Luis and his older siblings ate a simple rendition of the national meal in their apartment with their mother, and as night fell the siblings drove to visit their father while their mother remained behind. There, perhaps in reaction to the long silences and lack of effort on their father's part to have anything but a glum conversation, his older brother started punching his sister on the arm; his brother, when bored, generally hit nearby surfaces. She fought back and landed a fist to his jaw just beneath the ear. He didn't say anything, but Luis could tell he was simmering, and so Luis wasn't surprised when, as they were leaving, his brother locked the car door before his sister could get in. She pounded on the window and shouted. He laughed and refused her access. She climbed on the hood and glared at him. His brother started driving down the street, slowly, but with enough speed so that when he braked, momentum carried her backward off the hood and onto the pavement. She stood up with a bruised hip. His brother finally unlocked the door, and she climbed in gingerly and crossed her arms.

"Wouldn't have happened if you hadn't climbed onto the hood."

"Wouldn't have happened if you hadn't locked me out."

"Wouldn't have happened if you hadn't hit me."

"Holy shit you're a fucking asshole—you were the one hitting me!"

Luis was too preoccupied with laughing to involve himself. "I sometimes can't believe that this is my life," he said with affection.

Carlos was experiencing an unusually quiet Thanksgiving dinner at home. Typically, they went to his aunt's house. She was single with two daughters in their early twenties and a teenaged son. But no combination of the four people got along, so being with all of them together meant a web of screaming spun over the table: mother at daughter, sister at brother, brother at mother, mother at other daughter, and on and on. Carlos's own mother remained distraught three weeks after the election and didn't have the fortitude to withstand the noise at her sister's, and so the five of them, including his brother, ate at home.

When Jose had still been an APB student, he and Carlos would arrive a half hour early to school most days. They would sit on the floor in the hallway, ostensibly to prime themselves for whatever tests were coming up. But mostly they would just talk: about soccer, books, politics. Once in a while, they might reference the future, then an unknown. What passing teachers saw was a picture of an older brother pulling the younger along, while the younger brother pushed the older ahead. Carlos had felt not quite like a peer then, but close enough to have no airs, no compulsion to impress. Now his brother was firmly entrenched at Yale, and though he remained very much himself—controlled, confident, selective of words, humble—he was nevertheless maturing and evolving and now familiar with experiences that Carlos, even with his weeks at Brown, couldn't fathom. Carlos wondered how jolting it must be to travel back and forth across the country, between one place symbolic of America's highest promise and the other of its fixed poverty, to exist fully within these two disingenuous clichés. Over Thanksgiving dinner, they talked about work and weekend plans and traffic—in Los Angeles, always traffic—but for the most part they talked about family, and school.

Chapter 8

I'm exactly where I thought I would be, kind of to a T, it's ridiculous. I put in exactly the amount of effort I intended to. I'm friends with the same friends. I had exactly the dating experience I thought. Maybe it will add up to something, maybe not, it all just kind of is.

—Bennett

Bennett

Exams were the barrier standing monolithic before the beckoning light of winter break, as if in accordance with enduring mythological constructions by which the hero must overcome some final, mighty challenge before emerging battered but victorious and changed. Thanksgiving didn't help; no matter how well crafted the holiday assignment was with regard to preserving the knowledge gained thus far in the year, students were inclined to put that work off until the final hours of vacation and then realize in those hours just how much they'd forgotten. Particularly in subjects that were heavy on memorization rather than conceptualization, like chemistry and history, the setback could be severe: who remembered the valence of phosphorus or the date the Treaty of Tordesillas was signed, after a week off?

They were harangued for this tendency by parents, teachers, society—but the practical reality was that exams would be unpleasant regardless, and the idea of protracting that unpleasantness across the span of vacation stood counter to basic reason. Much healthier to succumb to the current moment, to do anything that was more enjoyable than studying—which was everything—and contend with the work once other alternatives had dwindled, typically the night before the exam.

Bennett was skilled at the last minute. For him, there was never a test in two or three weeks; the test always was tomorrow. Early in high school, he'd observed classmates manage this cycle in different ways. They pulled all-nighters. They accepted a poor grade, vowing to develop better study habits and make up for the score on later tests, which sometimes worked out and usually didn't. They skipped school the day of to provide more time. They invented new ways to ask for extra credit. They blamed others.

In order to avoid such apparent conceits, Bennett relied on a well-honed fusion of math and intentionality. Students at Beverly, and in most schools, had online access to their grades. On any given day, they could log in and see the numerical product of all the homework assignments, tests and quizzes, movie projects, class participation marks, absences and tardies. Teachers had different algorithms by which they weighted the factors. Some placed a high value on homework. Some used the final exam to account for 80 percent of one's grade. Some used steep curves. This information was all available with a high degree of precision to those desiring to track it. At the outset of each semester, Bennett gathered all the percentages alongside the assignment schedules and figured out exactly what he'd need to score at each juncture in order to end up with an NYU-worthy grade. Almost halfway through senior year, he'd hit all the numbers he'd aimed for, and he couldn't recall a time of being genuinely stressed—not about school. He was stressed about college, and about money for college. He was stressed about girls. He was stressed about open-mic stand-up comedy performances. He was stressed about potentially meeting his father for the first time. He was stressed about moving away from his best friends. But rarely had he stayed up later than he wanted to doing homework.

A friend once suggested that he might be missing out on some essential passage in life, that maybe he was moving through high school in such an automated frame of mind that he wouldn't remember anything notable about this time and age and place. Bennett's consideration of this idea was brief. Peering back over the last few years, he certainly had regrets—he could have been kinder to his mom, for instance—but he couldn't identify anything he'd grow old feeling as though he'd missed. The performative act of gasping over the magnitude of one's own course load did not feel to him like a precious and irretrievable marker of time. Of course, if NYU didn't accept him, then this meticulously orchestrated experiment he'd conducted over four years would turn out to be quite a grand failure.

Tio, Byron

Tio and Byron were both shocked by how suddenly their applications became a morass. For months, the deadlines had seemed comfortably situated after Thanksgiving, and now that day's passing gripped them with a singular fusion of panic and lethargy. The two boys had disparate personalities, but both were intelligent and driven—enrolled in multiple APs, active in student government—and had been well schooled by Ms. Reyes on the admissions process and its stages of demands. They shouldn't have fallen behind. But they also shared an unvoiced aversion to asking for help, particularly from adults, even as they were surrounded at this school by adults whose life purpose was in fact to help them. They struggled silently and very much alone.

Byron had contended with shyness throughout his school experience; the nature of schooling, of placing two dozen or more young people in a classroom and asking them to assert themselves in some way, was always burdensome for the quiet sorts. Byron felt that he'd assumed a healthy comfort with his plight in high school, mainly through his friendships, in which (beneath his suffering Luis's jokes) lay the intimacy and even, in brief glimpses, the vulnerability required for deeper understanding and caring for one another. Because Carlos and Luis were very much in command of the application timeline, he should have been at ease relying on them for advice: what form waived the application fees, sometimes as high as $50, from private schools; what form secured free food for low-income students living on campus in the Cal State system; which tax information mattered and which didn't. Either of his friends could have answered all of his questions without shame; that they could was in fact what caused him shame. At home, his parents couldn't help, not with essays, not with comparing and contrasting options, not with anything, really, besides imploring him to go to the best possible school for the least amount of money. He was very much on his own, and so engaging with the websites and paperwork brought stress, while laying them aside until tomorrow, and tomorrow again, and tomorrow after that, calmed him.

In addition, he chose to allocate most of the time he did spend on applications to schools like Cornell and Brown, schools he saw his closest friends applying to that were reaches for him—beyond reaches, really—while he passed over many of the tiresome steps required by schools like Cal State Long Beach, a campus he'd enjoyed visiting.

"You got to just sit down with Ms. Reyes," Carlos urged him, sensing his anxiety without obliging Byron to admit to it explicitly. "You know she's cool, she'll get through everything with you."

"Yeah, I know," Byron replied. And while he would knock on Ms. Reyes's door now and again, it was always to inquire about some extraneous detail of some specific form. He didn't alert her to the larger shadow enveloping him. One-on-one conversations, particularly those likely to hold disappointing content, made him nervous. So he avoided the chair in her office, and days passed, and deadlines grew closer, and he kept telling himself that it would all work out—that he was a good guy and a smart guy and he didn't have to trouble anyone.

Tio's confusion involved the specificity of his major and the way the mathematics of admissions in the California system changed drastically each year as the infrastructure strained against growth. He'd been determined to study engineering for much of his life, in part due to his admiration for a father who'd have preferred he not study anything at all. But the subsets of the broader field were manifold and highly specific: computer engineering, mechanical engineering, electrical engineering, aerospace engineering, civil engineering, chemical engineering, environmental engineering, industrial engineering, nuclear engineering, systems engineering, agricultural engineering, software engineering. Different UC, Cal State, and private schools offered different majors. Cross-referencing all that information was exhausting, and his parents didn't have Wi-Fi at home, so research was conducted on the school's laptops or on his phone with its cracked screen and iffy service provider.

He wanted to spend his adult life studying science processes in the mechanical, electrical, or chemical field, which were also projected to have some of the largest job growth numbers in the coming years and midcareer salaries in the low six figures. Not surprisingly, they represented three of the four most sought-after undergrad engineering majors. By listing them on his applications, Tio would be placing himself in competition with tens of thousands of others, most of them presumably well prepared and highly motivated, for limited spots in perennially over-populated programs. If he applied for mechanical engineering but received admission to some less compelling field like industrial or civil, transferring was said to be equally competitive and difficult. Tio was known outwardly for nothing if not his self-confidence, but this very first stage of trying to fulfill his aspiration seeded him with self-doubt.

Knowing what one truly desired to pursue as a profession at age seventeen was a preposterous notion, but it opened up numerous field-specific scholarships and was supposedly a positive with regard to admissions, signifying "direction" (or some such valuable quality), as opposed to applying undeclared. And Tio did know, or thought he knew now, with surety. Yet the undeclared option beckoned, because if he checked the engineering box and failed to gain entry, it meant that others who'd checked the same box had been deemed worthier. If he checked undeclared and wasn't ultimately able to enroll as an engineer, then he would be able to blame the bureaucratic machinations of a multibillion-dollar system with over two hundred thousand individual applicants each year. So very much of his high school education had been dependent on the arbitrary nature of judgment and the individuals wielding it over him in various ways. In December of his senior year, as the most consequential judgment yet grew imminent, he was weary.

In English class near the end of December, an English teacher berated him for not having his paper printed by the beginning of class.

"I haven't had time to get to the office today," he said, referring to the common printer they all used. "Is it cool if I send it now and go pick it up right after class and bring it to you?"

"Absolutely not, Tio. You were supposed to have it printed *right now*, and you don't because you didn't listen to the assignment, unlike everyone else in this room." She went on a bit longer. He nearly wanted to cry, maybe out of the embarrassing publicizing of his lapse, maybe because the teacher seemed to view it as a signal of some more defining flaw in his personhood. Later, when he overheard another student—quiet, female—make the exact same request of the teacher and receive warm permission, he simply felt mad—and madder still because of the fact that he'd been aware of the need to print the composition and could have easily done so during passing period, but he'd been talking to his girlfriend. His work hadn't been very good, at any rate. The overall interaction seemed like a perfectly appropriate metaphor for college admissions. Whether real or imagined, such metaphors abounded these days.

He loathed composition writing anyway, and not only because of the difficult difference between written and spoken language for bilingual students. In a deeper and more personal sense, his aversion had to do with the discrimination inherent to written exercises. If he performed poorly on a problem set in calculus or physics, he knew that the underlying concepts exhibited in the set had not yet aligned for him. Once they did—once he crossed that boundary of comprehension—the sense of achievement was real and lasting, as if his brain had grown a new fold of matter that would enable him to always solve any problem testing this concept. A correct answer contained no subjectivity. Dopamine aplenty surged through his head.

By nature, success in writing was more elusive and pained. When he scored poorly on an essay in government or English, the inherent takeaway was that his own ideas and his ability to communicate them were deficient—or maybe the grader just didn't like him as a person. Red pen marks that seemed accusatory

JEFF HOBBS

eliminated full sentences that he'd spent time constructing. Arrows and phrasings in the margins told him directly how his thinking was not advanced enough to "get" the material. And since writing held no triumphant instant of understanding that paralleled math, no objective and universally agreed-to formula for interpreting a poem and then crafting a flawless paper about it—since the only goal of writing was to "improve," and doing so meant expending huge portions of time and energy in order to encounter repeated criticism—Tio's tendency was to skirt the judgment that so tired him by mocking the material itself.

"Why should I give a fuck what some lonely lady wrote about her garden in, like, 1890?" (referring to Emily Dickinson's "There Is Another Sky"). "What the hell does it matter what I think led to the Cold War when there's already a thousand books about it and the shit ended forty years ago?" "Who even writes letters when we have email and text?"

He would direct such questions toward whichever unfortunate classmate happened to be nearby. But really, the scorn pointed inward, blanketing deeper questions of self-worth that he would never voice but were being exhumed by college applications—which also demanded a fair amount of writing that he couldn't dismiss on the basis of practicality. Though he did dismiss the practicality of the essay question for a $10,000 STEM scholarship: *If you become president, what would you change?*

He hoped to become an engineer; he was 100 percent certain he would never be president.

Jon

Jon's procrastinating tendencies infected each of his myriad obligations, but his classwork above all. He could explain his psychology in convenient ways—he performed better under pressure and so he intentionally created fraught situations for himself; he prioritized fun over work for his mental health—but each self-inflicted emergency stemming from his time-management habits, or lack thereof, demanded adjustments that he never seemed to make. His junior year included Ms. Kim's AP Language class—a notorious combination of one of the most demanding teachers and difficult subjects in school. The midterm paper represented a 40 percent portion of the final grade (first draft and revision accounting for 20 percent each). Though the paper had been an open, semester-long project, he didn't begin composing his first draft until ten thirty the night before it was due. Ms. Kim was delightful outside the classroom, eager to engage in conversation while exuding kindness through her bright eyes and distinct laugh, always walking around leashed to her French bulldog. In class, she could be frightening: high in expectation, rigid in results, unforgiving in her grading system. Jon worked for eleven hours and twenty minutes that night, crouched over the cluttered desk writing about the anti-vaccination movement and its portrayal in certain facets of American media.

As the first gray light of day began to penetrate the small windows of the condo, he continued poring through his literature and striking the keys. He finished his paper, or some shoddy semblance of a paper, at 9:50. His mother, who had been tracking his labor before she went to sleep and after she woke up, agreed to call the school and say that he was sick; her indulgence stupefied him with gratitude. Language class was at ten, and a physical copy was due, no emailed PDFs, no exceptions. He called a friend and arranged to send the document to her to be printed in the school library and then handed off to another kid in the class. (A benefit of being a good person, Jon was learning, was that others didn't mind going out of their way for you when asked.) Ms. Kim received the paper while Jon napped at home. She graded his work harshly, as she should have and as he knew she would. The most disheartening part of the situation was that he was fascinated by the topic of vaccination.

The result left him with the paper's revision and its half of the overall score due a few weeks later. Once again, these weeks passed and he failed to spend a single minute of them working on the paper. He also failed to account for the fact that the revised paper's due date, a Friday, was preceded by his AP Chem exam, the three-day AP US History classroom final, and the AP US History national exam. At the time, he was carrying an 86 overall in Ms. Kim's class and needed to reach 89.1 for an A. Amazingly, Ms. Kim granted him an extension for the weekend. He stayed up most of the night Friday and Saturday, then all night again on Sunday. Throughout, though bleary-eyed and feeling like a troglodyte in the faint glow of his laptop screen, he thought he witnessed the content come into focus as he altered the structure in places, excavated minute details of supporting evidence from the tall stack of books he'd amassed on the subject, and rendered his conclusion. The thesis had to do with the way popular media, in presenting the anti-vaccination movement as irredeemably ignorant, assumed a collective, undisguised tone of condescension that in turn further entrenched anti-vaxxers in their stances—that the media's active lack of nuance and respect perpetuated the precise behavior that it aimed to dismantle in the name of public safety. But he was groggy and not particularly confident in the work's overall coherence.

He cared about the paper, the subject, the class, especially the teacher. Yet he'd ignored this thing he cared about for an entire semester because he also cared about a dozen other time-consuming endeavors, and such was the incongruity of his life. Jon did get the A in the class, his score providing the floor of the curve's top bracket, an innocuous tenth of a point proving the difference between success and failure (which, in his mother's perception, was any other letter besides A). And he didn't change his habits. He wanted to, and he tried to, but he didn't. As senior year progressed, he managed his hours with even less organization while figuring that at this point, he'd just about earned all the grades that colleges would care about. But once he actually reached college, he would absolutely change his habits—or so he promised himself.

Carlos

Carlos was answering phones at the front-office desk at school, a part-time clerical job he did a few times a week. Between answering calls from parents asking questions in urgent Spanish about dates of events and why they were receiving absent notices when their kids had left for school every morning, a message from QuestBridge appeared in his email informing him that final results had been posted. He clicked the link and entered his password and waited for the slowish Internet connection to open the portal. Then he learned that he'd been matched with and accepted to Princeton University.

Chapter 9

It's hard, though, because it's like, damn, this is my future. Because once you submit your majors, you either get accepted or you don't. I was talking to some of the UCLA administrators, they were saying a lot of people are getting in with religious studies. So it's like if you just want to get in, you pick a random major no one cares about. That's what I should have tried to do but I fucked up.

—Tio

Tio

COURSE	GRADE	%	HRS
Academic Support	A+	100	5.00
AP Calculus AB	A+	98	5.00
AP Chemistry	A–	90	5.00
AP English Lang	A	95	5.00
English 12A	A–	90	5.00
Student Government	A–	90	5.00
U.S. Government 12	A	95.5	5.00

"It was difficult but it got done," read the caption to Tio's December 20 Facebook post, followed by an emoji of a bold, double-underlined *100*. He wasn't trying to be haughty, but rather he was advertising the fact that, even though he swore a lot and was called out by teachers and carried himself very much like the skate punk he was, he did care about school, and he did work hard. Thirty-four of his friends "liked" the post and left comments such as "Keep up the bad work PIMP," "Felicidades Tio!" "good shit," and "You going places." An ulterior motive of the post was the hope that it might prompt more Christmas presents from relatives.

He mentioned his grades—casually—to his parents. His mother was glad and asked to see the figures, which he brought up on his phone. She clasped her hands together and grinned and closed her eyes as if in thankful prayer for a blast of good fortune she hadn't anticipated. His father leaned forward and squinted at the screen as one might check a weather report. Tio had anticipated this or some like reaction, but foreknowledge failed to blunt the sheer spectacle of standing in his kitchen with the man who'd raised him, showing this man a set of straight A's, three of them in AP classes, and receiving nothing. He figured that there had to be synapses firing electricity and creating a response in this man's brain, there had to be personal memories whirling and merging into emotions. He wanted to know what those thoughts and emotions were, even if they were entirely negative. His father couldn't be so thoroughly, authentically apathetic as he seemed. Or maybe he could.

Tio had ultimately decided not to write his college essay about his father. Even though the man's sobriety persisted still, and Tio was very proud of him (a pride that would have made for a crowd-pleasing conclusion to the story), the passage of his sophomore year in high school was too excruciating to unpack publicly.

He'd written instead about the general plight of being poor and brown skinned in South LA.

A few days into the two-week winter break, he went to the Westminster Mall, just south of Long Beach, with his sisters, an uncle, and a few cousins. They went to Sky Zone, a cavernous room carpeted with gigantic trampolines, where they all bounded around pegging each other with rubber balls for an hour. Breathless, they went to the food court and sat by the fountain while the uncle went to Target. Tio gave his ten-year-old cousin a penny and motioned to the fountain: "Go make your wishes come true." The boy, overweight and adorable in his glasses, seemed conflicted as he stared at the water's surface, the hundreds of coins greening beneath. Tio laughed, "Must be some hell of a wish to take you so long."

"I don't know what to wish."

"Wish for candy. Or world peace or something."

The boy shook his head. "I *do* know, but I don't know if I should make it." His cousin looked up dolefully. "I wish my mom to die."

"I don't think you should wish that," Tio cautioned.

"She's the reason we're fat," the boy said.

"You dumbass," his brother replied.

The insult seemed to offer an affirmation. The boy closed his eyes and tossed the coin in with a soft plunking sound. His tight facial expression persisted as the uncle returned and they wandered around the mall a bit longer. At a certain point, Tio noticed his little cousin wiping his glasses: the boy was openly weeping.

"What's wrong now? You upset because they called you names?"

A hard, quick shake of the head, and then, softly, "I shouldn't have made that wish."

"Yeah, it wasn't that good of a wish."

"I think I just killed my mom." Salt water was trickling out of his face as he shielded it with his hand so that his brothers wouldn't see.

Tio leaned on his shoulder. "Listen, I have to tell you something. It's not a real thing—the fountain. It takes a whole lot more than a cent to make wishes come true."

The boy breathed out, grasping the conceit, and looked relieved.

Owen, Bennett

Small clumps of tar speckled the beaches of Santa Barbara. These were natural deposits washed in from the oil-rich coastal flats, where massive derricks rose from the distant waters on the horizon. The platforms were ugly totems to industry in the otherwise pristine setting where Owen and Bennett walked, the latter holding a camera and taking numerous pictures. The air was chilly but still, and the sea was a glassy, shimmering reflection of the gray sky. Pelicans glided lazily inches above the surface and a pod of dolphins cut precise arcs inches below. The Channel Islands loomed miles off shore with their whalelike shadows. The beachfront homes all had wide windows and sprawling decks on stilts from which their owners could absorb the scenery over coffee or wine. Owen stole weekends here at his family's house now and again. Santa Barbara was a calm and lazy place an hour and a half from Los Angeles. The small city held little to do for teenaged boys, and that was its draw. They walked and photographed wildlife and talked.

"Finding another person attractive makes me uneasy," Owen said, "whereas you find peace of mind in it."

"Of course: I like someone's picture online and our profiles say we both like Harry Potter books, let's go out."

"Is that the one you went out with sophomore year? She lived in, like, Egypt?"

"She was the closest I've ever been to my lifelong dream of having a girlfriend. But she lived near Six Flags—way too far to work."

"Nicole and I were walking away from rehearsal last week, and she came up between us." Nicole was his girlfriend and their inter-rupter was the head of the drama department, who had conceived of *Pericles* in space. Owen imitated the teacher putting a hand on each of their shoulders and speaking in a conspiratorial hush. "She was like, 'So you two have a big decision to make. What are you going to do next year?' Nicole and I looked at each other and laughed. 'Seriously, the long-distance thing never works.' We're like, 'Okay, let's lay it all out right here, thanks!'"

"Did you and Nicole actually talk about it?"

"We could chuckle about it, but no. It's still just kind of there."

He was referring to the timeless conundrum of whether he and his girlfriend would attempt to stay together once college began. The question still lay far off, like the oil platforms; but like the platforms, its existence was vaguely disturbing his momentary peace of mind. He had true feelings for her. Their senses of humor aligned in a way that drew out a lighthearted kindness and gave him a long-sought confidence. Losing both upon leaving home—the person he cared about and the self-worth he'd accrued—would be confusing and sad. And yet staying together across however many miles and experiences would separate them in college seemed its own predetermined disappointment.

Owen had been waitlisted by Wesleyan in Connecticut and had to wait until April to learn whether or not the other schools he'd applied to—schools in Boston, New York, Oregon, and Ohio—deemed him worthy (he had a strong feeling that the few schools that truly excited him wouldn't, being as their admissions standards were overall higher than Wesleyan's). Meanwhile, Bennett would hear from NYU in February. In eighth grade, they'd been warned that high school would drastically alter the social arrangement of their lives. Yet here they were four years later, walking on the shore, talking through and over and around topics of the moment, as they'd done then. But it seemed clear enough—much clearer than the thickening skies over the water—that though they still hadn't learned where their future homes would be, they would lose large pieces of their identities upon embarking there. They would lose people. They would lose simple frames of time like the one they were in now.

Carlos, Byron, Luis

Carlos and Byron had no real reason for wandering around the Los Angeles County Museum of Art. Their original plan this morning had been to visit a vintage music store in Highland Park, not too far by train from their homes, but they'd decided to buy day passes for the train and only spent an hour at the store, leaving a rare afternoon without obligation. They didn't have money for food or a movie and so they'd headed west by train and bus to Museum Row, as the well-trafficked area of West Hollywood was known. Most museums were free with student IDs. Luis was supposed to have joined but had opted out.

What are you doing instead? Carlos had texted.

Nothing, Luis had written back. *I'm doing nothing*. Then a *Zzzzzz* emoji.

The LACMA loomed over Wilshire Boulevard in great blocks of clashingly designed appendages. The boys approached the outdoor installation called *Urban Light*—a few dozen historical gas lamps from around the city placed in a square of dense rows in front of the museum's entrance. Little kids scurried around the bases of the lampposts while couples took selfies of themselves kissing. Behind was a shaded area with an outdoor French restaurant where idle yuppies ate charcuterie from marble cutting boards while drinking white wine. The museum grounds were interconnected with the La Brea Tar Pits, and the boys followed the footpaths there, past huge pallets of excavated earth holding the fossils of mammoths and dire wolves and other extinct fauna. In a black pond burbling with subterranean gases and ringed with natural tar residue, the statue of a mother elephant stuck in the sludge reached its trunk toward a father elephant and their baby, expressions fixed in panic.

"That's kind of scary—like for little kids?"

"It's scary for *me*," Carlos replied, thinking of the new president-elect and all the frantic neighborhood talk of family separations.

They toured the museum, cool and uncrowded and dim inside, and passed the Picassos near the entrance, *Toros Vallauris 1958* and *Jeune Fille Inspirée par Cranach.* The Monets were pleasing, as were Ruscha's *Standard Station* and Matisse's *La Gerbe.* The hall containing gleaming suits of medieval armor was awesome, the modern art wing less so.

"Feeling cultured yet?"

"I guess?"

Their favorite room contained a large installation called *Metropolis*, a complicated Erector Set–like latticework of Matchbox car tracks with hundreds of toy cars carried up a wide central ramp and diverging downward in dozens of directions. They watched these cars for a time and fell into a trancelike state: the constant motion, the dull hum of plastic in easy friction, the memories of filling whole afternoons with cars and ramps as young, simple children.

Carlos had been on the receiving end of complicated energies since the QuestBridge match. His extended family was elated of course, and they'd all gathered at his home for a small yard party. Since his brother had gotten into Yale two years earlier, the festivities contained feelings of casual familiarity. He hadn't posted the news on social media in an effort to reach winter break without a fracas; he didn't enjoy online attention the way some did. But teachers were talking about it, and news generally spread faster in high school than in any other milieu. Everyone in school knew within a day, and every teacher made a point of stopping him to offer congratulations. Carlos kept saying, "Thank you," repeatedly, and he meant it. Yet while these double-handed handshakes with his various educators were special, they also almost always took place in crowded hallways during passing period, in front of other kids, drawing their stares. And the stares were the hardest for him. Most of them, especially from the underclassmen, were completely benign and often admiring, accompanied by grins and head nods that transmitted a certain kinship as well as the unvoiced hope that, because they were also students at this school, they, too, could go places—maybe not Princeton, but somewhere that had seemed inaccessible until just very recently.

Certain students, however, projected the darker shades of human nature with regard to the achievements of others. These were few, all seniors and no doubt jaded by their own specific and uncertain college journeys—the endless applications, the impossible financials—but he caught them tucked amid the hundreds of faces. Carlos didn't necessarily know these kids, nor they him. He didn't feel angry and he didn't feel unsafe. He empathized with whatever the individual challenges were that might have engendered such resentment. But he carried their feelings with him.

"Eh, fuck those people," Luis advised with an eye roll and a shrug—Luis who possessed the sometimes enviable capacity to treat most any situation with an eye roll and a shrug.

College was competitive. The statistics of space and bodies and grades and money were daunting on their own for millions of prospective high school students in America, but numbers didn't account for the layers of emotion and their stakes. Sports notwithstanding, this was the first major contest in their lives, the first emphatic demonstration of their standing among greater society—even more so than SATs or GPAs. Throughout adult life, they would most likely never be asked again what their SAT scores had been; they were all sure to be asked many hundreds of times where they'd gone to college.

For all of the seniors, whatever transpired in the next three months would play a large and mysterious and hugely defining role in the next many decades—not just in job-seeking but in how they were to be measured and perceived in American society. Certain elements were within their control, or at least gave the illusion of being so, such as how well they organized materials and wrote essays. Many other elements were as governable as the physics of a faraway star, such as how admissions officers subjectively interpreted their materials and compared them with those of other applicants. Naturally, they paid attention to how their classmates were faring. Just as naturally, they critiqued and judged and suspected manipulation or even foul play: was this person listing Chicano studies as her major because she cared about Mexican culture or because it was less competitive than biology at UCLA? At the core of such compulsions was insecurity.

And so some surmised that Carlos had only gotten into an Ivy because his brother had done so first, or that he was the teachers' favorite and so they put more care into their recommendations, or that he possessed some inside channels from his summer camp. For those predisposed to such thinking, the notion that he'd simply worked damn hard while taking advantage of whatever good fortune found him—that notion tasted bad while they watched him receive his steady succession of high fives and fist bumps.

But Carlos couldn't control the feelings of people he didn't know, and he brushed them off in what could be called a Luisian manner: eye roll, shrug, fuck 'em. Princeton or no, he was still a student at Ánimo Pat Brown. He still belonged here.

He and Byron took the bus from the museum back to the Metro station, and the trains back to their neighborhood. Before parting ways, Carlos said, "Yo, we might take a hike at Griffith Park tomorrow, if Luis has his car. You coming?"

Byron shook his head. "No—I think I have to lay concrete tomorrow."

"Lay concrete? Where?"

"In our driveway. It's all busted up. My dad finally wants to fix it."

"How much is he paying you for that? Most contractors make, like, thirty bucks an hour."

Byron laughed and shook his head. He was mournful about losing a day of vacation to manual labor and anxious about his applications, due a few days after break ended, all in various states of incompletion.

"All right," Carlos said. "Well, hit us up when you're finished, maybe we can come get you."

The group didn't end up hiking—Luis's mother told him that she needed him to drive her to a doctor's appointment, so he canceled the outing. Then his mother ended up canceling the appointment at the last minute. Luis wasn't as annoyed as he normally would have been, as he'd learned on December 23 that he'd been accepted early to Cal Poly Pomona, one of two polytechnic schools in the Cal State system, prestigious in the sciences. The school had been his first choice at some point due to its strong engineering program, but he'd cooled on it after a cousin's friend who lived in the area had told him there was nothing to do there. But the security relieved him of the stress of regular applications. A more urgent stress involved Christmas presents. This year, friends at school had been giving one another gifts, something they'd never done before since everybody understood that nobody's family had excess money. But a sense of the ending of things, an early-onset nostalgia, had led to the proliferation of gift-giving—and having a lot of friends turned out to be expensive.

Latinos tended to celebrate Christmas Eve more so than Christmas Day. This was when families gathered, overate to the point of severe discomfort, and exchanged presents. Luis spent the evening with his cousins. They had pooled together some money to give his mother a gift card for rent, on which she was always a month or two behind. The sum wasn't enough to fully catch them up, but it was helpful and, Luis found, oddly touching. Last year had been their first Christmas since their parents had separated and had felt hollow, mechanical, a forced simulation of a way of life that had ended. This year felt more familiar, like they were young kids as yet ignorant of the chill of disillusionment. He and his siblings didn't argue the entire night. Luis couldn't recall a night in which they were all together that they hadn't.

Not far away, Byron's father and uncles had erected tents above the newly laid and dried driveway. His grandmother's birthday coincided with Christmas Eve, so it was a joint party laden with tequila and rum. When those bottles were finished and the adults were circled in chairs in the backyard laughing loudly at comments that made little sense, Byron subtly began asking various relatives for money. His attempt to take advantage of drunk people was unsuccessful but entertaining.

Farther south and east, Carlos stayed up until six a.m. with his cousins playing a soccer game he'd received for Xbox; he'd never pulled an all-nighter for schoolwork, but video games presented him no problem.

On Juniper Street in the company of his large extended family, Tio found that posting his grades on social media had not, in fact, garnered him more presents.

Across South LA, families gathered in small spaces and tried to stay awake until midnight, even the smallest children, as they did each year. Spaces changed as rent increases and job turnover and the unkind tides of commerce caused families to move constantly, but the food was the same as it always had been. The prayers were the same. The company was the same, or felt that way even though, as years accumulated, families fractured and merged, elderly people passed away, babies were born. For high school seniors, this was the final Christmas they would spend as children who could rip the paper off gifts with abandon and fall asleep on the floor, and so they savored the hours.

Jon

He'd never much cared for holidays. With school closed—the doors actually locked—Jon had felt interned in their condo during those two weeks each December. He equated school breaks with claustrophobia, and he played hours' worth of video games.

This year, in something of a concerted effort, he'd claimed a degree of independence for himself, and his winter break fell into a rhythm by which his phone would ding with a text, and a few minutes later he would hurry from his room to the front door, maybe pausing to call goodbye to his mom, maybe not. And then he'd be in a friend's car just heading somewhere without giving much thought to where exactly—maybe to drive along the Pacific Coast Highway, adjacent to the ocean, windows down and music loud, or to the UCLA dorms to play marathon Cards Against Humanity games with Aca Deca alumni, or to classic film screenings at one of the city's many vintage theaters. Upon returning, sometimes the following morning, he met any request from his mother for a description of his time with the words *Just out with friends*. And he was finding that being out with friends, doing nothing very productive, was pretty fantastic.

What surprised him was his mother's strange compliance with these new, slightly rebellious patterns; she never tried to stop him, never called his phone to check as to his whereabouts at midnight, never challenged his vague descriptions. The most she would do was ask with whom he'd been, and she already knew the answer since he'd been hanging out with basically the same people for years. In essence, she was behaving significantly further out of character than he, which left him in a state of absolute befuddlement. The obvious conclusion he drew was that she was outflanking him in some way, waiting for him to feel the lack of the attention that he was actively spurning—but such subterfuge seemed too alien to comprehend in a woman whose directness encompassed all her other traits.

As the actual holidays arrived, his friends became preoccupied with family and Jon once again remained mostly at home. His father wasn't a practicing Jew and the Chinese holidays weren't until February, so they had little to do. And still she didn't pester him regarding his final exam scores or preparation for college deadlines.

Jon remembered that she'd actually surprised him in this manner once before. Beginning at age five or six, Jon had begun piano lessons on their inexpensive but well-maintained upright; by her decree, piano was a mandatory part of childhood. His teacher was strict and technical, heavily focused on workbooks. She drilled and for the most part seemed to choose music specifically for its procedural monotony. For six years, Jon submitted to these weekly lessons, and as his playing skills became formidable, his interest in the instrument waned, and his mother's pressure grew more fierce. Such rhythms were common among the memory thread of Asian people he knew. Uncommon was the statement Jon made in sixth grade, sighting his way through another joyless song, listening to the teacher criticize his work ethic as his mother observed intently two feet behind him. Jon stood up and refused to play anymore. Yelling and accusations followed from all three angles. The teacher blustered her way out, his mother covered her face in humiliation, Jon remained steadfastly indignant the way twelve-year-old boys can, feeling like the victor in a battle in which he'd been grossly outnumbered. Then the piano sat there, lid closed, for two years: a testament to the disappointment he'd wrought. Though the instrument seemed to call to him from time to time, he'd created a predicament for himself in which playing even a brief jingle would be a concession.

As he began eighth grade at Beverly Hills, his mother quite casually stated that she was going to sell the piano. The instrument was worth at least a thousand dollars, so she wanted to be practical. It wasn't the suggestion that surprised Jon, but rather the tone with which she made it: calm and matter-of-fact, never accusatory, void of self-righteousness. Whether or not she'd planned to elicit a specific reaction, he was of course drawn back toward the instrument. Late at night, he began opening the lid and softly keying songs he liked, mostly soundtracks to video games like Final Fantasy. The talent he'd developed unhappily over his childhood still resided in his fingers, and the notes felt wonderful passing through them. He asked his mom, as offhandedly as he could, if maybe she wouldn't mind holding off on finding a buyer—if maybe they could instead find another teacher to begin lessons again. And so they did, one who let Jon pick his favorite classical songs to learn. Music, while failing to compete with video games in terms of hours spent, rivaled them in pure enjoyment. He tried not to dwell on the certainty that this had been his mother's goal all along.

Music had always been a primary bond between Jon and his parents. His mother loved old Chinese pop songs. His father treated his turntable and records with the care more often reserved for men with vintage cars, and Jon could sit with him through the entirety of a Springsteen album while they batted the words "So good" back and forth between them. (Invariably, his father would recount the time long before Jon was born when he worked at a radio station in Santa Barbara and, after a promotional visit from Springsteen himself, the station employees ended up playing a softball game against the E Street Band—and they won; Jon could recite the story from memory, verbatim.) They all loved classic rock and jazz. In the midst of any school-related conflict or simply the morass of taking one another for granted, their common language of notes and measures could always cut through and launch a grounded conversation.

Such moments caused Jon to wonder why he ever bothered to spend so much of his time unpacking the rifts he harbored with the people who'd raised him, why he searched for aggressive rejoinders in mundane exchanges, why he felt inhibited from positive thoughts while in their presence, why he could be so ornery with them when nearly all their time, thought, and money was spent on their ideas of what was best for him—even if he regularly disagreed with those ideas—and why music seemed to be the only passageway into unchallenging terrain.

Chapter 10

I'm stressed today.

—Byron

Guidance

To be a high school counselor was to be a teacher, administrator, personal therapist, family therapist, life coach, lawyer, secretary, police officer, financial adviser, diplomat, babysitter, mother, father, and general nag all collated into one occupation with ten-hour workdays and a mid-five-figure salary. The occupation itself was a conduit, ostensibly between high school and college but also between transcripts and admissions offices, students and teachers, children and parents, scholarships and tuition, individuals and dreams. They were the motivators who prompted young people to reach beyond the bounds seemingly imposed by class and by place. They were also the reason-voicers who had to impose the limitations of reality on the strivers whose raw numbers were prohibitive. Sometimes the hardest part of the job could be making sure kids were properly managing the straightforward task of tracking the status of their various applications and deadlines. Sometimes the hardest conversations involved telling a loving mother that her child's best opportunity might lie far away from home. The triumph of absorbing the expression of a student just accepted to their dream school was balanced by the task of sorting through backstop options for a student summarily rejected by the same. In low-income districts, counselors often found themselves sorting through dollar figures that were orders of magnitude higher than families had ever contemplated before. In any district, they were tasked with framing an adult decision, and all the manifold factors the decision encompassed, for young people who hadn't quite formed the capacity to perceive the breadth and consequence of it—and they had to do so without pressure or manipulation or any approach that might cause the young person to feel disempowered.

Counselors navigated these fraught emotional territories all day, every day, for hundreds of kids and their families, each with their own highly specific backgrounds and circumstances. The job was rarely as simple as shepherding students toward the institution they "liked" most, or the one that offered the most financial aid, or the one with the best programs in their intended majors. And the job was accomplished in an evolving competitive landscape that often felt geared toward ensuring that aspiration and reality were never, ever to align easily. Counselors were very, very adept at organizing computer files and emails.

Across the country, districts faced shortages of people in these roles and budgets to pay them. In the LAUSD, counselors on staff had an average caseload of 378 students, and as a result most of them lacked time to allot specifically to college entry. The students at APB were fortunate to have a dedicated college counselor in Ms. Reyes, and even more so that she'd been with the school since its formation ten years earlier. She commuted far from her home and infant daughter in Orange County, twenty miles of congested freeways distant. Any time logistics—or basic common sense—suggested that she work closer to home, the notion was exploded by the three hundred or so juniors and seniors in her charge, each of whom she knew personally on some level, all of whom came through her office constantly with hyperspecific questions, challenges, disappointments. Each new class presented her with a small handful of students who were not only in command of the admissions process organizationally but who knew instinctively what questions to ask when it came to summer programs, scholarship applications, and the general matching of particular interests with particular schools—students who understood the system's inherent gamesmanship (like Carlos). A far larger portion operated very much in the dark and were easily overwhelmed, with little room to maneuver through the unyielding, unfair intricacies of college admissions before they said, "Fuck it"—or some softer variation of surrender—and renounced any agency they had (like Byron).

They lived in California, where the public college system stated near the top of its mission that they were not just entitled to but deserving of a decent and affordable higher education. They went to a strong high school and studied under skilled teachers. If they earned high grades, or even just okay grades, then segueing into the next level wasn't supposed to be difficult, and it wasn't supposed to be complicated. But the transition was often both, and it was also intertwined with nuclear families who had emotional trouble with large changes, such as parting with children or restructuring monthly financial outlays, or both. Ms. Reyes could explain everything from the weight of APs to the value of lesser-regarded Cal State schools to the importance of community service. What she couldn't explain was the fact that admissions officers, regardless of GPAs and even SAT/ACT scores (supposedly an objective comparison), would always look at where they lived and how their surnames were spelled and wonder a little extra about their capacity to weather the many-layered rigors of high-level college work. Anytime an APB graduate dropped out of college for personal or family reasons, not a rarity, a mark was made on the stat line out in the electronic ether somewhere that further injured their cause.

The challenge for kids at Beverly Hills High School, where one dedicated college counselor worked alongside eight general counselors, each responsible for about two hundred students, was oddly similar to that of the APB kids when it came to selective colleges: the complicated stigma of preparedness. The assumption students like Jon had to disprove—subliminally, somehow—was that they were the product of an old school and system with presumably a large number of tenured teachers who were not inclined to adapt to the increasing specialization of the college landscape: the cushioned, old-money aura of the neighborhood writ over the school. Even for counselors, keeping up with what different college and university systems were seeking year by year in their incoming class was challenging. Small, private liberal arts colleges were dependable in their preference for "creative thinkers" who were very good at something—soccer, violin, interpretive dance. UC admissions were hypercompetitive in STEM fields, less so in humanities. Public universities elsewhere, like in Michigan and Arizona, varied in how many out-of-state students they accepted, where they accepted them from, and how much they cost. A suspicion existed that California students were penalized for hailing from a state that could seem a little (or a lot) obnoxious on the national level with its far-left politics and above-it-all ethos. Top-ranked universities—Ivies and other familiar, mostly East Coast names—hadn't historically accepted many Beverly students, maybe one or two a year, while they took dozens of kids annually from nearby private high schools like Harvard-Westlake and Marlborough.

The Beverly counselors worked with a fondness for their students, an aspiration to see them loosed from the shelter that was Beverly Hills, but they also worked with a knowledge that, for the most part, these students would be fine after they graduated from high school, wherever life found them afterward. The stakes were indeed lower here. But the most interesting cases were students like Jon, whose earnestness and fascinating nature no application could adequately capture, and Harrison, who yearned so deeply to do something in college that kids from Beverly Hills simply didn't do. These students and their counselors forever battled the solidified meaning that those words—*Beverly Hills*—carried in the world while battling for their place in it.

Luis, Carlos

"If you wait for the last possible second to send it in—like some of you do most of the time—then be prepared for the system to crash." Ms. Reyes was addressing the guidance period class, but she was looking at Luis. At least, he assumed she was, since he had no intention of submitting his final applications at any second other than the last possible. His Pomona acceptance padded a lack of urgency that was already present in him. He'd barely made it to school today, as he'd woken up late and made the simple calculation that rushing to dress and eat and drive would entail much effort, while staying in bed entailed none. Byron had texted him, *Where you at?* and then stated that he would pay Luis three dollars if he came to school in the middle of Mr. Snyder's class, just to see how he would react. Luis had made another, also simple calculation that three dollars was more than zero and had stridden into AP Government ten minutes before it ended. He hadn't prompted much of a reaction from the teacher, so Byron declined to give him the money. "I'll remind you again," Ms. Reyes said, "that over a hundred thousand applications will be going into the UC system on the same day, maybe even the same hour. So it's in your best interest to submit at least the day before. I know that's not good news."

Laziness wasn't the only characteristic in play with regard to Ms. Reyes's task of motivating Luis and others to take the initiative to complete their applications even marginally ahead of time; it wasn't even the most important one. When they were not in school with teachers constantly wheedling them, Luis and most of the people he knew were very much alone in the college process. His mother was no help at all, being busy and unfamiliar with official forms. Much of her income from her food truck job came as cash under the table. She didn't receive a W-2 or contribute to Social Security, and so the IRS entries on UC forms were confusing and fraught. He'd hassled his mom throughout the fall about gathering some stack of financial documentation that he could use, no matter how thin, but she refused because staying below-board was what allowed the family to live with relative comfort, certainly poor but a few notches above the level of stress known to others. They generally had money for groceries, birthday gifts, and leisure, if not always for rent.

"If you don't do taxes," he told his mother in exasperation, "they might not even let me into college. I mean, maybe community."

"I do my taxes, then you're paying for your own college—and video games," she replied, equally exasperated.

Luis engaged with the dreadful math of American poverty and upward mobility. At face value, when Cal Grants were pre-factored, community college cost around two thousand dollars per year. Cal State schools were in the six-thousand-dollar range, UCs were fifteen, and privates had reached astronomical numbers that required abstract thought to contemplate. He was in a position to qualify for many different sources of aid as well as compete for some scholarships, but in the end, nothing was free. His mother worked in a food truck. His sister was an assistant in-home care provider. His brother logged only enough hours as a store clerk to afford servicing his motorcycle. Luis worked summers in the

Green Dot charter network's IT department. Together, their budget worked relatively well. But the task of filling out one section on one college form threatened upheaval.

They'd decided that his older sister would list him as a dependent on her 2016 tax forms, which would save her money, while Luis would input her income of $18,000 as his household income without acknowledging that his mother earned around the same and his brother also contributed his wages to the family. Luis could be described in many ways—joker, loafer, slob—but he'd never cheated. He felt hugely nervous when typing the haphazardly concocted numbers. He considered the many other kids his age—in his school, in his neighborhood, in the country—who were also striving for a four-year degree. They were also picking through the numbers with anxiety, in the lamplight of small apartments, without much help. They were also asking their families to make great monetary sacrifices in the pursuit of the heightened prospects a college diploma promised but didn't guarantee. And they were competing for the same limited number of slots and the same limited allotment of financial aid. In gaming the system—not out of greed but out of what his family viewed as necessity—Luis knew that he was wronging these people, both known and unknown, on some level. The level was negligible in the great scheme, but he still experienced guilt as he clicked on the Submit button (a few hours before the UC system deadline, not quite the last second) and then prepared himself to wait—for admission, rejection, or, more ominously, a potential request for clarification regarding the unusual numbers he'd provided. In another section that asked for a hashtag describing him, Luis wrote, *#pleaseletmein*.

The following Friday, he wore a coat and tie to school—though mismatched and ill fitting—and he actually brushed his hair, somewhat. After school, Luis, Carlos, and a small group boarded a van and drove four miles north to the Stanley Mosk Courthouse, one of several blockish government buildings surrounding Grand Park in downtown Los Angeles. As they passed through the metal detector, they moved opposite a stream of Angelenos heading from the elevator bank to the exit on their way home from jury duty or court appearances or traffic ticket appeals. The majority, it seemed to the students, were Latino, and from their weary postures and narrowed, vacant eyes, their various legal experiences this afternoon had not been pleasant.

"Yo," Luis whispered to Carlos, "you're heading into the belly of the beast, how does that feel?"

"Shut up," was all Carlos could say in rejoinder. Luis was right, though: not many undocumented immigrants would voluntarily enter the city's prosecutorial center.

The 2016 national mock trial competition was an enactment of *The People vs. Awbry*, a fictionalized human trafficking case by which a restaurant owner was indicted for underpaying and later imprisoning an immigrant cook under his employ. APB's team had been assigned the defense role. For a few hours a week over the course of a month, they'd pored over the case packets and role-played lawyers and witnesses while being grilled by two professional trial attorneys who volunteered each year to help the school team. Carlos and Luis both loved mock trial—Carlos for intellectual arguments made amid murky contexts, Luis for the challenge of on-the-spot thinking and crafting counterpoints to the reasoning of others. Carlos's role was to make the pretrial argument, while Luis would play a defense witness. Their opponent was a half hour late. Bored, Carlos's eyes wandered around the unremarkable courtroom, which was hot and bright and plain. He smelled the residual body odor of those who had been here during the preceding workday. He thought about the people they'd passed earlier in the lobby, about how many judgments had been made here in the past eight hours; how many people had won or lost, rightly or wrongly; how many had spent their last moments of freedom waiting, bored, like the students were now; and how many had been ordered to pay money they didn't have or part with people they loved. The place felt like regret.

"They should fucking forfeit," Luis said just before the other team finally entered, all white and wearing expensive formal wear. They didn't apologize. Their teacher cited traffic.

Carlos made the pretrial argument, which he'd memorized. Though the case and its details, some of them sordid, were an invention, he still felt odd in his rational defense of a character who had by any objective definition exploited a poor foreign worker from a third-world country (the country was named "Tanterra" and its continent was unspecified, but certain details made it fairly clear that it was a stand-in for Central America). But Carlos spoke clearly about the controversial laws governing guest permits for workers. He didn't overly inflect his voice the way many students did when pretending to be lawyers. As in any academic argument, he stated a thesis, provided a slew of facts to support it, and then laced them into a grander conclusion. The other team objected to practically everything he said.

"The defendant was at the counter of the restaurant when—"

"OBJECTION! IRRELEVANT!"

"The apartment upstairs was up to par with housing codes—"

"OBJECTION! The statement is based on INCONCLUSIVE evidence!"

Carlos didn't lose his train of thought, but he grew angry at their apparent strategy of preventing him from fluidly conjoining two sentences. The stakes were low here—APB only had nine participants this year, most of whom were doubling up on roles, so they had no real potential to win—but he found himself caring disproportionately about representing Ánimo Pat Brown.

Luis was laughing when he sat back down. *"'My name is Carlos—' 'OBJECTION!'"*

With the tone set, the evening progressed as expected. Teammates who were more timid public speakers became rattled by the other school's confrontational tactics. Opportunities to assert key details were missed again and again. People grew nervous and forgot lines they'd been practicing for weeks. Luis had learned a new role right before the trial for someone who'd skipped school, and so lacked a command of the facts. Carlos couldn't help anyone since his job was finished. APB was shellacked.

Optically, the courtroom was reduced to a bunch of white kids from the Valley making a bunch of brown kids from South LA look wilting and unprepared—for mock trial and for professional adult life. Mock trial was inherently campy, with teenagers sometimes channeling *Law & Order*, but it was intended as a valid simulation of the future. One didn't need to be a lawyer to be put in a situation in which winning an argument by summoning—and sometimes bending—a selection of facts might prove a vital skill. If he or any one of his friends were to be stopped on the street by police— not an improbability—then presenting themselves with clarity and confidence could avert disastrous consequences. In interview settings, they would soon be competing for jobs and internships with people from more lauded schools with more refined preparation. When they began college in the fall, they'd be obliged to show that they belonged there, by virtue of their education and also by quickness of mind and force of spirit. Yet here in the courthouse, as the trial dragged on into the night, he and his friends didn't appear ready to rival whoever these white kids were. Watching the prosecutor invest particular effort in embarrassing a soft-spoken female sophomore who'd worked earnestly but whose memorized details were eluding her, Carlos had a meaner, perhaps unavoidable thought directed toward the courtroom's smug opposite side: *I bet none of you fuckers are getting into Princeton.*

Owen

Students poured onto the outdoor plaza on the third floor of Beverly's main building, the primary gathering place for lunch and passing periods. The long, wide concrete surface was dotted with picnic tables and ringed by benches and classrooms. On the Thursday before the presidential inauguration, as students were being released there for lunch, the sun was bright overhead and a cluster of students staged a semi-planned protest. The majority of those gathered at the outset were female, yelling, "My body, my choice!" Observing what must have felt something like catharsis for these fifteen-, sixteen-, and seventeen-year-old girls, no teachers intervened, and many applauded. The group of a dozen or so swelled to two dozen, then three or four. The plaza filled to capacity with joiners and encouraging spectators.

Owen was drawn outside as well. He remained confounded by the election, and by the fact that classmates with whom he'd argued about politics in the past were still, over two months later, milking the upset at his expense. "How're things at home these days?" was a common bit of snark. "Have you guys recovered yet?"

Owen stood on a concrete bench for a better angle, and he felt a rare positive energy regarding his school and its students—and this was when he heard the first incantation of, "Build that wall!" followed by laughter among a group of eight or ten guys, mostly underclassmen whom Owen didn't recognize. Whoever had said it was most likely trying to add some contention to the scene and make it more interesting; Owen highly doubted these guys gave much thought to actual walls or the people on either side.

"I think 'My body, my choice' is pretty tough to disagree with, don't you?" one of the original protestors said. The quite rational rejoinder elicited laughter and a louder, more unified *"Build that wall!"*

The two factions became clearly delineated and the "Build that wall!" group attracted more members, nowhere near the number of females but sufficiently formidable and raucous in matching them shout for shout. The principal (who was wearing a pink wig due to a non-election-related bet he'd lost) and a few other adults came to stand between them, arms raised to shoulder height in a preventative effort that arrived too late. Because this was Beverly Hills High School, there was little chance of a physical fight or anyone's being hurt; the students watching would eventually become bored and drift away, removing incentive from those inciting, and the agita would dilute into rash gossip. Owen was shattered by the scene.

The country felt hysterical and shitty across the spectrum. This had been the case for quite a while before the election. That he'd just seen the hysterics and shittiness refracted directly through his school—not just a heated classroom debate but through the whole of the place—angered him to a degree that gave more credibility to a dozen or two obnoxious contrarians than they merited. But his anger wasn't actually pointed toward those individuals. Owen and his friends had all spent a great amount of time telling themselves and others that Beverly Hills didn't resemble its image, that there was some level of diversity here, that people were basically grounded and open-minded, that the school wasn't much different from any other school in that its small handful of truly asinine people were far, far outnumbered by legions of the quirky and the nerdy and the goofy and the benign. They made such claims with humor, conviction, and shades of indignation.

After the plaza protest, Owen couldn't quite argue such a notion anymore, just as he couldn't quite imagine another school where such gross theatrics could have transpired. Beverly Hills High School was indefensible to him now.

His mother was tired from physical therapy that afternoon when he recounted the day, her voice distant, her jokes not quite hitting the way they normally did.

"All you can do is just be kind, be open, be funny—be yourself."

"Basically, *don't be an asshole*."

"Yes."

"Why do you think that's so hard for certain people?"

She didn't reply, but her hand fell on his arm and was a comfort. After a time, she added, "You know you can be a shit sometimes, too." Both laughed warmly. Then he lay in the bed beside her and they watched TV.

Jonah

A mile and a half east on that same evening, Jonah—Owen's erstwhile conservative tormentor in government class—was on the sofa in their small living room, sandwiched between his mother and younger brother, keyed to the TV screen. They weren't watching loud, endless news coverage of the coming inauguration (though they often did). Instead, they were watching *Scent of a Woman*, an Al Pacino film from the nineties about a blind war veteran and a boarding school student of humble means quite out of place in a milieu of wealth and legacy and entitlement. Jonah had watched hundreds of movies here, with his family. They were watching this particular one for the fourth or fifth time. Between the mother and two sons, they maintained a running commentary regarding the film's humor, character motivations, Pacino's patented scenery chewing, the very entertaining tango scene, the one-note awfulness of the boarding school set as depicted. In their small apartment in a five-plex building, they spent nearly all their free nights this way, together.

Jonah didn't mention aloud the degree to which he related to the student character's flailing travails among his overprivileged classmates. After his mother fled his father's home when Jonah was five, his entire school experience, from the Orange County coast to Beverly Hills, had involved feeling underprivileged—not just financially as his mother strived to provide while his father seemed determined to sap all her resources through court battles, but socially and academically as well. He'd come of age cash-strapped, raised by a single mother, Jewish in a community with very few, witness to verbal and physical confrontations, subject to the relentless crush of American family law—and so he knew intimately the worst of human frailty and cruelty. The past summer, they'd moved into a somewhat stable apartment situation—just a short block from school—yet the semblance of normality they'd found made him uncomfortable because all its previous instances in his life had ended at some point in disorder and trauma. The salve he carried away from those years—maybe the only salve—was the profound bond he shared with his siblings and their protective, nurturing mother. But still he awaited another unraveling.

His first entry into Beverly Hills High School freshman year had been similarly at odds with competing hope and anxiety. On the clean canvas that the grand school façade presented, he wished to paint a brand-new identity. His primary goal was to make the tennis team and claim the prestige that athletic grace granted. He was north of six feet tall and, while not a personification of sports excellence, quite coordinated overall and decent with a racquet. When his name didn't appear on the final list, he was left floundering for a means to stand out, to do something other than pass through the hallways anonymously for four years. He opted to attempt some kind of academic renown. He needed all four years of high school to attain it—because family upheaval had distracted him in elementary and middle school, because the handful of kids at the top of his class were exceptionally smart, and because he was a reticent person averse to speaking in class.

During that time, his social life revolved around his friend group of happily uncool outliers, video game marathons with his younger brother, incessantly prank calling his older sister's college boyfriend, and family movie nights.

The boy expounding authoritatively on unpopular conservative thought in AP Government class senior year had been willed into existence by a younger version of himself seeking sway in the world after a childhood spent largely with none. Because of the glasses (which he'd had to begin wearing in eleventh grade), the gangly limbs, the acne, and his unflappably wonkish manner of speaking in class, Jonah made a compelling target for those inclined to ridicule differently wired sorts. And peers certainly complained behind his back about his argumentative nature, particularly if he'd just expertly undermined the logic of an in-class comment one of them had made. But speaking at all was a newfound, hard-won skill—and he'd come to feel that a climate in which disagreement had become so nakedly, prohibitively emotional called for at least an effort toward reasoned and reasonable debate, even if it made him unpopular among the mainstream. He'd never been much interested in the mainstream.

Jonah didn't like the president-elect personally, but he could nevertheless argue in class that the uproar over the losing candidate's winning the popular vote was irrelevant because the existence of blue states such as theirs caused legions of Republicans living in them not to bother voting, and blue states were more populated than red states. Whether or not he was numerically correct, classmates of a different mind did not like hearing or being compelled to contend with such a deduction, and the dialogue grew quickly charged and unfocused, and any motion he made to return to facts was declared insensitive and annoying. The pattern was predictable and tiresome and universal. But at least he wouldn't be running into any of these kids at parties; he never went to parties. He watched movies with his mother instead.

Tio

In 1926, a landslide in San Pedro had collapsed a row of ocean-front homes down a tall bluff and into the sea. They'd never been cleared, and now the ruins hosted hikers and climbers during the day and clandestine parties at night. Jagged concrete platforms that had once been foundations were wedged into the rocks at odd but climbable angles, covered in graffiti as they formed a descent toward the blue water. Sunken City, the place was called.

Tio scrambled downward with two of his skateboarding friends. One had dropped out of high school, the other was about to enlist in the Marine Corps. They'd come for an impromptu gathering that had been circulated on Instagram, mostly of skater-type acquaintances, staggering uneasily along craggy ledges high above the ocean. They could hear the water but not see it, because it was eleven p.m., and the waves sounded offended as they crashed directly onto rocks thirty feet below. Earlier in the day, as they'd idled on a park bench nursing the bruises they'd earned from an afternoon on their boards, this had seemed like a good idea.

Once they'd located a safe-ish spot to sit, Tio gestured grandly to the kids drinking beer and smoking marijuana, laughing at exaggerated retellings of skateboard tricks landed and failed. He said, "Look at this American carnage. It's so terrible, so terrible, folks. It's the *worst*." He shook his head sadly, then laughed. He was imitating a phrase from the inauguration speech, which he'd watched four times, twice in school and twice later on his phone. They'd all easily mocked the new president's hair, the impossible shapes his lips made, the way he gesticulated with thumb and index finger pressed together. But the tone of the speech and of the particular day in America made for a grave revisiting of the election and what it meant for people who looked like them. To his military-bound friend, he said, "This is the American carnage you're going to be defending us against, whacking ISIS with your skateboard."

"It's a job I can actually get," his friend replied.

"It's gotta be safer than this place," Tio said, peering over the ledge to his right, where a row of twisted rebar rods thrust out like skeletal fingers from the concrete.

To the north, the homes on the wealthy peninsula of Rancho Palos Verdes glowed from their tiered rows high on the bluffs. To the south, floodlights lit the great machine works of the two busiest ports in the country. In between, the assorted young people hung out for a short while, bracing against the chilly ocean updrafts, wary of the danger here.

Chapter 11

FEBRUARY 1–FEBRUARY 20

The next person who calls me "Princeton," I'm going to kick his butt.

—*Carlos*

Byron

Over fifty thousand homeless people lived in Los Angeles in 2017. They lived in cars filled to the windows' midline with scavenged belongings. They lived in tents fixed in long rows against park fences, on overpasses and beneath underpasses, around transit stations and libraries and warehouses. They buried their torsos in recycling bins beside shopping carts stolen from Vons, Target, Whole Foods. They congregated outside of churches and missions. They trudged up and down traffic points of clogged intersections and freeway exits carrying cardboard signs pleading for money and mercy and jobs. They talked to themselves in confused and sometimes raging voices. They lay on the grass where they could find shade in public parks, such as the rose gardens in Beverly Hills and Washington Park in South LA. A third of them were mentally ill. A sizable, unknown number were addicts. Roughly four thousand of them were children.

For high school students, so many psychic layers collided when passing an elderly man with bare, swollen, cracked feet sleeping under a bus stop awning, or hearing the voices of a mother and child from within a wind-torn tarp surrounded by filthy blankets, or watching a man converse unintelligibly with the demons residing within him; the sight of flesh, dirty and burned and raw, and of eyes that saw a cityscape so far distorted from what most considered home. As humans, they felt. As young humans, they felt deeply and viscerally: pain, guilt, stabs at empathy. The aid they could offer came in the form of drives for soap, clothes, toys. As they filled those charity boxes day by day, they were subconsciously obliged to pair their own individual and unique aspirations for college and jobs in fields that impassioned them with whatever imperious sequence of events had found each one of these tens of thousands of individuals suffering: the terrible reality of too many bodies and too little space and resources.

One early evening, Byron was kicked out of his home following an argument with his mother over some topic he'd lost track of amid the argument's escalation. *"Go,"* she said. "You don't live here anymore." He laughed gently and tried to retreat to his room, but she was serious, following him with a garbage bag that she haphazardly stuffed with some of his dirty laundry on the floor before hurling the bag out the front door. With his dog on a leash, he grabbed the bag and slung it over his shoulder and walked slowly off into the neighborhood, muttering to himself about her irrationality, and his own, and the way reason was so often lost between people who shared a small space and little money. His mind constricted around the minutiae, the words and gestures, the rootless anger. The sky grew dark early and quickly, and the air was cold. He hadn't brought a jacket, and he had no money to stop and eat somewhere. The windows of homes and apartment buildings he passed glowed with the warmth of humans communing inside. He kept walking with the garbage bag and his dog, who strutted happily alongside his own shuffling sneakers. A wide loop brought him eventually back home, where his father was in the garage and casually motioned him inside. His mother had calmed. She shrugged away the argument, and the following day Byron's friends laughed about how, for forty-five minutes, he'd joined the city's homeless—not mocking him or making light, just nodding toward the farcical truths of being a kid.

"You're going to invent a bunch of shit one day," Luis told him, "and you'll get *paid*, and you'll buy them a house, and then, whenever you feel like it, *you* can kick *them* out."

Carlos

As Carlos's prospects soared further almost daily, he struggled. This current segment of the year had been fairly manic for his friends, particularly Byron, as they'd rushed to finalize essays and secure recommendations and input financials. They'd debated the merits of different Cal State and UC schools endlessly. February placed them at the front end of a wait that could last as long as three months before they learned where they would be and in what course of study and how much it would cost. Carlos had applied to other schools, including four other Ivies, but since December he'd known that he had Princeton secured and fully paid for. His quest, or whatever the years between kindergarten and twelfth grade should be called, was ostensibly over, its goal secured.

Yet every day that he walked to school in his blue shirt and khaki pants, he passed people scavenging for recyclables, breaking down tents at the behest of police, sleeping in alcoves beneath glaring sunlight so that they could be awake to guard their belongings at night. He passed other people consuming and selling drugs, mostly weed. People sold cut fruit from vending carts or drove delivery trucks, like his father. They worked in stores and behind food counters. They cut hair. They commuted for hours a day to neighborhoods with more jobs but no affordable housing. Life here was difficult, sometimes exhausting, and often painful to observe. But people living here were also very prideful. Carlos enjoyed saying that he was from Compton (technically, his home was a block north of the official boundary), because the word suggested a degree of exposure, and maybe some wisdom, regarding survival and resilience and the human condition. By allying himself with the one word, Carlos projected with authority a constellation of experiential traits: he knew what hardship was; he'd been discriminated against; he possessed a deep understanding of the kinship, loyalty, effort, and love that were necessary to thrive, here or anywhere; he was real.

The word *Princeton* had far different associations. More than the other Ivies, it seemed, this particular school's reputation was tightly braided with privilege and entitlement. The school was known for its exclusive eating clubs, an archaic dynamic by which one's status involved where and with whom one ate dinner. He'd heard that minority students there, especially nonathletes, had difficulty integrating with a culture that presumed and paraded wealth. The campus was nestled in an affluent, bucolic suburb far removed from urban life. The loud orange color emblazoning school sweatshirts and hats could invite strangers to casually murder him in South LA, where it was worn by the Hoover Criminals.

Carlos had never been to New Jersey, but he was quite fed up with people's calling him "Princeton." Its invocations were absolutely contrary to those of his home, and they unnerved him.

Carlos knew as well as anyone, and better than most, that the hearts of individuals were not determined by where they lived and how much money they had or where they were from. He'd directly experienced as much during the Brown academic camp last summer, where he'd excelled in class and fostered meaningful if fleeting friendships outside of it. He wasn't intimidated by wealth, nor did he disdain it. But he carried an unfamiliar stress that felt very different from that currently coursing among his classmates. The difference was, in fact, the stress's source. Early and spectacularly in this crucial year of their lives, he'd surpassed his classmates as well as the hundreds of thousands of young Americans who'd fantasized for years about a place like Princeton—who had geared all aspects of their lives toward it—but, in the stupefying algorithms of grades and money and support and race and ambition, had fallen short where he'd succeeded. And so he was different now. He was elite.

That's really what Princeton and other similar names signified in the end: *elite*, a status granted upon entry and crystallized upon exit. Carlos wasn't fond of this word or its implied status. When applied popularly in cultural complexes—airline rewards programs, college prep courses, and, yes, colleges themselves—the five letters didn't just suggest inequity, they flaunted it. The letters were now fixed irreversibly to his body, in bright orange, which meant that he was in possession of near-limitless opportunity but also meant that he was no longer the kid shaking his head while Luis stole some girl's shoe, or counting change in his pocket to see if he had train fare that day, or engineering a very sad Halloween maze, or watching Matchbox cars at the art museum. He did and would continue to do childish things, whimsical things, but he would never quite be that child again nor experience whimsy in the same way. Fading with his childhood, too, was his connection to his home: the small backyard shack and the streets surrounding it, the kids creating joy out of sticks and rocks, the parents laboring to provide stable homes for them and mine small moments for laughter, the uncles and aunts and cousins. He felt suddenly powerless to halt or even deflect the vector of the fading.

He knew classmates from previous years who'd traveled east for college. All of them had made some variation of the pledge to remain rooted here, somehow. His older brother had. Yet, Carlos had observed them with time's passing and sensed a peculiar distance, imperceptible at first and then widening, a dislocation from the spheres of influence that had formed them up until age eighteen as those spheres shifted to the lawns and dining halls and dorm rooms and residences of campuses far away. This transposition of spirit would happen to Carlos, and he was afraid.

His father was driving his truck route on a Thursday in early February. About to deliver a load of boxes to a stationery company in an office complex in Inglewood, he was startled by a collection of squad cars with lights flashing right outside the business. The attention of police and ICE officers was focused on the office adjacent to his delivery address. His family maintained a general self-assurance that their father was somewhat shielded from the sword of immigration enforcement because he worked for a reputable company, drove a truck with an official logo, wore a uniform, possessed a license. At a passing glance on a busy city street, he was clearly a contributing member of society. But a direct encounter with authorities was far different from a passing glance. He would have just continued driving if the street ahead weren't narrow with no outlet, if leaving the area wouldn't have entailed a cumbersome and conspicuous three-point turn. He now faced the difficult decision of whether to move along with his delivery and risk somehow being caught up in the immigration raid, or to veer away and possibly draw the eyes of some officer trained to be alert and suspicious. He chose the former, pulling up as far as he could from the cars, feigning disinterest. As he stacked packages from the rear of his truck and carried them inside, he saw in his peripheral vision a much tattooed, brown-skinned man being roughly escorted to a waiting van. A few cars pulled out with the van, a few lingered.

He asked the clerk at the stationery desk if she knew the story. She replied that she was certain the apprehended man was legal and was pretty sure he was noncriminal, but he dressed and carried himself in a way that drew that particular brand of attention. "He wears his Raiders jersey a lot." She wondered if maybe someone with a grudge had called in a tip on him.

"If he's got papers and didn't do anything, then I don't think they can hold him," Carlos's father opined.

"He's going to have a pretty bad day, though." She mentioned offhand that when the cars had pulled up, six or seven people had fled from the back of the complex and slid down into a drainage culvert behind it.

Carlos's father stayed for a few minutes cataloging the delivery in his handheld, and when he finished all but two cars had departed and the remaining officers were busy conferring with the neighboring business owner. He walked back to his truck and proceeded with his deliveries. He debated whether or not to tell his family that night. He didn't desire to scare anyone unduly over what had turned out to be an uneventful ten minutes, but he ended up sharing those ten minutes over dinner as a reminder. The average day was composed of moments and places. Not often, but once in a while, a bad moment intersected with a bad place. The decisions they made upon such a convergence were very important.

Carlos reacted with a shrug. They'd been schooled in this reality since toddlerhood. That reality had certainly changed following the election of a president who openly disdained them and devoted much of his rhetoric to ridding the country of them, but reality hadn't exactly been pleasant before this presidency. Their obligation was now and had always been to stay out of the way.

Carlos still had no knowledge as to the status of his DACA application, five months after submitting it, and the current political moment didn't feel like a wise one in which to inquire or complain. And in the meantime, here they were, eating his mother's lasagna, in a neighborhood where many people knew and cared about their family, and many teachers were devoted to elevating them. Carlos tried mainly to go to his small school and not dwell on the broader landscape too deeply. But he couldn't unknow the fact that innumerable families in the country whose kids had been rejected or wait-listed by Princeton would be beyond enraged to learn that he'd been accepted with a full scholarship. And he couldn't help wondering whether, even though he'd been accepted there, he would actually be accepted once there.

A few days later, after much discussion with teachers and his brother and Ms. Reyes, Carlos informed QuestBridge that he would defer the Princeton admission and await the results of his regular applications to other schools. He'd still have the opportunity to claim his slot in the early spring. But he wanted to know what his options would be. The decision somewhat raised his mood, because the fact that he would have options at all—which had been scarce in his life to this point—was remarkable.

Private School

Where options were concerned, the private college and university sector inhabited perhaps one of the higher planes of hysteria in the country, beginning of course with their tuitions, which could range from the middle to upper five figures when factoring in room and board, and continued to climb at a rate far exceeding inflation or national economic growth. Much research had been conducted regarding the financial math; little still was known outside of college boardrooms as to what market forces, exactly, accounted for it. Much research had also been devoted to representation, and in particular the extreme disproportion between the upper and lower class in typical student bodies; the numbers were predictable but equally confounding. As confusing as the dollar figures and demographics was the sheer volume of choices: thousands of private schools across the country, even as three out of four students attended public systems. Additional bafflements: how and why these institutions were ranked each year, and the degree to which attending them aided career prospects, and how exactly did the word count of research published in journals by faculty—a sacred metric—matter when it came to the learning accomplished by nineteen-year-olds, and what admission standards did each maintain—what alchemy of test scores and class ranking and teacher recommendations and summer programs and essays and hobbies made one a "good fit" in any given place? Inversely, what blend of course offerings and student demographics and size and location might make any given campus a "good fit" for a given individual? As a sprawling and amorphous body, private schools made for a highly enticing and coveted confusion.

An organic way for prospective students to obtain hard information, at least with regard to the latter question of fitness, was to physically visit a campus. Across great distances, campus visits could be too expensive or simply untenable in terms of time. Weather and architectural panache notwithstanding, campuses tended to look fairly similar anyway: quads, buildings, trees, playing fields, a library. The sustained marketing pitches that were campus tours also varied little in content: the dorms were vibrant with social life, the community was diverse and inclusive, the professors were available, the students were all focused yet laid-back at the same time. The moving tour was bound to walk past current undergrads en route to class in happy clusters.

Laying eyes on a place and interacting with its residents was a helpful luxury, but doing so didn't often answer what was perhaps the most pressing question of the current times, relating choice of school to general life prospects. "Go where you'll be happiest" was a tenet of the hands-off parenting set—a very nurturing one, especially when compared to the demands of its hypercompetitive opposite—but the words didn't apply, really, to first-generation students, or to families whose means did not track with inflating costs. In the context of discussion in high school hallways, counselors' offices, and around the dinner tables at home, the most useful dual metrics of college choice remained simple: name recognition and obtainable financial aid. But these factors often complicated the essence of the decision, for instance when schools of lesser name recognition offered the best aid packages. Few resources were available to quantify these decisions over the long term, or to account for the competitive element of the culture that drove individuals to pursue renown somehow—to attend schools that were farther away or more prestigious or just *different* from those attended by most of their peers, regardless of reason or expense or tangible benefit. Again, the confusion.

Admissions officers at these schools were the mysterious gatekeepers, taking on a great prominence in the waking and sleeping anxieties of the students who existed, during these post-application "reading seasons," as small files uploaded to their online databases. As a whole, they were not a well-loved or much-admired element of the process. Generally, they were perceived as, if not totally soulless, then at least immune to the emotions of those whose fates they determined with a mouse-click. The harshest renderings painted them as pawns of the rich and the legacies and the sports dynasties that wielded outsized influence in any given private school's orbit. In reality, the job of an admissions officer was to read a tremendous number of applications, do the simple algebra when it came to scores, highlight the essays and teacher recommendations that felt special to them personally, then present their conclusions to the admissions board for holistic review. The job was tedious and involved the friction of many contrasting personalities trying to reach some kind of unanimity—a tedium and friction common to many jobs. They carried the added weight of being obliged to play God in some sense—to decide subjectively, based on their own knowledge of student experience and outcomes, that a certain student might well qualify for admission and generous financial aid by the base metrics, but maybe some factor (comparatively low SATs, faulty grammar in an essay, the absence of extracurriculars) indicated that this student might be more likely to flourish elsewhere. Any admissions officer experienced great, genuine triumph at having located a student who might never have considered a top-tier private school, ushered them through the process, and lobbied successfully for their admission. The same admissions officer experienced huge, also-genuine heartbreak when, during the last step of that same narrative, some obscure gear within the number-crunching apparatus rotated enough to nudge this rare, cherished, fought-for student from the final admit pile. Like everyone else at all levels of the process, they experienced confusion, too, and the foreknowledge that the majority of the effort they made, no matter how positive or compassionate the intention, was reduced in value to the dichotomy of "Accepted" and "Rejected" stamps.

The UC system was massive and daunting and competitive, but at the very least its guidelines were fairly clear in terms of grades and scores, and its costs were somewhat discernible. Privates seemed able to operate in a far more obfuscating way. Even as most all of these institutions repeatedly pronounced a desire for diversity, and a few of them with sufficient endowments had transitioned to need-blind admissions, the names of families who had donated buildings were still engraved over the front doors, and the private high schools that had historically fed them—schools that charged tuitions in the same relative zone as the universities—continued to feed them, and the rare kids from low-income schools granted access continued to struggle at them (and had become increasingly vocal regarding these struggles). The overall admissions process had over time been streamlined by the Common App and increased access to information, and by a genuine desire of private schools to recruit from broader reaches of the country, but the reality remained complicated and agitating for teenagers working late at night on the fine points of their applications, dreaming of the possibility that these boxes might one day soon translate into a new and boundless window of life, or might not.

Jon

Stanford had rejected Jon's application, a not-so-crushing blow for which he'd already steeled himself. The school was incredibly competitive and was also one of the roughly one hundred private schools with need-blind admissions, making it even more so. Over forty-five thousand prospective freshmen applied each year, and less than two thousand were accepted—about 4.5 percent. He'd known and discussed with counselors the fact that Stanford was a reach for him in terms of his own standing in the class, the high school's standing in the landscape, and the city of Los Angeles itself. Jon was fourth in his class academically, but the few ahead of him were formidable talents, and one of them had already been accepted to Stanford. (Jon was genuinely happy for and proud of this classmate, whom he admired.)

Universities like Stanford, by virtue of their mission, labored to draw elite students from all spaces and races in the country and the world. Jon happened to live in a city of almost five million people, with tens of millions more in the surrounding counties. Some lived in South and East LA and other areas with low incomes and high diversity. Others went to prep schools known for funneling students into the top-ranked schools. A few had national profiles based on sports or other achievements. A few were legacies. Students with tremendous grades and a variety of standout activities attended schools all around him. All inhabited a packed city that could only be permitted a limited proportion of admits to any given institution.

Jon remained even-keeled, confident that the early spring would arrive with multiple desirable alternatives. (The University of Chicago was his second favorite destination—though its admission rate of 8 percent, while almost double Stanford's, did not inspire great optimism.) At the same time, he'd earnestly wanted to get into Stanford. Jon was not a competitive person and didn't mind that he had never really won anything before, in all the competitions he'd entered and teams he'd joined. But winning this particular competition would have felt wonderful—heroic, even. Instead, he was informed by way of an online portal's rote language that they had noticed and appreciated his virtues, but not as much as the virtues of others.

He continued metabolizing the feeling while sitting on the dais during a Tuesday-night district school board meeting—a particularly contentious one regarding recently circulated gossip suggesting the possible closure of one of the four district elementary schools, due to its severe vulnerability in the event of an earthquake, and the hundreds of millions of dollars that would be required to fix the structure. A board member had said something offhand to the local press about maybe not needing so many school campuses for so many fewer students. Vast outrage ensued across the flats of Beverly Hills, and a litigious crowd had appeared tonight to fume and vent.

As student liaison to the board, Jon was fascinated by these moments in which numbers and practicality crossed paths with sentiment and tradition, when slow tides of change suddenly undermined what had always been taken for granted. The packed lecture hall resounded with the murmurs of two hundred or so residents waging what they clearly, collectively saw as a righteous fight. Person after person took the microphone during the public session to call the board members cowards and wolves. They decried the property taxes they paid (their rates were among the lowest in the state of California). They flung accusations of decades of money mismanagement. They prompted their young children to say, in meek voices, how heartbroken they would be to not have a school anymore. A camera filmed in the back of the room.

No actual plans existed to close the elementary school—it was just one of many ideas by which to address the compelling dual problems of failing infrastructure and falling enrollment. The access to education was not in question, nor was its quality—only geography (the three other elementary schools in the district were within a mile). But the feral defensiveness on display orbited something more than education, some instinct residing deep inside of people, some accretion of nostalgia and pride and fear of change and suspicion of authority that summated in a furious sense of disenfranchisement. People rarely reacted calmly to the pairing of school and change. He figured that the reason had to do with the memories people carried—carried from the exact passage of their lives that Jon was near completing. To remove the school would be to tarnish the memories.

Jon arrived home after ten that night, and only then began his homework. His father worked in the marine glow of his computer, and his mother was asleep. He sat at his desk and began marking up pages of *Madame Bovary*, tracking the ways by which the eponymous character's excesses led to the ruin of self, spouse, and child. The book had shaped much of Western literature, and it was also really boring.

Byron, Luis, Tio

Very few undertakings were made easier or less expensive by virtue of living in Los Angeles. Grocery shopping, getting to school, getting home from school, playing pickup soccer, recycling, fixing a leaky roof, finding a summer job, paying rent, renewing a license, celebrating a birthday, finding childcare, filing taxes, turning left: all made for various degrees of toil in a city built horizontally, densely packed and growing by fifty thousand people per year, with terrible transit. The physics of the place had no recourse, so one grew accustomed to the difficulties while also complaining all the time. Traffic was the emblematic problem, but deeper, more affecting disconnects between people had been laid over decades. The city was spread out over five hundred square miles, while the majority of white-collar jobs were concentrated in a few small building clusters, creating severe disparities in housing costs, commute times, and upward mobility. Most important with regard to the formative years of young people, the city was relatively segregated economically, racially, and culturally. Many cities in America were, but Los Angeles, with its incomparable congestion, rendered the simple act of leaving one's neighborhood a considerable and expensive feat in itself. On a broad scale, Los Angeles harbored great riches of diversity within its markers, and at the same time made interface with people of different experience a labor. Interface did occur in the sublime public spaces of shorelines and state parks, at parades and concerts and Dodgers games and the annual Festival of Books—but not on a daily scale, and certainly not in most schools. Aside from traffic jams and the film industry and nice weather, Los Angeles had little in the way of a unifying identity.

On a Wednesday evening in early February, after ninety minutes spent on two trains and a bus, Byron entered a Starbucks on Robertson Boulevard, a West Hollywood street known for its high-end clothing and furniture stores, restaurants, and a baby boutique catering to new parents in the market for thousand-dollar strollers. The city's dissonance was loud to him here. He was tired and a little nervous as he sat down. A while later, and twenty minutes late, a woman in her twenties, nicely composed in a long skirt and dress shirt, found him.

"You're . . . Byron?"

He stood and shook her hand. She told him she worked for a film agency and a meeting had run over. She apologized for being late.

"I'm late all the time," he said, and then realized he shouldn't have said that in a college alumni interview; this woman had volunteered with Cornell, her recent alma mater, to interview prospective students—a formality widely presumed to have little bearing on admissions, but still another box he needed to check. She asked if he was eating or drinking anything, and he said no. She offered to buy him something, and he said sure, scanning the menu of frappés and lattes and other high-calorie caffeine carriers he'd vaguely heard of. He pulled a lemonade from the refrigerated rack. While they waited for her complicated order, she asked, "Is Cornell your first choice?"

Byron said, "No," and again realized he shouldn't have said that, silently commanding himself to stop being honest with this person.

She seemed taken aback. "What's your first choice?"

"San Luis Obispo."

She made a face as if she'd just bitten a lemon or rotten egg. "Over *Cornell*?" Byron nodded and shrugged. "Why?" she asked.

"It has the best engineering and aerospace programs in Cal Poly."

She was shaking her head as her foamy drink arrived, and back in their chairs she proceeded to tell him with fluttering hands how much better Cornell's programs were in those areas, and in all areas, than any Cal State school.

"Cal Poly," he said, correcting her. He didn't know why this was going so poorly so quickly. He didn't really know why he was here. He had only a minuscule chance of being considered by Cornell, but Luis and other friends had called it their top choice, so he'd mimicked them and applied. He'd heard from someone that students there committed suicide by jumping off a certain bridge into a gorge.

When she finished denigrating California schools, she asked, "What's your second choice?"

"Dartmouth."

Dartmouth was another profound reach for him, and he didn't know much about it except that it was cold. She performed again the animated routine of explaining why the ranking he'd made was wrong, and he listened under the body-lock of a surging anger while thinking: *You don't know me, so why are you shitting on my choices?*

After her spiel, she stopped asking him about school preference and retreated to the pattern more typical of these interviews: *Why do you like Cornell? What subjects are you interested in pursuing? What are you most proud of in your high school career?*

He didn't have any answers he considered interesting, and he didn't think she cared much anyway. He made little effort to engage her beyond her questions. When he mentioned his interest in aerospace, she informed him with a sober face that it was one of the hardest programs to enter. After twenty minutes, her last question was, "What's your goal?"

Byron blurted, "I want to be Iron Man."

She laughed so hard that a few drops of coffee splattered onto his side of the table, and he couldn't gauge whether she was laughing at or with him. He couldn't gauge most of the dynamics within this interaction. She seemed like a nice person, like she wasn't intentionally trying to hurt his feelings repeatedly. He clarified that he actually dreamed of helping design high-tech armored suits for the military, and that a few members of his extended family were on active duty now, and she apologized for laughing. She even appeared to entertain his idea seriously. The meeting lasted a third as long as the time he'd spent traveling there, and the time he'd spend returning home. It lasted about the same amount of time as she was late. The sky was fully dark once he thanked her and said goodbye, and he walked with hands jammed in the pockets of his Ánimo Pat Brown sweatshirt, down the clean slate stones of Robertson Boulevard, past the Petrossian restaurant, where Owen often ate with his father, past shopwindows glowing with soft yellow light and embossed with French names in dramatic script, behind which adults idly perused racks of clothes and showrooms of kitchen fixtures, to the bus stop, to go back home. On the train amid people commuting from work to their farther-flung neighborhoods, he began his English reading homework while wondering if the disastrous interview was a result of him, or her, or simply the wide experiential chasms that separated people.

Luis's Cornell interview was much easier. He met with a man in a tall office building at Seventh and Broad Street downtown. The man was in his thirties and handsome in his suit. In a nice conference room with a view over the diamond district, the man began with, "First things first: this isn't an interview. Cornell couldn't give less of a fuck what I think. They don't even look at it. So let's just try to have a fun conversation."

"For real? They don't even *look* at it?"

"I could write that you're a psychopath and it wouldn't affect your chances of getting in."

Luis chortled. "So why do you do it? Wouldn't you rather be home right now?"

"I can help add a few more things to your application, and it's a fun way to meet interesting people. And if I volunteer for this gig, then the university won't hit me up for money—at least not as much."

He asked a couple of stock questions and suggested that Luis pad his application a bit, a recommendation from his summer job supervisor, for instance.

"I think it's too late to add anything at this point," Luis said.

"That's one place where I can actually be useful, just forward whatever to me and I'll forward to them and they'll add it."

"Damn, you've got pull."

They talked about Cornell and the weather of upstate New York and physics. The man took notes and seemed quite interested in Luis and his experiences. They talked for almost an hour, laughed often, and when they shook hands Luis felt as though he'd just met a nice, cool guy who happened to wear a suit and work at a bank and be a white Ivy League graduate.

Tio's Cornell interview was worse even than Byron's: At 4:11 p.m. on a Thursday afternoon, after waiting for notice of the place and time for over a week, he received an email telling him that his interview had been scheduled for 4:15 that day at an office downtown. He forwarded the email to admissions@cornell.edu explaining politely that four minutes was not quite enough time to travel from his neighborhood to downtown. A few days later, he received a reply stating, with apologies, that interviews missed without prior notification could not be rescheduled due to the interviewers' time constraints.

Chapter 12

You can do a million great things, but everybody's always just going to remember the one mistake.

—Luis

Owen, Bennett

Two totaled cars, both white sedans, faced one another at the intersection of Moreno Drive and Lasky Drive, directly in front of the high school. The grilles were smashed, the hoods tented, and large holes had shattered from the windshields. The bent metal was ugly and severe, but more haunting were the teenaged human bodies inside and outside of the vehicles. One girl lay facedown on the hood, the hind section of her body draped over the dash of the passenger side. Another was belted into the driver's seat with her head slumped forward. A young man was propped against the side of the car, with bright crimson smears across his face and stains on his T-shirt. The same color cut a wide swath diagonally across the crumpled front section of the other car. A girl knelt on the pavement beside the boy, holding his hand and sobbing while a crowd of hundreds of Beverly students and parents and teachers watched from beyond yellow tape. Firefighters began easing one of the bodies onto a yellow stretcher. Police surrounded the area.

A helicopter flew in tight circles overhead. A man came forward whose uniform read, in bold letters, *CORONER*. Owen was supposed to be the driver of one of the cars but wasn't.

Every 15 Minutes was a biennial event in Beverly Hills. This year's incarnation had been planned by the ASB and was one of the most grueling weekends on their slate. In their well-funded effort, the group orchestrated elaborate sets, student actors, and real police and firemen in a two-day presentation intended as a reflection on student drinking. The production had been conceived many years before, by a father who'd lost his daughter in an accident, and was regarded by students to be very important and moving.

A small interruption in the realness came in the form of a student, dressed in black with white face paint, circling the perimeter slowly and silently, looking on with a mournful face: Owen.

Owen had been volunteered for a lead role in a short film that was the event's centerpiece, a fictional depiction of the events before and after this fictional crash, in which a student receives admission to his top college, which leads to a party, which leads to drinking, which leads to the crash, a funeral, and courtroom scenes in which the party hosts are held liable.

Owen had woken up the morning of filming with the flu and so hadn't been in the movie at all. But someone on the planning committee had decided that he deserved a role in the event, and so he'd been bidden to play the ghost of some unspecified teenager who carried a sign that read, *I was killed in a texting and driving accident.* Owen did as told, and the result totally belied the carefully constructed realism surrounding him, leading to a certain amount of heckling from bystanders.

Then the dozen students in the scene, including Owen, were obligated to disappear from campus for a day and turn off their phones; this was to simulate their actual deaths. They stayed four-to-a-room at a nice hotel, and the following day were given a tour of the police station and later a mortuary. After briefly visiting Marilyn Monroe's grave for some unknown reason, they were assigned to write a hypothetical posthumous letter to their parents. He invested a fair amount of thought in the work.

That evening, in the same space where nationally televised awards shows like the Golden Globes were held, the short film played on a large screen, and then Owen and the other actors filed onto the stage past framed pictures of themselves as part of a faux memorial service. The atmosphere was suitably somber until the last person accidentally knocked a picture over, which caused a domino effect, flattening all the frames. Half-stifled laughter sounded across the crowded space and was quickly tamped. The principal, teachers, students, and parents made speeches from a podium regarding their fictional losses. Owen had been selected to read his letter aloud, still in the odd role of the unassociated dead person.

"In the past, whenever I've contemplated death, I've always attached a certain romance to it, like it would happen in front of a firing squad or driving off a cliff into the ocean, at sunset, while saving a small town from a bomb. But instead, I died because someone thought an intersection was a good place to check their Snapchat. This person didn't just take my life, he took my death. Sorry, Mom and Dad. I love you."

The long day ended and he was permitted to talk to his friends and girlfriend once again. He immediately learned that a few kids, and even a teacher, were criticizing the letter he'd read, calling him disrespectful, cheeky, an asshole who had undermined the event by turning it into "Owen's Comedy Show." Some combination of the ghost costume and the not-suitably-mournful letter—with which he'd been aiming for a minorly profound reflection—and the slightly sardonic tone with which he spoke generated a consensus among small groups that he hadn't taken any of the epic two-day program seriously.

"So I give up two days of my life for the event, sit through an hour-long question-and-answer with a mortician, try really hard to be earnest about the whole thing—all of which the school basically ordered me to do—and now that makes me an asshole," was his takeaway. He was aware that he was being sensitive but somewhat astonished by the capacity of people to find something to be shitty about.

"I think that it couldn't have ended in any other way for you," Bennett replied, not entirely joking.

Bennett had been tapping his phone screen constantly. For weeks he'd been waiting for an alert from NYU. He wasn't a superstitious person, but he'd been wearing his lucky under-wear, and he'd been kicking his lucky tennis ball along the side-walk to and from school. During one such walk a few days after the event, he received an unremarkable email instructing him to check the university portal, which required signing in and clicking on a succession of small-type links. Overexcited in the thumbs, he kept clicking the wrong buttons and navigating out of the wrong web pages. When he finally reached the status of his admissions, he found no exclamation points, no congratulations or exhortations, just a short sentence informing him that his long-held, meticulously orchestrated dream of getting into NYU was now realized. He kept walking along the wide, shaded street, head downturned, rereading this sentence over and over. When he did look up, he noticed the soft wind swaying the palms and the birdcalls and the squirrels spiraling their way up tree trunks, and the fact that aside from a construction crew working a tear-down site, he was the only pedestrian on the long block. He was glad to be so absolutely alone in this moment.

His mother was in the kitchen when he arrived home, and his particular knowing smile broadcast the news to her instantaneously, so she was already in motion toward him when he said, "I got in," and her arms gently wrapped him, and his her, and they both held the embrace for nearly a minute.

"I'm so proud of you," she said, words she'd been practicing and praying she'd have the chance to employ. The moment was a quintessential piece of the whole of Bennett's imaginings, singular and timeless, pure and paramount and also very fleeting, one of a handful shared between parent and child over an average life's span: college, marriage, childbirth, not many others. When the moment ended, he said, "Now we'll find out what it costs."

Money had forever been the screen dimming the beacon of NYU, one of the most expensive universities in the country, in the most expensive city in the country. His mother had a successful career in television production and other enterprises, and years earlier she'd moved them from the home she still owned in the Hollywood Hills to a rental apartment in Beverly Hills because of its public school district (she'd found the general behavior of private school parents abhorrent beginning in kindergarten). But the cost of tuition and boarding at NYU, plus related school, travel, and living expenses, had surpassed $70,000 per year. Because of where they lived and the property they owned, they couldn't expect much in the way of financial aid. She'd always been internally conflicted over her son's collegiate version of Gatsby's green light across the harbor, not because she couldn't afford it—with some well-thought-out financial planning, she was confident that she could—but because, based on her own experience in the entertainment industry, she didn't believe that the massive outlays demanded by film schools aligned with the opportunities such schools provided, nor did she care at all about the esteem that her son's prestigious placement lent her (which made her something of an outlier in the entertainment industry). To do what Bennett wanted to do, she believed, he simply needed to keep doing it: work, write, create. She didn't say as much now, as he continued to glow. And she promised herself to refrain from such commentary in the months ahead. He'd bound himself to a pursuit, and he'd obtained it, and the glow itself felt worth its imminent price.

In the short term, Bennett played the role of third wheel to Owen and his girlfriend at a Mac DeMarco concert, a performer with a cultlike fan base who sang slow, offbeat ballads while scaling the venue walls and ripping layers of clothes off and genuinely acting like a heavy metal rock star. His performances were bewildering and strangely hypnotic; they went to see him whenever he played near Los Angeles. Bennett basked in these hours while observing others in the crowd, a weird, dense assemblage of alternately young, punkish music aficionados and middle-aged people who wore polo shirts and looked like they handled urgent matters during the day. The latter group all appeared so glad to be there, smoking pot from vape pens and dancing badly and acting juvenile throughout this reprieve from family and work and daily obligations. Bennett studied them and their different versions of happiness and somehow felt a rare clarity that night, the kind only great live music had the power to grant. He felt like life would be pretty good.

Luis, Carlos, Tio

The red and blue lights flashed in Luis's rearview mirror, paired with a short, shrill squawk: among the least wanted colors and sounds for a brown person to see and hear in a car in South LA. He was idling at the curb outside a friend's home—Tio's girlfriend—after she'd asked for a ride to school that morning. Across the street was an elementary school, and while waiting Luis had seen the two policemen ticketing people who had walked their kids inside while leaving their cars for a few minutes in a loading-only zone. He considered that to be a dick move—a move probably never attempted in rich school districts—but hadn't thought much more of it. Now, while tracking the officer from the squad car to his driver's-side door, he was terrified—and more so once the second officer took a position to the right of his rear bumper, hand planted on his holstered firearm, a standard precaution with terrible associations.

He had reason to be alarmed. He was driving his brother's car, which was a maroon lowrider of the sort driven by gang leaders in films. The car had tinted front windows, which was illegal. Its plates were still branded by the dealership his brother had leased it from, months past the ninety-day grace period (the registered DMV plates had arrived by mail in time, but they'd been misplaced in their messy, frenetic home and eventually forgotten about). And Luis had not yet obtained his provisional license; he'd been driving with a learner's permit that required an adult to be in the car. He'd fucked up.

"License and registration."

In the clutch of his fear, he did his best to remember all the rules of behavior that he and everyone he knew had been taught and retaught specifically for situations like this. He kept his hands visible on the steering wheel—that was a big one.

"Sir, do you mind—what did I do?"

"You're obstructing traffic." Luis didn't understand what he meant since the car was idling in a legal space on the residential side of the street, whereas the police car was now in the middle of the street and blocking a line of silently seething parents. But he wasn't going to protest. As if anticipating an argument anyway, the officer added, "You're beyond eighteen inches from the curb."

The officer was terse, just shy of antagonistic, as he asked Luis questions about the car and his destination. He softened somewhat when it became apparent that Luis, with his navy shirt and glasses, was just a schoolboy. When his license failed to match the registration, he was ordered to get out. Taking care to keep his hands visible even as his shoulders slumped in compliance, Luis obeyed, and he felt very much like a child. Much radio back-and-forth ensued with various dispatchers, along with some grave-looking interface between the officer and the laptop mounted in the squad car. The windows, the plates, and the learner's permit were all severe problems. The officer wrote him a citation and told him where to find instructions to schedule a court date. Luis learned that he wouldn't be able to obtain a real license for at least two years after completing additional, expensive traffic courses. The car was to be impounded—and at that point Luis pleaded for permission to call his brother. The officer granted him the use of his phone, flashing a quick glimpse of pity, and his brother then rushed to the address to prove legal ownership, calculating that the fines he would receive for the car's condition would be cheaper and easier to deal with than the impound lot and its layers of fees.

"Drive safer," the officer said in parting, about forty-five minutes after stopping Luis, who hadn't actually been driving at the time.

Once the squad car turned out of sight, Luis thrust his middle finger in its general direction and shouted, "I didn't fucking do anything!" Then his brother commenced screaming at him. The whole incident and its costs had occurred over three inches and a friend running five minutes behind.

He arrived at school late and livid. Luis could be loud, baiting, and condescending, but his friends rarely saw him upset. "I was pulled up somewhere and a cop decided to be a dick," was his explanation. They were in chemistry class.

"You were pulled up somewhere in your brother's tricked-out, tinted, no-plates car, without a real license, and you have no fault in all this?" Carlos proposed, partly in observation, partly because opportunities to challenge Luis's antics were rare and not to be deferred.

"Fuck that—I was parked!" He stretched his arms wide in indignation, an eighteen-year-old crucifix.

"I'm just glad as hell that I wasn't in the car with you," Carlos said, shaking his head. "I'd be locked up on a bus to Tijuana right now." He was exaggerating, as Carlos had practiced his potential interactions with authorities to a degree far beyond what Luis knew, and he possessed the tenuous screen of his Washington State ID. He sympathized with his friend for the vulnerability they all shared due to race, location, and age, but he also questioned Luis's outrage at having gaily placed himself in a position that could so easily doom others. A more appropriate response, in Carlos's estimation, would be relief.

Neither of the two attended the Caballeros con Cultura dance the following night, which Tio had been widely billing as the *baile del año*—the dance of the year. Luis was still stewing over the car misfortune, though surprisingly, his mother wasn't angry, categorizing what had happened as a simple inevitability and taking a portion of the responsibility herself. Carlos had to be home with his younger sister because his mother had been working the four-to-midnight shift of late, and on Fridays his father worked until ten packing box shipments to Miami. Tio had invested tremendous effort in the party, desiring it to be different from typical school dances—more sophisticated than a perimeter of gawking people surrounding a cluster of dancers. He aimed for an atmosphere reflective of the group's core discussions about culture and masculinity. Instead of a DJ playing pop hits, he'd hired a live band to play Mexican dance music. He'd gone to great lengths for permission to use the outdoor grounds of the campus. Families were contributing *sopes* and *pupusas* and other essentials of their various ancestral regions. He strove to create an ambiance that, for a few hours on a Friday night, would give the people there a connection to a world broader and deeper than the one they knew in South LA. The inflatable bouncy house that their friend Victor had contributed didn't exactly serve this purpose, but bouncy houses were always a value-add.

Leaving the apartment, wearing slacks and a pressed white button-down and tie, he called goodbye to his parents. His mother was cooking and his father was watching Spanish news. They both knew vaguely about C3 and the dance. His mother had expressed pride at his initiative. His father had seemed a bit flummoxed over the group's values equating manhood with sensitivity; the two were mutually exclusive to him, and the whole notion of men discussing feelings together struck him as effeminate.

"You look nice," his father said tonight. "It's good that you dressed up for this dance."

"Thanks, Dad."

His mother emerged from the kitchenette with approval. "You look grown-up."

"Thanks, Mom."

"Your father used to dress up like that, when he was courting me back home. He was your age but didn't look so grown-up as you, wasn't nearly as tall as you, but he'd take me out to dance in the plaza."

His father smiled to himself, surely remembering those days long ago, far away.

"Were you a good dancer, Dad?"

He nodded and his smile widened slightly. "Yeah, I was great. And I dressed up nice, too, even if I wasn't so tall."

On the way to school in the dusk, he thought of what his parents must have looked and felt like during those nights, and the image made him glad. Even though his father lived in a rigid binary world—one in which women cooked and men watched TV—and Tio did not aim to inherit this binary, the fact of their resemblance, this passage through time between them, still propelled his heart.

About two hundred students came, and throughout the night Tio mingled among them. Like a regal host, he introduced himself to people he didn't know, thanked them for coming, made sure they were fed. He looked around the small plot of grass beneath the soft light, the young faces laughing over food on the picnic tables, couples illicitly attempting to make out in the bouncy house, the rows of bodies performing energetic, hip-centric dance steps, and he was proud of himself. In his pride he thought not at all of fathers and applications and uncertainties and the future.

The thrill of the dance and the closed chamber it had placed around his anxiety faded quickly, as most thrills did. People were acting strangely across the senior class, arguing for no reason, commandeering student council meetings with irrelevant and melodramatic complaints, growing suspicious of various methods students may or may not have employed to increase their chances at competitive schools. In mid-March, they were nearing the end of another long stretch of school days. Spring break was two weeks away, and so was the massive dump of acceptances and rejections it portended. Schoolwork had all but ceased to carry meaning for the senior class, causing a collective stir-craziness. Days passed slowly.

In the meantime, the college board loomed on the prominent, mitered hallway corner opposite the administration offices. On the large sheet of cork would be pinned the miniature ensigns of every school that accepted an APB student. Its surface was mostly empty now. The most artistic member of the student government, a boy named David, was spearheading the background decoration. He was soft-spoken and had grown up in the foster system with his older sister while their mother dealt with substance abuse. Now he lived with his mother, but she was barely speaking to him since he'd begun dating boys the previous summer. In the midst of life's confusion, or maybe as an antidote to it, he'd been devoting an inordinate amount of time to painting the college board. In the next month, this mural would fill well beyond its capacity with small flags and would become the spiritual centerpiece of the school.

"You know what that looks like, don't you?"

Luis was standing ten feet behind him, with his head tilted to one side, squinting at the delicate floral pattern.

"It's not really any specific thing," David said. "It's just supposed to be kind of peaceful."

Luis waved him over, and David backed away from the painting to stand alongside him. "Now look at it."

David tilted his head also and squinted through his glasses. When he saw what Luis saw, Luis laughed in a loud and cathartic bellow.

"Oh, yeah—that's not what I planned."

"But now you see the big picture." From afar, the drawing looked very much like an anatomically detailed vagina. "So, our very own Georgia O'Keeffe, that's got to symbolize something—right?"

"I don't want to know what it symbolizes. A space vagina."

"What are you going to do now?"

"I think I can . . . blend it? So it won't be so . . . obvious?"

Luis patted him on the shoulder. "Okay, uh, good luck with that?"

"It'll eventually be covered over with colleges."

"I hope so. If it isn't, we're all kind of fucked."

They both knew that it would be. What they didn't know—what no one really knew, and what was the driving force behind the recent, school-wide angst—was what those colleges would be, and who among them would feel triumphant, and who would feel left behind.

PART III

Spring

Chapter 13

I sometimes fantasize about being a hermit in the middle of Switzerland or some random place. Just take all the people away, all the things we have to do, the scores and degrees and people telling you things, and kind of screw it and write poetry or something. But—I'm not going to do that, obviously . . . right?

—Jon

Jon

"Uuuuuuuuuuuhhhhhhh . . . *what?*"

Jon had initially been wait-listed by the University of Chicago, which felt akin to asking a girl to a dance and being told that she would go in the event that someone she liked more couldn't. The day prior, he'd received an email from the university's local admissions representative asking to speak on the phone, and so he'd stepped out of his first-period class to take the call in his counselor's office. They'd exchanged a few pleasantries, and Jon answered a handful of stock interview questions ("Why do you want to go to the University of Chicago?") while he waited to be informed that either his packet was incomplete or his admission had been declined from the wait list. Instead, he learned that he'd been accepted. His reaction was one of low-key bemusement while his counselor met his eyes from behind her desk, her face animated with a thrill that, at least outwardly, far exceeded his own.

His counselor had been at Beverly for almost thirty years, helping a quarter of the student body with their schedules, their extra-curriculars, their day-to-day grades, and the trials of admissions. She maintained an aerial view of each individual whose thickening folder filled her hard drive; she'd once had Jon come to her office to explain a flubbed but largely meaningless pop quiz on *Othello*. He didn't know exactly to what lengths she'd gone behind the scenes on his behalf, only that she'd guided him with meticulousness and a distinct confidence—which he'd assumed had been performative—through the wait list process. She'd helped him craft a letter reaffirming his interest in the university and had prompted the principal to call the admissions department directly to ask for a re-review of Jon's application. Jon had been grateful for all of these efforts, but he hadn't presumed any actual results would come from them; he'd felt that these were kind educators doing what they could from the outskirts of a system beyond their influence. Now, as he thanked both the admissions representative and his counselor profusely and then made his way to second period, his mind reeled a bit at the way small moments and random people had a capacity to alter one's life.

The second half of March swelled with emails from admissions offices, all containing some variation of the message *There is an update to the status of your application.* The past era's anxiety of checking mailboxes and determining a physical envelope's weight for some indication of its contents had been replaced by the tapping of a phone screen or laptop trackpad. These subtle movements then transmuted the past months of uncertainty into future weeks of deliberation. The unveiled choices were not always those previously imagined or hoped for, but they were all but locked. Three and a half years of high school were culminating in these first few weeks of spring, loaded with a pressure students had abstractly conceived of but not fully understood until now. Not only were their educations being determined, but also in some way their future homes, friends, careers, marriages, children—every component of their lives, really.

The winter had been a fairly wet one, alleviating for the moment a historic five-year drought, but the weather had for the most part been warm and bright. It was warm and bright now. It would be warm and bright for the rest of the spring, the atmosphere of Los Angeles not at all reflecting, or seeming to care about, the colossal goings-on.

As Jon processed his Chicago admission and its ramifications (he would need warm clothes), he wondered on a macro scale whether this inflection point was in fact so colossal, whether it mattered at all if an individual person went to college in Chicago or Michigan or Oregon or Southern California, an Ivy or a state school or a small liberal arts college, to study history or gender studies or math or developmental biology. Jon, his classmates, his friends and his acquaintances and strangers, were simply part of a cycle, repeated every single year and experienced by multitudes. These web portals and the messages they contained—beginning with either the words *Congratulations on your acceptance* or the words *We regret to inform you*—were lifetime markers that were also enwrapped in American machinations of commerce and presumed upward mobility and perpetual inequality and the mysterious, vexing metrics by which individuals and their experiential souls were judged. They were also just words generated by computer inputs, concerning people who were just growing up, making decisions—mostly innocuous decisions—as they strove to make sense of the world unfolding and discern a vision for how they wanted to inhabit that world. This particular stretch of time was at turns illuminating, heartening, crushing—but mostly just strange.

The weekend before spring break, Jon and his Aca Deca compatriots flew to Sacramento for the state competition. They left on Thursday evening and began cramming the moment they reached their hotel just off the Sacramento State University campus, four to a room, drilling each other on the music, math, literature, sociology, and politics of the early 1940s. Starting at two a.m., members began splintering off to sleep. Jon stayed up the latest. As was his tendency, he'd ignored much of the preparation over the course of the winter. But now that the competition was close, his mind and competitive spirit were activated, and his focus was total. These efforts, of course, manifested too late to alter any outcomes.

On Saturday, the campus was kinetic with hundreds of groups of high schoolers moving from building to building for their tests on various subjects, fifty questions per. They wrote essays. They each gave a prepared speech regarding a designated topic, followed by an eight-minute interview. Jon thought he'd done okay, but he missed the presentation of the final results because he had to leave early for an LA Youth Orchestra rehearsal on Sunday. He heard later that Beverly Hills had placed sixth in their division of around fifty schools, which was a quite decent result after the hundreds of extra hours they'd spent at school over the course of the year. He also heard that, as expected, the ardent cheers that greeted each team as its name was announced in the auditorium—*Torrance High School! Folsom High School! Cathedral High School!*—had fallen into silence when Beverly Hills was called.

Carlos, Tio, Luis, Byron

The Westfield mall in Santa Anita was busier when they walked out of the Red Robin restaurant than when they'd walked in. Tio, Luis, Byron, Carlos, and Victor had gone for dinner, feeling flush after spending the day working for Victor's parents at the racetrack carnival. UC acceptances had been sliding out over the course of the week preceding spring break, so the large plates of deep-fried food in which they profligately indulged had a cathartic effect on their minds while taxing their digestive tracts. They also were loath to return to their various apartments to spend a weekend night refreshing and refreshing college Web pages.

Tio was feeling confident; earlier in the week, he'd been accepted to Pomona, the Cal State polytechnic school that had accepted Luis in December. But his financial aid situation there remained unclear. Based on what he'd learned from Luis, he wasn't feeling optimistic about the money. Luis had been given substantial need-based aid relative to full tuition but would still be responsible for upward of $10,000 a year, a prohibitive figure. But Luis had also been accepted to UC Santa Barbara the day before, and that news had leveled Tio's frenetic interior: he had better grades than Luis, better attendance records, better leadership accolades due to his Caballeros con Cultura role, and only marginally lower SAT scores. His girlfriend had just been accepted to UCLA, and Tio had been helping her with schoolwork for three years. The college board at school was rapidly filling with the full range of UCs and Cal States. The delay with learning his own status bothered him a bit, but the system's servers were notoriously overloaded—at least, that's what he was telling himself.

"Let's hit up that massage chair," Tio said. Outside of the Sharper Image store, the wide, deep piece of electric furniture beckoned with its coin and dollar slots.

"I'm going first because I can barely walk after that meal," Luis said.

Tio replied, "I think Carlos should go first, because Harvard."

Carlos had heard from Harvard at the very beginning of the acceptance window. He'd also gotten into Columbia. As when the

Princeton news had pulsed through school, he'd spent the past eight days shrugging his way through ceaseless praise streaming toward him from all angles, and he felt even more tightly wound than he had in December.

"I'm not putting my body on that thing," Carlos said. "You could get lice and bedbugs and shit. Who knows who's been sitting on it?"

"I've been sitting on it." Luis plopped on and fed two dollars in. The motor began its work, and though his body didn't seem to be moving, he began to hum and the vibration cut up his voice. *"Thi-i-i-i-i-s thi-i-i-i-ng i-i-i-i-i-i-t i-i-i-i-i-i-tche-e-e-es a-a-a-a-and fe-e-e-e-els fu-u-u-u-u-ucking w-e-e-e-i-i-i-rd . . ."* An elderly Asian woman was staring from across the walkway. The boys noticed, but no one could tell whether she was doing so in disapproval, curiosity, or amusement. The chair turned off in a stunningly short amount of time considering the dollars spent. Luis half sat up. "That kind of sucked. Anyone else?" No one had any interest. Luis proceeded to feed in two more dollars for another session.

They meandered into a Korean-themed arcade, where they each continued to deplete their day's earnings on racing games, basketball contests, and military shoot-'em-ups. Tio caught Byron gawking at a young woman, an arcade employee, cleaning the screens and buttons with antiseptic wipes.

"Man, you found the woman of your dreams." Byron nodded stupidly, and Tio prodded him: "You can't just look at her like that, she'll get, like, a restraining order. Go talk to her."

"No, I can't do that," Byron mumbled.

"I'll go, then."

Byron grabbed his shoulder to hold him back. "No, don't."

"Maybe it's better this way," Tio said. "The courtship, the marriage, the home and family and growing old together—it's better if it just stays in your mind, like the ideal version. The real version's always way worse."

Few leisure activities consumed cash at the rate of video game arcades. Within thirty minutes, each was down to his last ten dollars. They huddled around Carlos as he finished a decent run on a virtual motorcycle—he finally crashed and exploded in a sad little puff of smoke and flame—and then took what reward tickets they had accumulated to the prize counter. Stuffed animals, plastic tchotchkes, cheap Dodgers hats, and superhero-themed paraphernalia were all priced upward of five hundred tickets. None of them had earned more than seventy.

"At least we'll score some candy," Luis said. But even a small pack of Asian-lettered gum cost seventy-five tickets. "Fuck this."

Walking across the parking lot, Tio produced a pack of the same gum from his pocket and fanned out a few sticks in his hand like playing cards. "You guys still trying to chase that gum? I got three packs in my pocket."

"You just took it?"

"I finessed it."

"You stole it, bro?"

Tio reasoned: "I spent, like, twenty bucks at that place, for fourteen tickets. Each pack of gum's worth, like, fifty cents. End of the day, they still stole from me."

Luis drove them west on the I-210 toward the setting sun (his mother had been generally lax in her enforcement of his car privileges following the citation). The mountain chain that stretched from the Inland Empire to the Pacific Ocean rose high on their right, and to their left the mat of suburbia stretched into the haze. About halfway to Pasadena, where the CA-110 would dogleg them south toward home, Luis pulled off the interstate.

"Five Guys," he said in explanation, nodding toward a sign for the burger joint towering high on a thin pole. "I've never had it before. Have you?"

"We just ate burgers an hour ago," Byron said.

"It was more like two hours." Compton was culinarily limited, mostly fast food and taco stands and *mercados*. Whenever they traveled beyond it, they were inclined to binge.

"I've only got, like, four dollars left," Carlos said.

"That'll cover a burger. I'll spot you fries."

Luis pulled into the lot and they stood in a long line. With their last dollars from the carnival job, they ordered their burgers with bacon and fries and shakes. Luis added bacon to his milkshake, because the option was listed and he couldn't not take it. They sat and ate and made various exclamations regarding the way these particular burgers seemed to melt on the palate.

"It really is an unbelievable sensation," Luis said analytically, through a mouthful.

Byron sat in his chair, moaning quietly to himself, "Mmm-mmmmm . . ."

"You look the same way as when you saw that girl cleaning the games."

Their talking ebbed into the pure, primal contentment of eating. Carlos used the bathroom, where the walls were plastered with vintage-style photos of beautiful women in bikinis eating hamburgers, one staring at him from above the urinal, a foot from his face. The day had been long, unremarkable, and as much fun as he could remember having. He couldn't picture college being this fun, couldn't picture being part of a group of people who could sustain such ease around one another. He couldn't imagine that the Ivy League education stretching ahead of him would include a single day like this one.

"You fuckers!" Upon returning to the table, Carlos learned that his fries had been doused with hot sauce, which his weak stomach would punish him for eating, which his friends all knew.

"Sorry," Luis said innocently. "I'll eat them if you won't."

"I was looking forward to those." Carlos now looked mournfully at the mound of sheeny yellow strips, streaked with red.

"Then you made the mistake of leaving them here unattended. How can you call yourself a Mexican if you can't eat hot sauce?"

Carlos pushed the fries toward Luis, who upturned the batch into his own.

"You go to the East Coast, no one to watch your back—you best learn to protect your food. You'll thank me."

The sky was dark as they passed southwest through the center of downtown LA, beneath the fifty- and sixty-story glass towers with lettering across the brows reading, *US Bank*, *Union Bank*, *Deloitte*, *Omni Hotel*, and the massive luxury condo complexes under construction, the unfathomable cranes suspended above them. Then the highway pivoted due south, past the eastern flank of USC with its bell towers and clean brick façades, and entered the low-rise sameness of South LA.

Amid all the talk and activity, Tio hadn't checked his phone since they'd entered Red Robin a few hours earlier. He did now, scanning through some annoyed texts from his girlfriend, who'd expected him to be home right after work, some more from various skateboard friends telling him which spot to be at and when. He refreshed his email: Twitter feeds he subscribed to from CNN and NPR, some logistical notices he had to deal with regarding the Caballeros con Cultura camping trip that he was organizing for spring break, junk mail in Spanish, and tucked among them, a message from UC.

Tio didn't say anything to the others in the car. The music was playing loud—Kendrick Lamar—and they were all wearily nodding their heads to the bass, stomachs filled to capacity, talk exhausted for the moment, staring out of windows at the streetlighted sprawl. Tio's phone reception was always spotty because his phone and network were both cheap. The device took minutes to load the

UC link, then process his password, then follow his thumb-taps to the message center, where he found separate messages from UC Berkeley, UC Irvine, UC San Diego, UCLA, UC Riverside, and UC Santa Barbara.

He clicked on the messages, one by one, as the Century Boulevard exit approached, and learned that he'd been denied entry by all except Riverside, which offered him a space in its College of Natural and Agricultural Sciences. "Aw, fuck," he murmured to himself, unheard over the music.

Chapter 14

This is your life. You get nervous. You just want to finish.
You're just like, damn, what's going to happen?

—Tio

Owen

Owen was practicing the midshow song-and-dance number for the Beverly Hills spring musical, *The 25th Annual Putnam County Spelling Bee*. He was playing one of the leading roles, William Morris Barfée, an overly confident nerd, complete with short shorts, suspenders, glasses, a part down the center of his grease-flattened hair, and knee-high socks. The number was called "Pandemonium," and the actors riffed on the randomness of spelling bees, by which one contestant might be given the most elementary of words while the next might receive a complicated obscurity. Pop quizzes, life obstacles, relationships, college admissions: all the pressing facets of teenaged existence seemed to fall within this metaphorical zone.

He'd been choreographing his intentionally clunky dance moves in his mother's bedroom during the evenings, testing out movements of his rangy limbs and sharp joints while she directed him from a nest of pillows set against the headboard. She was

very skilled at this—if sometimes harsh—and the ridiculousness
of the scene in the room lent them a disproportionate joy. He
loved this woman so very much.

Owen had decided during the winter that if he were only to
gain admission to his safety schools, then he would definitely
spend a year focused on his acting, most likely at one of the many
well-regarded conservatories within a short drive of his home.
He'd somewhat rooted for this to be the outcome. Now he'd been
accepted into two schools that he'd assumed to be far reaches: NYU
and Kenyon College. NYU had always been an entity associated
solely with Bennett. Owen had applied on something of a lark
after having spent part of the previous summer in Manhattan.
The acceptance brought with it a flurry of warm projected images
involving him and Bennett exploring different neighborhoods,
using bad fake IDs to enter underground rock clubs to see cult
bands in the nether regions of Brooklyn (not quite having grasped
the level of gentrification in that borough), continuing to act in
Bennett's offbeat films, experiencing snowfall and the library and
mature women and Central Park and the oddly alluring loneliness
of living in a city as densely packed as New York.

Kenyon, though he'd never been there and had only applied
on the offhand recommendation of his counselor, was on many
levels the opposite of whatever an NYU experience portended.
Kenyon was a small school, in a village called Gambier in central
Ohio. The student body there numbered around 1,600, the same
as Beverly Hills High. According to pamphlet pictures, the campus
was wooded and serene, with a small main street of shops and cafés
its only semblance of urbanity. The college ideals were presumably
liberal even as the campus was nestled in a highly conservative,
working-class area. Classes were small and taught entirely by professors. The weather would be frigid, the location isolating, and
he'd have no friends there.

He spoke constantly with his brother regarding the dichotomy in his mind, the very different bubbles he was choosing between. His brother was, as ever, generous and thoughtful and measured in his advice. And yet all forms of guidance were starting to matter less now, as options and unknowns expanded widely from the single shelter of his high school. He was older and he had to make choices—and then he would have to contend with those choices, the paths both taken and not taken. He would no longer have the security of relying on others' advice at each juncture—or the security of being able to lay part of the blame on that advice for his own misjudgments. He somewhat had to stop ruminating and get things right.

In the meantime, he struggled in rehearsal to contort his arms and feet and torso with some degree of artistry: *"Life is random and unfair / Life is pandemonium . . . That's the reason we despair . . ."*

Tio

The acres and acres of tiered asphalt that composed the Dodger Stadium parking lot were filled with over twenty-five thousand people, and Tio had to poop.

"I'm nervous as hell," he told his girlfriend. "That's why I have to go so bad."

"You're disgusting," she said, pushing him away. "Stop talking about your business and go deal with it."

The same thing had happened to him last year before the marathon: nerves firing throughout his gut during the bus ride as he considered the physical pain the next four hours held, followed by an urgent bodily need for expulsion, followed by a frantic search that led only to long and unmoving lines jutting from each of the dozens of rancid port-o-potties the city provided—which were what he encountered now. He couldn't deal with the lines, and there was nowhere else to go. The initial waves of faster runners had begun the race half an hour ago, and the Students Run LA group was already moving toward the chute soon. Tio decided to wait and figured that there would be kinder facilities along the marathon route.

The scene was a colorful madness. Most people wore sleeveless racing shirts with either spandex or short, loose-fitting shorts. Others wore superhero capes, clown costumes, hats with water bottles fixed to the sides, pajamas. Some people appeared absolutely focused, others intense and red faced, others in a Zen-like trance. Some looked hungover. Tio now felt like he had to throw up as well as defecate.

Their starting slot came fast, and soon they were on the route, penned in by bodies on all sides, heading southwest toward the downtown skyline. Less than a mile in, Tio's thighs began aching with a stiffness he'd never known in practice. He was unsettled by the early-onset hurt, and he stayed close to his girlfriend for the downtown segment, claiming that he wanted to keep her company. Really, he just sought the slowness of her pace. She grew irritated with him, because he wouldn't stop making fun of the other runners around them: their outfits and facial expressions and running forms.

"Look at the way that lady's feet kind of swing around instead of up—doesn't that look ugly to you? And that fat dude—he's not making it 26.2, damn."

"He's running faster than you," she said.

"I'm just running the pace you're at."

"Go on ahead, then," she said. "Don't worry about me. You're running against yourself."

She knew that his machismo now gave him no choice but to leave her behind—and leave her alone. She was right.

"Ah, damn," he said, reluctantly accelerating. "I'll wait for you at the finish line."

"You don't have to wait for me."

"You're the one who gets mad anytime you don't know where I'm at!" he called as he weaved ahead, through the crowded downtown canyons, until he caught up to a group of male runners from APB.

He'd had less than a week to metabolize the UC emails. He hadn't made much progress in doing so. He'd been pissed off for four days before falling into a malaise of depression and futility. Taking his girlfriend to the movie theater to see *Logan*—a super-hero movie about the loss of invincibility with age—had left him bawling tears far more complicated than the plot of the film merited. His skateboard had always been the remedy for such psychic downturns, but though he'd been masochistically layering bruises on his knees, hips, and elbows, skating's enchanting power was failing him.

"Tio, you're going to be a *farmer!*" had been the joke most often deployed once the news had circulated about Riverside and agricul-tural sciences. Tio, who had never been restrained in mocking the travails of others, had no retorts and no choice but to absorb the gloating barbs, which alluded to not only the high ambitions he'd failed to meet but also their collective heritage. Most all of them had descended from farmers of one sort or another.

He wished that he'd taken AP Government and English. He wished he'd done better on the SAT verbal section. He wished he hadn't posted his straight-A first-semester report card on Facebook. He wished he'd written his personal essay specifically about his father's alcoholism instead of the less specific struggle of growing up poor in South LA; he wished he hadn't been too ashamed to tell the central moment of his own story. That final regret had him dwelling constantly on the sharp drop in grades he'd experienced sophomore year, during the drinking spell, and what those numbers must have signified to people who knew nothing about Juniper Street during the year 2015. In the harsh light of retrospect, he was wondering why he hadn't been strong enough to maintain his grades despite the trauma at home—why he hadn't proven himself more resilient during those months.

Classmates were giddy over acceptances to Berkeley, Irvine, San Luis Obispo, Santa Barbara, and others. Luis in particular had been loud about his intention to be in Santa Barbara next year, while Tio simmered inside thinking of all the C's from which Luis had recovered at the last moment, all the days Luis had skipped school for no reason.

His parents, even his father, had been congratulatory about the news. They didn't tier schools the way students did. To his mother, they were all the University of California, they were all part of the American narrative of immigrants cementing their valid place and improving their status generationally. She'd hugged him so warmly, and he'd looked down at her head pressed against his chest. For a moment, he'd forgotten his own despair. His father had nodded and mumbled something. Perhaps there'd been some modicum of approval if not pride set within the throaty sound. Tio couldn't tell, but he chose to believe there was. Regardless, Riverside had made for the very floor of the ascending bars he'd set. Practically, this perspective derived from his observance that high-performing students, straight-A students like him, didn't go to Riverside. Psychologically, Tio saw himself as a leader, a role model, a caballero. In the context of South LA and beyond, he saw himself as elite. Elite people didn't go to schools that accepted half of all applicants, a high percentage of them first-generation. Nor did elite people study agricultural sciences. This was how he felt, no matter how shallow or disingenuous or outright incorrect such feelings were.

You want to be an engineer, then apply for engineering and go be an engineer. He'd heard this message dozens of times over the last six months, from teachers, counselors, friends. They'd sounded so confident that they'd worn down his impulse to apply in some other, less competitive field, or just apply undeclared. The encouragement had brought him to override his own cynicism, layered over eighteen years of life, regarding the idea that a system that had rarely worked in favor of people who looked like him might have begun to change. That it had in fact changed for Carlos, Luis, his girlfriend, and others in the hallways at school, but it hadn't for him, further concentrated his melancholy.

At least his legs were loosening as he coasted along Sunset Boulevard through a wide corridor formed by hundreds of cheering Angelenos. He'd latched on to a group of four friends moving at a quick clip through this gentrified section of the city, past vintage music and furniture stores, cafés emanating strong smells of warm bread as a small, special torture while the temperature climbed toward eighty degrees. His thighs felt strong and reliable and his lungs were serving him well. He listened to a mix of electronic dance music, and six miles passed with relative ease and even enjoyment. On Hollywood Boulevard, where long lines of tents lived in by homeless people were staked just behind the tourists browsing in and out of novelty stores, he began to hurt: lungs and calves, simultaneously. He switched the soundtrack to Metallica, hoping the heavy metal would distract his brain from processing his overtaxed body. It didn't, really.

His group lost two members, either moving ahead or falling behind, he couldn't keep track. The phone holder around his arm began chafing his skin. He called his girlfriend, who was three miles behind now. She told him not to call her again. He had to go to the bathroom and couldn't suppress it this time, so he stopped, and when he emerged from the awful cubicle, he was alone on Santa Monica Boulevard in West Hollywood, with a straight nine miles remaining to the beach, where the finish line was. He tried to resume that pleasing pace again, but his body failed to respond, and he walked a few miles beginning at the sign marked *17*. He didn't like being alone generally, but particularly here. The primary fulfillment of the marathon had always resided in finishing together. He changed the music to a Mexican *corrido*, soothing in its quiet redundancy, the opposite of heavy metal. He walked past a long row of gay bars with names like Rage and the Abbey, where strangers who'd been drinking all morning urged him along. "C'mon, kid! You can finish! Go! Go!"

He raised his arms at his sides and said with a scowl, "You think it's fucking easy running a marathon? You try to do it!"

He passed the green sign that read, *Welcome to Beverly Hills.* This stretch was flat and only a mile and a half long, from Doheney to Wilshire. A manicured rose garden ran the length of the right side. On the left were a succession of parking lots servicing the high-end shopping district. He began jogging again. Residential streets curved north off the boulevard, large colonial homes with their porticos disappearing under the shade of maple, alder, sycamore, and juniper trees. Palms rose like stilts above everything. The street was wide and lovely. Straight ahead, though it was not yet visible, he could begin to sense the expanse of ocean at which all of this ended. He pressed on, Beverly Hills making for an unmemorable few minutes of his circuit through Los Angeles.

Carlos, Luis, and Byron had planned to utilize an informal aspect of the race that permitted people to run the last five miles even if they weren't registered; they were going to jump in and both encourage and mock the APB runners. But they hadn't coordinated well with the train schedule—all had overslept—so they took the Expo Line all the way to Santa Monica and made their way to the finish. Luis was tall enough to pick out runners over the crowd as they came down the final stretch. Their plan was to celebrate with friends from student council, eat some free food, maybe all go to the pier roller coaster together and then sit around on the beach. But the APB runners coming past the line to receive their medals and their silver thermal blankets were on another plane of existence that had no place in it for these boys who'd slept in until halfway through the race. None of Luis's jokes could penetrate their armor of exhaustion, no bit of praise could bridge the 26.2 miles between them. The runners just wanted to be together. Tio wasn't answering his phone; no one knew where he was. The three boys quickly reboarded the train to go home, considering the afternoon a waste. A woman who appeared of unsound mind sat across from them, clutching a heavy, tattered backpack in her lap. As the train started moving, she began counting down in a shrill voice, *"Ten . . . nine . . . eight . . ."*

Other riders stared at her. Some distanced themselves. Luis whispered to Byron, "Oh my God, shit's about to go *boom*."

"What the hell is going on?" Carlos asked.

"She is counting our life down," Byron replied casually.

"Seven . . . six . . ."

Luis channeled characters from a generic disaster movie: "Carlos, Byron, you guys are my best friends, I've always truly admired you, I'm sorry we didn't have more time to reach our dreams together . . ."

"Five . . . four . . . three . . ."

"I'm grateful to have known you fuckers. It was a good journey while it lasted . . ."

The train dinged and the next stop was announced before the woman reached *one*. When the doors opened, she exited the train.

"Damn, this city."

Upon finishing, Tio had weakly taken his medal and walked in the direction in which the herd seemed to be walking. His breathing was measured, his legs numb. The finish was on Ocean Avenue, high above the shore. This westernmost sliver of Los Angeles was one of its most objectively gorgeous, and the cool sea breeze padded the endorphin-rich feeling. He passed a food table where volunteers doled out bananas, granola bars, energy drinks, doses of Advil. He took two of everything. He called his girlfriend a few times to say he would wait for her, until she started yelling at him because she had two miles left and he kept bothering her during the hardest stretch. So he forgot about her. He vaguely remembered that he was supposed to gather at Santa Monica High School with other SRLA runners to sign a sheet that proved he'd finished. The campus was another mile away, slow step by slow step. His mother was waiting there, and he hugged her.

"Where's the car?" he asked.

She shook her head. "No car."

"Shit."

They walked the mile back to the Metro station near the finish line; he was nearing thirty miles for the day. On the train, he texted his girlfriend that he was heading home, and she was mad at him about that as well: *You said you would wait for me!* He fell asleep at some point, and his mom jostled him awake for the change to the Blue Line to South LA. Saliva had drooled from his mouth onto his running shirt.

At home before dusk, he showered and lay down and found that neither his mind nor his body would relax. In fact, he was suddenly feeling antsy and energized and loath to be alone after this day of traversing his native city. His legs burned with a kind of electricity. He texted a skater friend. Thirty minutes later, they were at the park. Tio squatted on his board, steering toward a ramp, pushing for the velocity to carry him upward, rising, falling, landing, over and over and over, in the twilight.

The next morning—a school day—he found that he couldn't walk at all.

Harrison

Harrison spent the first half of the LA Marathon running as fast as his body was capable: repeat sprints on the Beverly Hills football field, alone on the expanse of bright green turf two blocks removed from the marathon course. Unrecruited in football due to the low caliber of play by the Beverly Hills team, he was sustaining his dream of playing for a Division I college team through sheer, solitary training. Twice a week he ran sprints up Runyon Canyon, a paved fire road that curved up a steep grade in the Hollywood Hills. He lifted weights six days a week. He performed complicated plyometric drills with a personal trainer whom he paid with money he earned installing light fixtures for parties and events. The statistics for walk-ons, particularly in Division I football programs, were not encouraging. And Harrison's choices grew more limited each day: Tufts, Boston University, and Michigan had each rejected him, and he didn't understand why he wasn't being accepted to places that hadn't necessarily felt like reaches when he'd applied. Michigan in particular had flabbergasted him, as his SATs and GPA were well above the mean there, and the idea of wearing those iconic blue and gold helmets, even on the practice team, was thrilling. He must have been docked points for being out of state, and his other passion behind football, filmmaking, hadn't been something he could put forward on his applications since it was only a hobby; he'd recently been working on a short action film in which two characters defended themselves from a home invasion by goons quite generous with their machine-gun fire. Projects such as this one—and the video he'd made for an English class mashing up *Othello* with a *Real Housewives* reality TV show—gave him tremendous fulfillment but did not much elevate the résumé of a prospective physics major.

Harrison had been accepted to two big football schools, the University of Colorado in Boulder and Purdue in West Lafayette, Indiana. Though he'd never played on a competitive team or in a competitive league, and the probability of even being permitted to try out for one was low, he still spent most of each day absorbed in the image of it, his entire dream and its pursuit a kind of celebration of youth, each sprint and lift and jump a declaration.

After his exercise, Harrison drove his mom's car about an hour southeast to La Mirada, where his father lived. His parents had never married, had in fact separated while Harrison was still in utero. He had a strong relationship with his father and the family his father had started with his current, very kind wife. He spent every other weekend in their quiet town, and his father came to as many sports games as he could, but Harrison had never known a nuclear family. The night of his life that he remembered most fondly was when his older half brother had woken him up around midnight, and they'd driven up into the hills to a pull-in lookout off Mulholland Drive, which traversed the crest of LA's bisecting mountain range, and they'd sat on the hood looking down a thousand feet across the many glowing miles of the San Fernando Valley, not talking about very much—because they were guys, and guys usually didn't—but mainly wondering aloud how the world, their unremarkable everyday world, could appear so cosmically stunning at night, from a distance.

Later that week, back at his mother's apartment, she knocked gently on his bedroom door and peeked in. The hour was late, and he was happily engrossed in the editing of his action film project. She had just binged a few episodes of the popular Netflix series *13 Reasons Why*, a show that addressed the issue of teen suicide and all its many strands (depression, stress, bullying, sexual abuse, adult negligence, attention seeking). Fully caught in the narrative's grip, she began to wonder if all American teenagers were just frail, lost, cruel, maladroit beings, and she was compelled to ask her son, with extreme earnestness, "Are you okay?"

He looked confused. "Uh, what?"

"I wanted to ask if you're okay. Is everything good?"

He shrugged and replied, "Uh, yeah, I guess?"

"You're sure?" Her voice quavered emotionally.

"Yeah, Mom. Totally sure. Totally okay."

"Make sure you get some sleep," she said. "I love you."

"I love you, too," he said, smiling and shaking his head at the peculiarities of parents as she closed the door.

Chapter 15

Some teacher was giving advice on how to get through high school and how to succeed and what we should be doing. He said, "You have the rest of your life to goof off, so you shouldn't be doing that now, you should just be keeping your head down and working on class." And I was like, "Holy shit, you are so wrong."

—Bennett

Carlos, Byron, Tio

The Yale website wouldn't let Carlos log in, even after an email informed him that acceptances, rejections, and wait lists were online. The admissions office, three hours ahead on Eastern Standard Time, was closed for the day, while the small, error-red text kept telling him that his name did not exist in the system. Though he was already in possession of acceptances from four other Ivy League schools, he was anxious and frustrated.

Carlos had been acting like kind of a dick lately. He'd become withdrawn, reluctant to participate in classroom discussions as college placements seemed to leach those discussions of practical meaning. When he did put himself forward, the purpose was as often as not to undercut the reasoning of a classmate who didn't read as much as he did, didn't think as concisely. After a tenure at APB spent being patient and supportive, almost limitlessly so, this slight intellectual pugilism tasted good.

At the same time, the antics of friends had come to seem less entertaining, more childish. He simply could not bring himself to care whether or not Luis could embed a pencil ninja-style in the fifteen-foot ceiling, his volleys of unsuccessful attempts raining points of lead upon the unsuspecting heads of classmates. He didn't see the value in spending his time refereeing student government negotiations in which small alliances filibustered decisions regarding the prom location (they were looking at a venue in Glendale that was offering a decent rate but, from the outside, at least, looked like a strip club). He'd ceased worrying about work or high school in general anymore, and his characteristic humility was sloughing off with surprising ease.

A low-resolution but nagging anxiety that had plagued him throughout the year, even after he'd heard from Princeton, had to do with the question of whether any triumphs he might experience would be based strictly on his own merit or rather on some undefined amalgam of his brother's path and progressive liberal sympathy toward his undocumented status and quotas that called for high-functioning Latino enrollees—whether he was representing a demographic condition more than individual merit. Yet presently, no one anywhere could justifiably state that Harvard, Princeton, Columbia, and Cornell all wanted him due to optics, and he couldn't help feeling now as if he'd outgrown APB. In some way, perhaps he was in the process of outgrowing all of South Los Angeles. He'd certainly outgrown the undocumented jokes.

"Does a Harvard diploma come with citizenship?" Luis asked.

"Fuck you," was Carlos's basic reply. He felt ready to graduate and move on from these people in this place and time. The mind-set had washed over him as sudden as it was consuming—even if it was really an armor against the imminent grief of losing all three: people, place, time.

His family tolerated exactly none of this attitude at home. His mother made him clean and babysit his sister and keep his phone out of her sight. His father made him listen to his mother. His sister tormented him in the usual ways that younger sisters did. Harvard admission did not alter the hierarchy in that backyard home—and neither did Yale, once Carlos finally learned that he'd been accepted (there'd been a glitch in which his middle name had been switched with his surname within the Yale server). Carlos had come to expect this admittance, not in a hubristic way, but as the completion of some fantastical cycle by which his parents had come here together, alone and moneyless and without the faintest inkling of prospects, and now, almost twenty years later, there was a chance that the sons they'd brought with them might both attend Yale University—together.

"The thing is not to feel like you have to come here," Jose told him over the phone from New Haven, calling in response to the news. "The schools are going to organize a trip for you, because you're low-income first-gen. So just go to each of the places, pay attention to what they offer and what they feel like. Meet people and think about how you fit in, or don't. See what the money is, obviously. Then choose."

"Yeah," Carlos said. "That makes total sense."

His immediate compulsion was not to go to Yale. After these years of being somewhat tagged to his brother no matter what he himself accomplished, pride dictated that he aim his path clear of the shadow Jose cast. He knew intellectually that pride should not be in play where major life decisions were involved, just as he knew that the Ivy League banners on his sector of the college board did not make him a worthier person than any of his classmates, just as he knew that this fleeting, momentous passage in life would be best spent cherishing his school and his friends rather than resenting them. He was confused and constantly weighing who and what mattered, and why. Doing so shouldn't have been this difficult. Playing video games was much easier, and that was primarily how he spent the hours throughout spring break while his friends toiled over their coalescing options, or the lack thereof.

Another layer of confusion lay in the degree to which his heart broke for Byron, who'd been declined not just by his extreme reaches such as Dartmouth and Cornell, but by all the UCs and Cal States to which he'd applied as well. He didn't have a four-year school, and so his options for the following year were now community college, a job, and the military. In his own inward way, he was seriously considering the short- and long-term merits of each. Outwardly, he projected casual resignation as he scuffed his sneakers across the laminate floor from class to class, backpack slung low off his shoulders. Carlos wanted to be present for him as a friend, but he struggled to summon words that might strike the proper balance between consolation and encouragement and realism. He'd thought spring break would lend them time together to analyze options and cement the best route forward, but Byron had ended up traveling to Guatemala for a large family reunion, where he spent a week in cramped vans and small rented homes with aunts and uncles and cousins. Gorgeous black-sand beaches lined the coast of Monterrico where they stayed, beyond patches of jungle and open-air cafés with live music and performers dancing the Palo Volador, but he mostly remained inside, lying on a mattress playing games on his phone while the adults drank and told old jubilant stories of growing up on and around these rutty dirt roads. His downloaded virtual worlds provided some small buffer against reality's cruelty.

And Carlos felt equally for Tio and the admissions climate that found a 4.6 GPA and multiple leadership roles insufficient at four out of the five state schools to which he'd applied. Nothing he could say, no framing of UC Riverside as a very fine four-year university, no invocation of Tio's gifts and how they would ensure his success regardless of place and program, provided catharsis for his friend's hurt. Carlos's accolades made him a celebrity, but they also rendered him useless for the moment in the precise measures that had always carried them through school: shared experience, mighty aspirations, and empathy. No longer could he authentically feel what Tio felt. He could only observe Tio's bitterness, and now and again lay a hand on his friend's shoulder, let his eyes fall toward the ground, and say that it sucked and he was sorry.

Carlos was unprepared for—and stunned by—this new futility. Always, he'd given his friends advice. Always, he'd accepted it from them. Usually, the advice had involved calculus or biology or the clanky machinations of American government. Sometimes, it had touched on romance, or conflicts with parents, or tensions between young men. Counsel in all its forms had sustained them and conjoined their paths and delivered them here, to the brink of manhood—where those same paths were diverging in rapid and uncontrollable and possibly unbridgeable ways, both physically and emotionally. The impending rift—and their foreknowledge of its opening—released a mournfulness over them all.

"It's going to be okay," Carlos told Tio over and over. "You'll go and do the work and get the grades and get a degree. Riverside's good. You're good."

"Yeah," Tio would reply unconvincingly. "I know I'm good."

On a Friday before the end of spring break, Carlos's mother opened an ominous piece of mail from the Los Angeles Department of City Planning. The authority had discovered—or had most likely been informed by some anonymous area resident—that their home was unzoned and their residence illegal. The family had thirty days to move or else face court proceedings.

Owen, Bennett

A Beverly Hills senior prank of lore involved farm animals. No one knew who had conceived of the idea and carried it out, or what year it had been, or if it had even happened at all. But according to the story, on one spring night seniors had brought in three chickens, three goats, three ducks, three lambs, and two pigs. They'd numbered the animals, one through three, with marker on their flanks. The two pigs they'd numbered one and three. So when school employees had begun the unenviable task of rounding up the animals, they spent days searching for the nonexistent number two pig.

This year's graduating class weakly tried to come up with some memorable equivalent—bring shopping carts instead of backpacks to school, hire a mariachi band to follow the principal around for a day—but the effort quickly waned, really just a way to distract from the more consequential choices closing in.

"I'm clearly going," Bennett said, regarding NYU. "I keep saying to my mom, 'I'll figure out how to pay. You shouldn't have to.' And she keeps saying, 'I'll pay, don't worry, it's your dream.' But I know it's just a lot—like, objectively obscenely a lot—for a thing she doesn't necessarily believe in. Like for the price of tuition, we should be guaranteed the very best internships, that kind of thing, which of course is not how it works."

"Does she say stuff like that?" Owen replied. "Like, to make you feel guilty?"

"No, she's totally, completely cool and supportive about it all the time, which probably makes me feel more guilty." He added, "The only negative thing she's mentioned is that NYU is effectively a multinational corporation at this point, and being beholden to one kind of freaks her out."

"I think a lot of them are now," Owen replied. "Universities. I mean, right?"

Both had been accepted to NYU and were reasoning their way through the marvelous appeal of remaining classmates. Yet the exchanges, during the few times they'd attempted to broach the subject, were inflected with awkwardness—and the awkwardness was more than a little jolting for two people who had in some way been maintaining a fluid, ongoing, stream-of-consciousness conversation together for over a decade. Bennett's pursuit of NYU had consumed almost half of his life, while for Owen the idea was just a recent, unanticipated bit of manna. The cost twisted Bennett's consciousness into knotty loops while Owen did not have to factor money into his thinking at all. Bennett was absolutely excited about moving to New York City; Owen found the place a little too chaotic and overstimulating for his sensibilities. The gap in perspective involved specific numbers and logistics, but it also signified a greater current in their lives that neither could quite identify and neither desired to voice out loud.

Owen felt guilty, too, as he'd been largely apathetic toward the fallout of college admissions that now dogged millions of current high school seniors, including his best friend—he'd had the privilege of apathy—yet now that the results had worked for him, college was simply dangling as an option.

"New York, I don't know, it might just not be my thing," Owen managed to express. "But at the same time, you'd be there, my brother's probably moving there next year, my girlfriend will probably be on the East Coast. That would all be cool, I guess."

"My worry is, you know, college is supposed to be this time where you branch out and meet all these different people and whatever. And I kind of doubt that if you're there that I'll be making an effort to hang out with that random kid from Wisconsin on my floor. That's all hypothetical, obviously."

Owen concluded, "I guess I should see how this Kenyon visit feels before really thinking in concrete terms."

"Yeah, same, I need to talk to my mom some more. I've been being kind of an asshole to her, for no reason."

Bennett was being honest about treating her poorly, and he didn't know why he was. He would go through a school day, in a fine mood and generally pleasant to everyone, and then he would return home and his mother would ask him some innocuous question or make some mundane comment, and he would fail to restrain a sarcastic, sometimes hurtful rejoinder. Afterward, he would regret it. In their apartment, his bedroom was connected to the central living room, which contained her work space, by an open portal. The apartment had a pretty view and was spacious, but still only a few yards generally separated them. Yet he could not quite summon the will to cross those yards and apologize, or ask how her day had been, or thank her for her unwavering advocacy for a path that caused her such valid skepticism. Maybe the impasse had to do with the stress of possibly meeting his biological father over the summer, or some kind of roving resentment of the dependence he had on her. Maybe it was fear of losing that dependence, such that he was tabulating in advance the imminent continent-wide separation from his only parent. Maybe he was an ungrateful little punk. Or maybe it had to do with the way his dream had, upon its fulfillment, so quickly begun to weigh on and confound him.

This parental realm was yet another in which Owen was losing the ability to relate to his friend, as he'd lately settled into a state of deep kindness and self-conscious honesty toward both of his parents. He hadn't always been so pliant, and he was as capable of parental deception as anyone (in order to attend a big New Year's Eve party sophomore year, which he'd pitched to them as "a small family barbecue" at a friend's, he'd enlisted his brother's girlfriend to play the role of his friend's mother on the phone with Owen's mother, and she'd sustained the ruse masterfully). But for many months, he'd been telling himself in different ways that he wouldn't go to college, that he would take that drama teacher's advice and join a conservatory and remain not just close to home but deeply involved with home. Now he was nearing commitment to the opposite, and the world was feeling a little bigger than he wished it to be.

While conscientiously not challenging his parents at home, at school he continued to be astounded by the arbitrary power that adults seemed to enjoy wielding over children. In English class on the second Tuesday in April, they were accomplishing very little and he happened to look down at the face of his phone screen tucked within his open backpack. A text from his girlfriend appeared: she'd moved up off the wait list at her first-choice school. He reached down in order to respond quickly. The teacher noticed and promptly confiscated his phone. Owen sighed and was polite about his infraction, but after class the teacher informed him the phone would be taken to the front office to pick up later. The situation was feeling needlessly laborious when Owen went there to retrieve the device, and it grew even more complicated when an assistant principal emerged from his office flaunting a wide grin. "Nope! Sorry, Owen—we're keeping it in the safe. It's in the vault until Friday!"

Owen tried to reason, "Really, it's my first time getting caught with a phone. I do a lot for the school—I did the *15 Minutes* thing, the radio station, I give a lot of tours for new parents, anytime you need a performer for assembly, I'm good for it. Three days is a long time when we're dealing with college stuff."

"Nope! Can't open the safe unless you talk to your teacher."

So Owen did, interrupting the English teacher's lunch. He seemed annoyed, as if Owen were propelling this disruption, but said that he would call the office to sort the matter.

Later: "Nope! It's already in the vault! Friday's the day!"

"My English teacher called it in."

"Not yet he hasn't—can't open the vault unless he calls with a compelling reason."

Owen replied, because he couldn't help it at this point, "This vault seems to really excite you; you're getting a lot of enjoyment from this whole vault situation. I don't totally get that, as it seems like a weird thing to celebrate, my phone being in your vault."

"Come back Friday, sir. The sound of that vault opening will be music to my ears, let me tell you!"

The front desk phone rang: the English teacher with permission for Owen to reclaim his phone. The assistant principal made an extensive production of pulling keys from his desk and disappearing into the office, presumably hauling open this real or fictitious vault, and bringing Owen his phone sealed in a plastic bag as if in evidence or quarantine. "I'm sorry to deprive you of your vault symphony," Owen muttered while turning to leave.

He didn't even care very much about having his phone over the next three days. He'd been trying to untether from the thing anyway, and all the text messaging could be done via computer. He was just stuck marveling at the fact that he was eighteen years old, he could legally vote, work, travel internationally by himself, but he hadn't as yet earned the status of being treated as a somewhat functioning adult—a facet of high school that felt like part of the persisting joke that all the grown-ups were in on, and to which Owen and most of his classmates had long since become painfully wise. Devices were just one incarnation: he and his friends and all teenagers were given a lot of shit for owning phones and paying too much attention to them, and in turn teachers seemed to carry a righteous mandate to rid them of this addiction. But he felt that maybe there should have been some acknowledgment of the fact that the adults they saw in store lines and cars and restaurants and business meetings and every other space, who were all staring intently at their little screens all the time, weren't just checking work emails.

Jonah

Jonah was alarmed when he heard the shouting at their front door on a Sunday morning. In the five-plex in which they rented, various branches of a multigenerational Persian family surrounded their unit, and they had never much liked his family and their late-night movie marathons. That morning, his mother had accidentally dropped the TV remote on the floor, and a middle-aged woman now stood in the doorway, yelling at her loud and fast, accusing her of making all sorts of racket exercising in the middle of the night (Jonah knew that he was the only one awake in the middle of the night, and not exercising). The sight of his mother being verbally belittled recalled tiers of seared memories from his child-hood. The defining characteristic of these memories was his own terrible powerlessness as they unfolded. Now he donned a bathrobe and grabbed a coffee mug from the kitchen. The mug was empty but he felt that carrying an adult morning drink would make him appear more authoritative. He came to the door, towering above both women.

"What seems to be the problem here?" he asked casually but with a deepened voice. The neighbor explained her imagined plight. He laughed amiably. "Oh, no. There's been no noise like that here, we wouldn't ever do anything disrespectful like that." He fake-sipped from the mug in his gambit to come off as a mature, convincing male presence. She seemed to measure him for a moment and then softened. He added, "It might have been the garbage trucks that I heard, way earlier than usual. I was quite bothered as well."

His mother stepped aside while he carried on their conversation, using big words, complimenting the neighbor and her family profusely. The neighbor finally nodded and even smiled. She told Jonah's mother, "You have an amazing young man here," and left. His mother hugged him and thanked him for intervening. "Always, Mom," he replied. He hadn't come across many opportunities in his life to play a hero like those in the comic book movies that enthralled him. He wasn't sure how often he would in the future. This moment felt nice.

Jonah had accepted admission to UCLA, where his older sister went. (As part of an oral presentation for a certain scholarship, he spoke about *Scent of a Woman* being one of his favorite films; he was later awarded the scholarship.) He would continue to live at home with his mother and younger brother in their apartment. The school setting would be much vaster in every sense, but his family movie nights would continue. He was glad to be keeping his world small—particularly after a UCLA visit had left him a bit unnerved because all the premed students he met exhibited different degrees of hysteria.

Before freshman year, his mother jobless and his father continuing to render their lives a ruinous legal chaos, the image of his mother serene and proud as he looked forward to high school graduation had seemed whimsical. But he saw her that way now. She was over a foot shorter than he, yet her earnest warmth crested over him from within her spirit.

Jon

The disbanding of Aca Deca for the year was the end of something greater for Jon. For three years, he'd had reason to remain in the hallways and classrooms beneath that grand clock tower until eight or nine, sometimes ten or eleven at night. For the small group of kids who, for various reasons, sought this extraneous mastery over a randomly designated zone of knowledge, Aca Deca was a strangely intimate secret that they'd shared, and that they shared no longer. He wondered if—when he hopefully had children, and when they hopefully went to high school and hopefully found their respective places of solace—he might mention all those afternoons and evenings he'd spent at school. And if he did, he wondered whether those hours would feel significant, twenty or thirty years removed—whether they would feel formative and vital at all, or simply a distant residue, an insignificant component of a version of himself that no longer was.

Jon's acceptance to the University of Chicago brought with it an apogee of pride but also a reckoning with the fact that his family couldn't pay for it. The school was indeed need-blind in its admissions, but his zip code, as ever, muddied the segue from aspiration into aspiration's cost. "You are not to worry," his mother told him when he raised the issue. "You did this. We will find a way." That she spoke the words in Chinese lent them a flavor of mysticism. He'd grown up on the outer periphery of the layers of historical, political, and social history that had created such a firm cultural confidence in providence. Being thoroughly westernized and subject to America's foundational belief in self-determination, he'd questioned Chinese block thought extensively and certainly didn't consider himself a part of some cosmic chain coursing through millennia and geared toward his own matriculation at the University of Chicago. But in this moment, in early April of his eighteenth year, as his achievements converged with his mother's expectations, he saw in her eyes the beauty and simplicity and even the humility of her vast, rich doctrines.

"Yes, Ma," he said. "We'll see how it works out."

During this last stretch of school, Jon consciously decided to eat dinner at a table with his parents—something he'd rarely ever done—and talk about their days, mundane as they tended to be. This rite felt peculiar and underwhelming at first, laced with regret that the togetherness was only happening because of the end of a time of life. But in the face of this particular end, he tried to summon aloud his memories of all the Little League baseball games his father had coached, all the evenings his mother had driven him through Los Angeles traffic torments to reach places he needed or just wanted to be. He made a point of crediting them with his love of baseball and piano, two devotions that sustained him. He tried to communicate that while he could be haughty at times, he was well aware that the University of Chicago was a beginning that he shared with them, and he was grateful. His expressions were clumsy but genuine. After dinner, he and his father would sit in the living room, evening news blathering in the background, and listen to records on his father's turntable—Savoy Brown, Moon Martin, and (always) Springsteen—and they'd talk about the music's progressions while his mother, as ever, cleaned. "You know that time," his father would begin, "when Bruce and his band came to my radio station . . . ?"

Tio

"That's why I feel like life is unfair. I worked my ass off. I'm not saying other people didn't, but they didn't try as hard as I did or do as well, and some of them got accepted to the schools I wanted. That's all types of fucked up. I'm depressed on that."

"I get it, man," Mr. Sandoval replied. "I've been there, too."

"But you got into UCLA. I could have gotten C's, just straight C's, all four years—could have *not* busted my ass all four years—and I'd still be going to Riverside, for fucking farming."

Mr. Sandoval struggled to conceal his grimace with a smile as he shook his head. "No, Tio. That's the thing. No you *wouldn't*.

I don't know what you'd be doing, but you wouldn't be going to a four-year, UC school. I don't know what I can tell you to make you understand that, but you need to understand that." Mr. Sandoval truly didn't know how to elevate Tio's sour thinking, how to frame his matriculation at Riverside as really a wondrous turn in his life, and in the narrative of his family, rather than as a betrayal by the system. He couldn't offer the platitude that many of Tio's classmates would have been thrilled to be going to Riverside. Nor could he put forward the notion that Tio remained very much the determinative factor in his own future, once he overcame his defeatist thinking and applied himself to college—that if he forged dependable friendships, asked for help when needed, and invested the hours necessary to thrive, then he could will himself into the top tier of his college class as he'd done in high school. But to reach that point, Tio would first have to endure this one, with all its pain and all its damage to his self-worth.

For now, the teacher could only say that Tio was wrong to consider himself a failure.

They were on a bus curving along the Pacific Coast Highway, beachgoers strolling along rocky shores to their left, tall jagged hillsides rising vertically to their right. Soon they made a sharp turn onto an impossible road that shouldn't rationally have existed in this topography and definitely shouldn't have been open to buses. The vehicle's engine brayed as they carved long, scary switchbacks up into the Santa Monica Mountains.

"I'm just a shit writer, is what," Tio persisted. "My essays were shit."

"You wrote how it is. You didn't try to tailor it to anyone or use any tricks. You should be proud of your essays."

"Yeah, see where they got me." Then: "Aw man, now I'm getting carsick."

The ocean had quickly receded down slopes covered in scraggly mustard flowers, and then it disappeared behind a stand of mesquite forest. How the bus driver was realizing these hundred-twenty-degree turns, Tio had no idea; each seemed to send the nose of the vehicle out over the precipice while the front wheels hugged the asphalt's outer rim. To settle his stomach, he fixed his gaze upward toward a long row of multilevel mansions draped over the ridges above, braced by stilts.

"You're going to be good, Tio," Mr. Sandoval said. "Just work, like you do. Talk less than you do. The world's about to get a whole lot bigger. And so are you, man."

The campsite for the Caballeros con Cultura retreat that Tio had organized and raised money for was a tiered series of wide, flat dirt plots set deep in the hills, with trailheads branching off into different directions of wilderness and some large wood-and-rope contraptions resembling military training exercises. The group's main goal for the weekend was to hike together five miles to the Backbone Trail, which would take them to the highest point in the mountain range. Two hours after unpacking in the spider-infested cabins of twelve bunks each, their first attempt at the summit was disheartening. Tio led the way until he noticed small groups of classmates simply stopping behind him, then turning around. They blamed the heat and thirst.

"That's what water bottles were invented for," Tio yelled down the slope.

"There're mountain lions out here, bro!"

"Damn, you all are unfit."

"We didn't just run a marathon like you, okay?"

Tio returned to camp with them, exasperated.

No one among them had ever really camped before, so the process of starting a fire and cooking rice and beans for almost thirty hungry people was fairly pathetic. The rice ended up undercooked, the beans a mush, the ensuing s'mores a charred mess. Most of their homes were crowded with siblings and parents and filial squabbling in small spaces, and the vast openness and enveloping silence here felt eerie at first, an emptiness to be filled with school gossip and admissions updates and complaints about teachers. Tio overheard people far below him in class rank talk of next year at UCLA, Irvine, San Diego, their generous Cal Grants and other financial aid, how it was all working out. Bitterness surged up a channel in the back of his neck. But as the hours passed and the fire diminished into a short pile of faintly glowing embers, the group as a whole grew more comfortable with the quietude. They seemed to embrace it, and even to cherish it. They talked more softly, then not at all. And Tio looked around at the dimly lit faces and grew astonished that they were here, surrounding an exhausted fire in the dark, far enough from urban light pollution such that a few dozen stars were actually visible above them, because of him.

"C'mon, man, I really got to shit." His friend Rogelio said this hours later, at two or three in the morning, after rustling Tio awake. He had to use the bathroom urgently but was too afraid to leave the cabin alone.

"There's no animals here going to mess with you," Tio groaned.

"It's not animals—it's fucking psychopaths, yo."

"Dude, how many people been shot within five blocks of your house this year?"

"Five blocks? I don't know, one or two."

"But you're scared of the woods?"

"It's so fucking dark!"

Tio accompanied him from the cabin, and they groped around the site for a few minutes before finding the bathroom. Then Tio endured the indignity of listening to his friend put the hole in the ground to use.

"Beans," he muttered—and then heard a distinct shuffling in the dirt nearby. That rapid swell of alert—honed by his youth spent skating around South LA looking for decent ramps and rails in areas where mortal threats could appear instantaneously—poured from his amygdala and heightened all his senses as the point of a flashlight trained directly onto his face.

Mr. Sandoval said, "What are you doing out here, Tio? Smoking weed by the bathroom?"

"Nah," Tio replied, shielding his face from the beam. "Rogelio's taking a shit."

Rogelio called from the bathroom, without embarrassment, "Yeah, I really am."

Mr. Sandoval laughed. "Well, hurry it up, then—it's fucking scary out here."

"We know," Tio said, and knocked an elbow against the thin wooden walls of the toilet. "Come on, man, get finished already so I can go back to sleep."

Chapter 16

APRIL 17–MAY 12

One takeaway from high school is thinking about all the nearly catastrophic things that nearly happened but didn't.

—Owen

"Magic foot, take me to the final round . . ."

Owen pranced, hands flitting about at his sides, striding legs reaching unnaturally far ahead of his body—all the movements he'd spent hours perfecting at the foot of his mother's bed. Before what might be his final moments onstage, he'd undergone his usual ritual of vomiting in a trash can before the curtain rose. Now his left leg performed a swing dance while his right foot scribbled imaginary letters on the floor. He couldn't really see anyone beyond the stage lights, but his father was among them, somewhere near the back and on the aisle due to claustrophobia. In moments, Owen could hear the man's low, distinctive laugh apart from all the others. His mother was home, either awake and thinking of him or asleep and dreaming.

A week later, he was riding a shuttle bus through uniformly flat land and a succession of small working-class towns, past industrial buildings overrun by weeds and rust, yard sign after yard sign blaring support for Republican candidates ranging from the president (five months after that election) to the local school board. The sky was gray and cool, the roadways isolated in meandering

JEFF HOBBS

cuts through woodlands. The whole of the landscape was at once beautiful and decayed.

The two-day trip to Kenyon College as part of a group of sought-after students paid for by the college involved the usual rounds of school tours, classroom visits, and student presentations. The campus was small and tranquil, with tall spires looking down on tree-lined footpaths between clusters of gothic and colonial buildings. Open space spread out everywhere. A class discussion of Plato's Allegory of the Cave predictably pivoted toward the matter of people who had voted for the current president—such people, of course, being the ones "in the cave, looking at shadows," while the liberal young people debating the topic at Kenyon clearly stood out-side, in the full light of reality. Owen, still shaken and flummoxed by that January protest on the plaza, found himself being more out-spoken than was probably polite, activated by the current progressive zeitgeist, truly desiring to share his experiences and observations at Beverly—experiences and observations that strangely seemed to feel more vivid the further he was removed from them.

A prominent section of their introductory packet contained the transcript of a much-celebrated commencement address that the late author David Foster Wallace had given at Kenyon in 2005 entitled "This Is Water: Some Thoughts, Delivered on a Significant Occasion, About Living a Compassionate Life." Owen wasn't nec-essarily an avid fan of the author's, but he knew that college-aged intellectuals in particular—such as those idling beneath the oak trees all across Kenyon's campus—held him in high esteem. He read through the address in its entirety. Then he read it again. Owen was predisposed to treating such brazen self-promotion—the college appropriating as its ethos the independent words of a great thinker they'd invited to speak there once—with skepticism. But the work drew him in to the point where, awake late at night in his assigned dorm room, he brought the actual address up on YouTube and watched that twice as well. The point was simple: that human beings have a particular tendency to become so absorbed in their own day-to-day immediacies that they forget or even disparage the immediacies of others. And while the author turned some disingenuous literary wheels during the course of the speech (humbly professing to lack any resounding knowledge that might benefit the audience and then proceeding to make a series of proclamations directing them how to think and lead their lives), Owen was genuinely moved. The simple essence of the message intertwined with many of the questions he consistently, sometimes manically, posed to himself, most centrally: How best to be a decent, healthy, worthwhile person in America right now?

The author's eventual suicide seemed to haunt the document, as if to suggest a final and definitive answer.

Carlos, Luis, Byron

Princeton spread out along rolling grassy hills, the dorms and class buildings like fortresses overlooking the wealthy, pastoral suburb that surrounded the grounds. The 270-year history of the university was a powerful specter as their guides recited lists of famous people who taught or had taught there: John McPhee, Elena Kagan, Alan Blinder, Toni Morrison. The content of the classes they attended in physics and political science was appropriately expansive and profound. Princeton was an objectively awesome institution when viewed up close. But a feeling of disconcertment tailed him in the whirlwind, and it wasn't solely due to the eating club they visited, which, true to lore, looked and felt like a plantation manor. Maybe its bucolic setting—one of the core allures of the place—was in fact the source of his unnerve: the absence of concrete and asphalt and dilapidated family storefronts with truants loitering outside, the scarcity of any working person who did not work for Princeton, the well-maintained cars that moved along in an orderly fashion and always stopped for pedestrians. He felt far, far away from home here.

Along with a few dozen other low-income, first-generation students, Carlos had been invited on an expenses-paid tour of the East Coast schools that had accepted him: one of many current efforts being made by Ivy and other elite schools to reduce the stress and isolation that campus life often generated for students who were transitioning—or, as it could sometimes feel, being displaced—from the communities in which they'd grown up.

And then, ninety minutes after they departed Princeton, New York City loomed across the Hudson River as their shuttle inched toward the Lincoln Tunnel, and from a distance its myriad skyscrapers seemed to be rooted there not for commerce but for their dreams and their dreams alone—though less so once they joined the maelstrom of uptown traffic. The Columbia campus on 116th Street was small, spanning just a few blocks of longitude and latitude. Though cloistered by fencing from the likes of Broadway and Amsterdam, this place felt familiar: the vehicular white noise and hurried people not inclined to slow or change direction for anyone, the simple truth broadcast from all angles that he didn't matter all that much in the schematics here. That brand of urban anonymity was pleasing to Carlos. More tours touted the diversity of the student body, more low-income kids talked about their enriching experiences, with tribute paid to professors and class sizes, the access to museums and jazz clubs and theater. Carlos wondered if any college student actually went to the theater or jazz clubs.

Los Angeles was so broad, its many neighborhoods jammed together at odd angles dictated by farm plots and corrupt land grabs and racism, the proliferation of cars and construction of freeways. New York felt so cleanly determined in comparison, by waterways and bedrock and parkland and a sense of potential that, with a little hustle and good fortune, could be easily realized. He knew empirically the way real estate, just as in LA, did in fact centralize the very wealthy here in Manhattan while marginalizing all others farther and farther outward in the boroughs and beyond, and how the quality and reach of its transportation system somewhat masked the disparity at street level. He knew that the state of feeling like a pioneer with much rich territory ahead on which to stake a claim was the primary draw of the city and also its primary illusion. But he found it impossible to escape from its sway while here in the center of the island.

Then New Haven, where his brother met him upon arrival, and simply the sight of him seemed to ground the whole frantic, strange trip. With Jose, Carlos managed to part from his group to take an actual tour. Jose had told him much about Yale, the good and the bad, the weird and the surprising, the people, the frats, the cultural houses, the general alignment of the place and culture. Carlos had promised himself not to let his proxy relationship with the school bias his appraisal. That promise was easily made when Yale was just an entry on his travel itinerary, easily forgotten when walking beside his brother through the arched entryways with Latin inscriptions, past the grass quads flecked with students reading and holding hands and throwing Aerobies. He and Jose used to walk together to Ánimo Pat Brown every morning, a little over a mile north on San Pedro Street, in South LA. Now they were walking together on Elm Street, in New Haven. They used to eat together in the crooked nook in their backyard home from which their parents were currently being evicted. Now they ate dinner in the ornate dining hall with arched ceilings thirty feet high, beneath portraits of elderly white men, while the chimes of nearby Harkness Tower cast "Pachelbel's Canon" across the campus. They talked over the very same subjects they always had—music, sports, girls, school—and yet being together really was profound, leaving Carlos to consider how ignorant he had been, how blithely prideful, to underrate the magnitude of blood in making his college choice.

He had heard his brother talk about feeling uneasy here sometimes—here where so very few of his five thousand classmates could conceive of living in a shack in South LA, being undocumented, having a father who delivered packages for a living. But his insecurity seemed nonexistent, or at least well disguised, as his brother moved smoothly through the afternoon and evening, which found them at an a cappella concert in which a dozen male students dressed in tuxedos sang and danced their way through a mix of show tunes and current pop hits. Later, at a short-order counter in the dorm basement, they ate grilled cheeses and French fries at two a.m. They hadn't really ceased talking all day.

Harvard was the last destination. He was tired from the travel schedule and decision fatigue and from having to act interested in what everyone was telling him throughout. He paid semi-attention to the tours and classes. He found the campus to look and feel as Harvard-y, in all respects, as people said that it did. By that point, he'd already made up his mind where he would be in the fall.

Returning home, he downloaded the trip to his parents using vague teen-speak—"The tours were cool . . ." "Everyone was really nice . . ." "Food was just okay . . ."—before pivoting quickly toward their housing situation, which had weighted his mind throughout the sojourn. They had little legal recourse to contest the eviction; undocumented families had little legal recourse to contest anything. His parents were looking for another rental, but the ballooning citywide housing costs had begun infiltrating South LA as well, and they had yet to gain a line on any remotely affordable unit in any remotely safe area. The balance between the two—money and safety—was a challenging one. They'd been paying $1,000 per month for years, without the standard 2 percent annual increase. The average price in Compton for a two-bedroom was now $1,500. The one place they'd been optimistic about had turned out to be a scam, and they'd been grifted out of a $200 deposit. They were assuming now that they would move in temporarily with Carlos's aunt in Gardena a hundred blocks south, which would be cramped and make for a torturous commute for everyone, but it was family and a reliable interim solution. Part of the fabric of South LA was the interim solution of family.

His parents had come to this country with less than $100. They'd worked very hard at difficult jobs while raising children and relying only on themselves. One of these children was an Ivy League student, another was about to be. If he were ever to write an editorial about his family's experience, Carlos could argue without exertion that his parents had contributed as much to their country as anyone, short of serving in uniform—though such a public stance would of course invite a crush of furious, belittling counterarguments. At the very least, he could reason that their story represented exactly the immigrant narrative that had been celebrated through generations as central to American ideals— except that this narrative was neither celebrated nor idealized when the flesh of its central characters was not white. In a few weeks, he and his parents were likely to be sleeping on mattresses on the floor.

Astonishing to him was how calm his parents remained—his mother in particular had been far more distraught after the presidential election than she was now—and how much more interested they were in his own looming decision than in losing the home in which they'd raised their children. His mother cooked and cleaned; his father clumsily helped her to the extent that she would allow before ordering him out of her kitchen; small gestures of affection passed between them; the usual. Neither could understand much regarding the last week of his life, the sheer wackiness of being fêted by America's most estimable intellectual centers. Further, they knew that they couldn't understand, and were familiar with the sadness of that—of being invariably left behind. But still their questions were ceaseless and energized and loving.

"So have you chosen?" his mother asked, a bit overzealous in her nonchalance. This was the question whose answer she truly cared about.

Carlos smiled. "I'm going to Yale."

She released a strange, unsubtle *yip* sound and squeezed his shoulder, which was at about the level of her glowing, slightly moist eyes. His father grinned and nodded like a hitter who'd called his shot. They'd never before betrayed the degree to which they desired their boys to be together.

The next morning, he was glad to join Luis, Byron, and their friend Victor on a bike ride along the Los Angeles River in order to shop for their prom suits (arbitrarily, Luis's mother had decided that he wasn't allowed to drive today). The natural river had once been the primary water source for the entire region. Now it was an ugly fifty-one-mile concrete culvert that on most days ushered a small trickle of street runoff from the San Fernando Valley to the bay in Long Beach. The bike path along the western flank, though foul smelling, passed through South LA free from cars and traffic lights and pedestrians staring down at phone screens— free from the general hazard navigation that defined much of life in the city. Small but lush flora grew from the excrement-rich sediment deposits along the center. Herons, red-tailed hawks, and hummingbirds swooped about the trees. Small clusters of tarp tents and lines of dirty laundry were strung by the homeless between branches. The street debris left by winter flooding clung high in the branches. The stretch was beautiful and rank at the same time, and in that contrast, something like sublime.

A group of teenagers sat just off the entrance as they began their excursion, drinking and smoking, and one of them pointed to the boys as they passed, considering them in succession: "That dude's gay, that dude's *definitely gay*, that dude's probably not gay, that dude might be gay . . ."

The air was ninety degrees and breezeless. Luis was sweating through his shirt and shorts within minutes. Victor's bike seat had been stolen recently, leaving a hollow pole; he had to ride the entire way standing up. They passed beneath Compton and Lynwood and South Gate and Bell Gardens, maintaining a hollered, over-the-shoulder conversation with one another about whether or not prom would suck and why did they still have homework and how certain people were still spazzing over the schools they did or didn't get into. Now and again, bike enthusiasts speeding in their ridiculous, brightly colored spandex getups would swoosh past with a terse warning of *"Left."*

Seven miles later, exhausted, they locked their bikes at the destination mall and slumped into the various stores, like Ross, Marshalls, and Men's Wearhouse. As in so many areas of their collective lives—dwelling places, legal representation, college—a fundamental axiom held true: the best suits, the ones that fit well and made them look strapping, cost far more than they had to spend; the suits they could pay for looked and felt awkward, if not terrible. Salespeople were less than accommodating toward the group of sweaty teenagers. After an hour, discouraged and suitless, they rode the bus home.

"I feel kind of bad I stunk up so many good suits," Luis said.

"Don't," Carlos replied. "Those suits were shitty and overpriced. The people were assholes."

"True. I guess I don't feel bad, then."

Carlos asked about Luis's own real estate travails. His mother's landlord had recently informed them that he was selling the building and that he would give them three months' free rent in order to save up for and have sufficient time to find a new home. But then he'd found a buyer faster than predicted and reduced their time and rent abatement to one month. Incensed, his mother had hired a lawyer. But the man she hired turned out not to be a lawyer, but rather a clerk for a lawyer. Or something like that. He'd been ignoring their calls but had cashed the $400 retainer she'd paid him.

"So she's freaking out. It's just a whole ordeal."

"What are you going to do?" Carlos asked.

Luis shrugged. "I don't know what the hell we're going to do. We all sit down to try figuring it out and then we all just end up in the kitchen laughing."

Harrison

He pointed to Kendrick Lamar onstage and hollered in the girl's ear, but—though their bodies were pressed closely together—she probably didn't hear his words. She nodded and kept dancing.

Harrison had driven to the Coachella music festival two days earlier with his mom, and the hours since spent jumping and screaming and vaulting his body around the outdoor space crowded with scantily clad, drugged-out yuppies and hipsters had for the moment relieved him of the frustration of having only two college options—Colorado and Purdue, both of which he'd considered his safety schools when applying. He was leaning toward Purdue because of Colorado's reputation as a party school. The vexation was that the Purdue football program didn't even permit potential walk-ons to try out for the team. His stream of emails to the head coach pleading his case didn't seem to be gaining traction.

But the festival had been dreamlike, and Kendrick Lamar was performing less than twenty steps away from him, and he was dancing with a gorgeous high school soccer player from Los Angeles who seemed to be as enamored with him as he was with her.

When he reconvened with his mother to drive home—she'd been with her own friends throughout the festival—he was giddy to report that he was pretty sure he had a new girlfriend. The pure and energetic glee that activated his face resembled what she saw in him during football games, which was why she'd let him play football at all, and why she indulged his current, quixotic quest to play in college. As they drove home through the desert exchanging fantastic Coachella moments, she nurtured hope that this girl he'd met wouldn't break his heart, and that this Purdue coach would give her son a chance to play, and that college would work out for him. At this point in life, after raising him almost entirely on her own and after marveling at the strong, curious, loving young man he'd become, she felt as if the extent of what she could do for him had now dwindled simply to hope.

Luis, Byron

Arctic ice cover was at its lowest level in recorded history. The Russian state had undoubtedly influenced the American presidential election. England had just initiated its formal separation from the European Union. North Korea was nearing capacity of a nuclear strike on the West Coast, or so it claimed. ISIS was withering but remained the center point of geopolitical dread. The White House had banned all travelers from seven Muslim countries from entering the United States, which had been massively protested, overturned, appealed, and overturned again. Pemex, the Mexican state-owned oil monopoly, was nearing bankruptcy; gas prices in the country were destructively high and rising. Hundreds of Mexican people were kidnapped and murdered each week by drug cartels, while thousands sought entry into the United States through both legal and illegal pathways. Individual murders in America were falling year by year while both mass shootings and minority fatalities at the hands of the police remained chronic. The contraction of the middle class persisted and the education system continued to reflect the nation's disparity. Months after the election, presidential politics still dominated the partisan news cycle, rendering any kind of clean demarcation between fact, fiction, and opinion opaque at best.

The unfolding events of the world were cataloged in columns of links on various news sites, the headlines worded bombastically to reflect the site's political leanings, the adjoining thumbnail images selected for the same purpose. The world's happenings felt far beyond individual influence, as they always did (though actors and actresses and athletes—people who pretended to be other people for a living or accomplished dazzling feats involving spherical objects, respectively—sent tweets under the premise that fame and wisdom were interwoven). These happenings were constantly being edited by assorted ideologues, as they always had been (though politicians and newscasters were becoming harder and harder to tell apart). And the era's particular brand of imperious, impetuous intellectual certitude presumed that where you lived, what color you were, what industry you worked in, and what god you believed in dictated precisely the standpoint you took in any debate. According to the ordinances of social media, any contrary stance, no matter how infused with reason, was a damnable betrayal carrying a sentence of public shaming.

Meanwhile, young people were led to believe by their educators that if they pursued knowledge and kinship, if they took advantage of all the opportunities America presented them, if they strove to become compassionate and impactful members of society, then they would be "causes of change" or "drivers of change" or "stewards of change." Seniors were told this over and over and over, with increasing emphasis as graduation neared. Having just been subjected to the ungentle machine works of admissions, the tidy phrases were hard to ingest with the seriousness they seemed to demand.

In this global context, Luis held a stapler vertically, the slot aimed at Byron. He was squeezing the trigger repeatedly. Staples dribbled out and ticked onto the desktop.

"What the fuck are you doing?" Byron inquired.

"Shooting at you."

"Ha ha. Stupid." They were in guidance period, which had shed all traces of utility at this point.

"I'm bored so I'm gonna staple your ass."

Byron suddenly slapped his hand onto the table in front of him, palm down. "You want to do something with the stapler, fucker, then come on. Do something."

"For real? You want me to staple your hand?"

"I want to show how you talk shit all the time, but you won't actually do it."

Luis thought a moment, his face slightly perplexed at first, then suddenly assertive. Casually, he brought the stapler down on Byron's hand, and with a closed fist gave the apparatus a pump. Byron flinched, just a little, and he didn't make a sound. Neither moved for a moment. Luis raised the stapler and they both stared at Byron's hand. The staple was cleanly embedded in the skin over his middle metacarpal. Tiny twin beads of blood had emerged around the teeth.

Luis breathed out in amazement. "*Holy shit*, I just stapled your hand, yo!"

"Jeez," Byron said in an even, observational voice. He brought his hand close to his face and just kind of peered at it.

"You told me to do it, sort of," Luis said, now defensive.

Byron pulled the staple from his hand, drawing more blood up through the exit wounds. He flexed his fingers in and out and shrugged. "Doesn't even hurt," he said.

"That's still the greatest thing I've ever done," Luis replied.

That night, playing video games in the apartment from which his family would be decamping at some point soon, Luis received a text from Byron: *We done fucked up.*

What?

I can't move my hand at all.

The fuck?
It hurts like hell.
You think it's infected or something?
It's possible. It's all red and purple.
Put ice on it?
I tried.
Fuck, why'd you make me do that?
I said we fucked up!

The next day, Byron came to school cradling his hand near his armpit. The two pricks looked like a venomous snakebite left untreated too long. Now he couldn't move his wrist in addition to his hand.

"You should show the nurse before you have to amputate that thing," Luis urged. "I don't want to be responsible."

"I'm sure it'll be fine. It's just stiff."

"It's all fucked up, bro!"

"It'll be *fine*, Luis."

By fourth period, Byron regained the ability to bring his fingers halfway into a fist. By sixth, he could type on a keyboard. By the end of the day, he could close his hand and also hold a pencil, albeit painfully. He demonstrated for Luis.

"See? I said it's fine."

"You're a dumbass."

"I'm a dumbass for putting myself in the position to get my hand stapled. You're a dumbass for stapling my hand. It's all good."

A new poster board had been mounted in the hallway for the last weeks of school, with the header, *My favorite memory is . . .*

Seniors had begun pinning entries on index cards: *When my friends were there for me; When Mr. Snyder fell down in the basketball game; When I got a 93 in AP Chem; When I got into UC Davis.*

Luis offered his entry: *When I stapled Byron's hand.* And Byron offered his beside it: *When Luis stapled my hand.*

Chapter 17

I'm afraid this school has carried me a lot for four years, and I'm scared that after this, no one else is going to carry me. But I'm hopeful, too, that maybe I can do it myself. I know a lot of shit.

—*Tio*

Tio, Carlos, Luis, Byron

Tio grabbed his friend's cell phone from across the McDonald's booth, over greasy wrappers and cardboard containers. "Trust me," he said. "I'm going to take care of this for you."

His friend—Rogelio, the same who had begged Tio's escort to the campsite bathroom—was on his third prospective prom date. The first two he'd asked—one via an elaborate "promposal" involving a mirror and an unfortunate *Beauty and the Beast* reference—had said they would consider it but only if other guys who they suspected might ask them didn't. His pride damaged, he'd wooed a third girl, and she'd said yes—but then she'd learned through the usual high school information networks that she'd been only his third choice. They were texting back and forth regarding this complication when Tio usurped the phone. His friend grasped for it back. "I can handle it," Rogelio said. "I've got a line."

"Nah," Tio replied. "Keep your no-good lines out of this. I'm going to help you."

The girl had asked directly and angrily if she was in fact a desperation choice, because if so, she purported to have other options herself. Posing as Rogelio, Tio wrote her, *No girl, I've been thinking about you for a long time. I only think about you. Other people are just talking shit. I luv u.*

"You're good now," Tio said, handing the phone back with ample self-satisfaction.

The girl then texted that another guy had in fact already asked her, and she couldn't really decide, but she was now leaning toward the other guy. Rogelio sought further counsel from Tio.

"Oh shit, you're on your own now. I didn't know about that. That's fucked up."

Rogelio moved his fingers rapidly, his mouth an irked straight line. He asked her if she'd said yes to the other guy. She replied that she had. He reminded her that she'd already said yes to him. She wrote back, *Sorry.* He threw the phone on the table. Tio laughed and shook his head pityingly.

"This shit ain't funny," Rogelio said.

"Actually, it's truly hilarious."

"I'm about to have no prom date!"

"Which is your own fault for talking shit to everyone. You needed to play this much cooler."

Rogelio proceeded to go home and record a freestyle rap on his phone, profanely insulting each of the three girls, which he then publicized on SoundCloud, and as a result received a four-day in-school suspension. Tio absolved himself of the situation, telling Luis, "Hey, I tried to help someone who didn't want to be helped. What more could I do?"

Tio was having his own prom-centric issues in that his girlfriend was upset with him, not an uncommon state in their relationship.

The promposal ritual had become de rigueur over the previous years: boys were expected to construct complicated, clever, and expensive modes of asking girls to prom. Signage, videos, music, costumes, props, volunteer actors: anything less than an outstanding effort signified that the boy didn't care enough about the girl to deserve her as his date.

Tio had eschewed the whole formality as a waste of money that he didn't have anyway. He'd proudly done nothing.

"Guess you don't love me," his girlfriend told him. "All these guys love their girls except you."

"I do love you," he replied, exasperated. "I'm gonna take you out to a nice dinner and a show. I'm gonna take you to Six Flags with the money I would have spent on a fucking *sign*."

"For once, Tio, why can't you just follow the crowd?"

His voice was desperate with notes of condescension. "I've got a summer job at NerdPhone. I'm about to be making two hundred dollars a week. I'm going to spend it all on you. What the fuck is a promposal about anyway?"

"Maybe we just shouldn't go to prom together."

He put his hands on his forehead. "Damn, girl, who the hell else are you going to go with?"

His outward petulance mirrored hers. In his mind, he was feeling much more exposed. In three months, she would begin her freshman year at UCLA. He would be at Riverside. The schools were only sixty miles apart, but somehow the distance felt much greater. She would be in Los Angeles. He would be in the Inland Empire. She would be studying engineering. He would be studying agricultural science. She would be surrounded by people from Bel Air and San Francisco and other centers of wealth and privilege in California and beyond. He would be surrounded by a lot of people striving to be the first college graduates in their family; almost 60 percent of the student body there was first-generation. Whether or not they stayed together—and Tio very much wanted to—their experiences were going to diverge quickly and sharply. And he had no idea how long the commonality of Ánimo Pat Brown, the little high school that had brought them together via ninth-grade math class, would serve to bridge the space between them. He guessed that, as meaningful as high school had been, it wouldn't remain binding for very long. So prom and graduation felt to him like their very last moments uncomplicated by growing up. But he still wasn't keen to waste money on a promposal.

She ultimately acquiesced. As his first post-non-promposal ges-ture, Tio pledged to pay for a car to drive them to the prom site in Glendale.

"Are you crazy?" she replied. "That's a waste of money. My dad will drive us."

Tio groaned from deep within the young man's universal plight of not understanding women.

The transport was even less romantic than it sounded, with Tio in his tux in the front seat flailing to make small talk with a some-what intimidating man who communicated mostly in grunts and was still skeptical of the relationship after three years. His girlfriend, enjoying this minor torment, stared out the backseat window in her shining blue dress and the small corsage he'd given her. The venue did in fact resemble a strip club from the outside, with opaque windows and a weather-worn awning over the entrance. In the vestibule, a photographer was taking pictures of couples against a white screen, but the line was long and they slipped past into the ballroom. Aside from the low ceiling, the space was pretty, with floor-to-ceiling mirrors along the walls and glass chandeliers and ornate moldings. Round tables surrounded a parquet dance floor. The DJ was playing pop hits. The few people dancing this early were the same people who always danced early, including two girls in matching dresses who'd come to prom together. Tiered trays of salmon and chicken and asparagus, all lathered in the same Parmesan cream sauce, crowded tables in one corner, with a dark red punch bowl the centerpiece of the opposite corner.

Luis, Carlos, and Byron had all come dateless. Luis had spurned the effort and rumors and potential embarrassment required to ask a girl out; Carlos was still maintaining his long-distance relationship from Brown (though a girl from student government had jokingly offered him a promposal: "The US isn't taking you as a citizen because I'm taking you to prom!"); Byron was still too depressed about not going to college to have thought much at all about prom besides getting his body dressed and there. They sat along the wall together in the suits they'd eventually scrounged from a consignment store, wondering what odd national tradition had designated these hours so precious and costly, why the food had to be fancy rather than good, why forgettable songs from the eighties and nineties were suddenly sacrosanct. An array of pinpoint blue lights circled the room.

"Check out Tio and his girl." Luis pointed at the couple as they made their way from group to group. "Campaigning for prom king and queen!"

"People already voted," Carlos replied. There had been some contention regarding the ballots, as Tio and his girlfriend's names had been listed at the top of the boy and girl columns, respectively, which had led to a bitter faction claiming that the vote was rigged in their favor.

Byron spent the first hour leaning forward on his chair, elbows on knees and head resting on hands, watching the evening unfold with a sober expression. He'd procured a summer job at the Los Angeles Metro headquarters at Union Station, which would give him a modicum of security while he continued to unearth education options that didn't equate with what he'd accomplished in high school. One of the perks was a free Metro pass, already active. He'd ridden here with Luis, but if he desired to leave early, he could take the train home alone at no cost. Carlos put his hand on Byron's shoulder, attuned to his silent woe, but said nothing.

A local South LA newsletter had recently requested an interview regarding Carlos's accomplishments, and he'd agreed because his extended family would be proud, the local notice would benefit APB, and he knew no one would really read it beyond these blocks, so immigration enforcement wasn't much of a concern. The resulting piece was well written, fawning, and inspiring—for the community in highlighting what one of its own was capable of, and for Carlos personally in the sea change it signified: no longer would discretion have to be a defining undercurrent of every choice he made. With the Ivy League as an armor of sorts, he had the nation's permission to begin telling his story. (Though when the *Los Angeles Times* contacted the school shortly after about doing a larger profile, he'd instantly declined; there were limits to the exposure he could undertake in order to be heard.)

He couldn't quite describe the burden that had lifted from his consciousness upon notifying Yale of his acceptance. It wasn't as simple as expectation or destiny or legacy or perceived human worth. It involved the sudden dissolution of the rigid structure he'd been contained in all these years, the derby in which a small few bright kids from his neighborhood—a small few out of many, many bright kids—vied for an annual allotment of entrances into the ivory tower. He resented the structure and those who'd built it. He hadn't much enjoyed climbing within it. He'd at times been alienated because of it. And now, for the rest of his life, he wouldn't have to consider it. He could just focus on making the outcome meaningful.

A classmate whom he didn't know well but considered a good person had recently lost his best childhood friend, who hadn't gone to high school, to a gang dispute. The entire school seemed to mourn for this loss, though only one or two had ever met the murdered young man. They all had childhood friends who hadn't gone to high school and so were more vulnerable to violence, unemployment, drugs. Carlos had many. This latent sorrow for a stranger was binding and grounding and transcended the many flags on the college board. He'd spent his last weeks of school focusing on what he loved most about school: the people within it.

And so these weeks had felt simple, as freshman year had: just a string of school days, each one presenting a succession of low-level challenges and obligations and annoyances and disagreements and pleasures and wonders, each class giving way to the next, each day giving way to the next, no singular piece of it remarkable but the whole of it a kind of enchantment. Aside from award ceremonies, at which he'd been well lauded, and AP exams, on which he'd performed well, the days and weeks didn't feel like an ending, not yet.

Tio and his girlfriend were eventually crowned prom king and queen—of course they were—and handed crowns and sashes to wear before taking the floor for a solo slow dance. The scene was antiquated, gracefully so, and Tio's friends watching from the edge of the floor could see all the angst and bitterness and worry that he'd been clenching so tightly seem to peel from his face. He mugged the way he always did, actively striving to drain the moment of any semblance of gravity. But his spirit visibly rose. At the same time, Carlos was feeling his stomach tumble into a terrible queasiness. He eyed the salmon that he'd eaten, and the cream sauce that had seemed far closer to room temperature than it should have been.

An after-party had been arranged at a house on Fifty-Third Street in South LA that someone's aunt and uncle had given over for the night. But Luis stopped for fast food on the way there—he stopped for fast food on the way anywhere—and at this point Carlos was in the opening salvo of food poisoning. He spent almost an hour in the bathroom, and by the time he came out—pallid and sweaty and exhausted—Luis and Byron had jointly decided to take him home and skip the party.

"My memory of prom when I'm, like, fifty years old is going to be Carlos heaving his guts out in a disgusting Carl's Jr. bathroom," Luis said in the car. "And that's the best memory I could have possibly hoped for. I'll tell my grandkids about it."

In the backseat, Carlos just moaned miserably in a fetal position, holding his stomach in as best he could.

Owen, Bennett, Jon

The alarm began chirping when he opened the door, initiating the sixty-second window the system provided to enter the passcode. But the one he knew did not work; he keyed the sequence eight times with increasingly aggressive fingers, looking helplessly at his girlfriend, who stood behind him. His dad must have changed the code recently. The chirps accelerated, the clock hit zero, and then the horns brayed throughout the house. It was almost midnight. His girlfriend stood outside covering her ears while Owen flailed around with the buttons, the strident and awful noise shattering his ability to think clearly. Now the security company would call his parents and send a car here, and his parents would know that he'd come to the Santa Barbara beach house without asking permission. They would have to go straight back home and then it would be two a.m. and he'd be in a preposterous amount of trouble—and that would be his conclusive memory of high school. He shrugged toward her in contrition and waited.

Earlier in the evening, they'd decided a bit reluctantly to submit to the whole national decree of prom, from the pre-event photos to the chartered shuttle buses to the formal dance to the sanctioned after-party to the unsanctioned after-party to the Beverly Hilton hotel, where each year groups pooled money to rent strings of rooms. And the dance had been lovely, the ballroom space at the Pacific Design Center in West Hollywood huge and lavishly decorated, the students showing up fashionably late in gowns and suits and clinging to their cliques while cluster dancing, the music-aided nostalgia prompting people who'd been friends in middle school but had drifted apart in high school to embrace and make breathless invocations of treasured memories.

From there, they'd taken an Uber back to her home to change for late-night events. On the way, he'd turned to her.

"What if we just bagged the whole after-party thing?"

"We bought tickets and everything."

"But it's not something either of us have ever been interested in. And it's prom. So maybe it's the kind of night where we just do something we want to do, without kind of basing it around what everyone else is doing." Though they'd still only tangentially parsed the subject of staying together next year, tonight was quite possibly their last real, formal date.

"Okay," she'd said. "What should we do?"

Owen asked the driver, hypothetically, how much it would cost to take an Uber to Santa Barbara. They agreed upon a healthy off-the-books rate that was still cheaper than the fees for the remaining slate of prom events. Two hours later, they were at his parents' house in Santa Barbara in a state of utter panic and regret.

After a time, the alarm shut off of its own volition. He waited for the landline to ring, but it remained silent. He waited for a squad car to pull up outside, but none did. He waited for a neighbor to knock, but the homes on either side were dark. He waited for the ominous word *Dad* to light his cell screen, but the three letters never appeared. The system must have been disconnected, somehow.

They spent the evening sitting on the oceanfront deck, listening to the waves shifting small stones beneath their quiet, grounded talk. Away from people and influences and places they were supposed to be, with no one else in the world aside from an Uber driver knowing they were here, sharing some cheese and crackers they'd packed, they felt at once grown-up and absolutely juvenile at the same time; such a feeling was kind of entrancing in that it could really only occur in this precise, evanescent intersection of childhood and adulthood. They savored it while watching the ocean (though less so when Owen's father called him the following evening, while they were riding the last train back to Los Angeles after nearly missing it; Owen fibbed a bit and said they'd only come to Santa Barbara that morning for the day, and his miffed father replied in that penetratingly accusatory tone only fathers commanded: "So I guess you're just doing whatever you want now, and that's the way it is?")

Around two a.m. after prom, Jon was watching the same ocean. He was with friends who'd also steered clear of the after-parties, where the alcohol and the inevitable police visits did not strike them as enticements, and had instead gone bowling for a few hours in Santa Monica before finding a McDonald's and then walking two blocks to the eternal siren song of the beach. They skirted the high-tide line, still in their prom getups, bow ties sagging, dress shoes in their hands, pants rolled up. They kicked sand and let the cold waves cover their feet while laughing about other fading memories, grateful for the rhythms of their own prom night, willing to do anything, including sit in the chilly sand in formal wear for hours, to hold off the night's ending.

Two weeks later—two days before graduation—blankets and chairs covered the red-zone turf of the football field. A lectern stood near the uprights. The latter half of rush-hour traffic heading west to east blared horns along Olympic Boulevard, on the far end of the field. The sun had arced behind Century City, and the stunning orange light would fade fast now. The format of Senior Sunset was simple: a keynote speaker gave remarks, and then the microphone would be free for any departing senior who so desired to address the class. Year by year, the event inspired vastly different reactions. Some past seniors had recalled it as one of high school's most meaningful and beautiful experiences. Others had deemed it a campy instance of mandatory, manufactured nostalgia.

Owen and Bennett had come without much expectation, just thinking that it would be interesting to hear kids they'd never gotten to know reflect a bit on their time at Beverly. There was also the off chance they might witness some manner of spectacle. They intentionally sat apart from the cohort of kids who'd come mainly to snicker at the earnestness of others, and the night unfolded unmemorably with a succession of seniors thanking friends and affirming the degree to which these years would be cherished: heart-felt and—aside from an outlandish story involving a kidnapped girlfriend—mostly void of drama.

Two days later, Owen stood in the school parking lot removing his graduation gown from the box a few minutes before they were to file onto the football field for their last two hours as Beverly students. He situated the garment and noticed people around him pointing and giggling in their shiny white floor-length gowns.

"Nice one, Owen!" someone called, giving him a thumbs-up. "That's classic!"

"What is?" he asked, confused.

"Awesome joke."

"I kind of like to be in on my own jokes—what's going on?"

He looked down and saw that his gown only fell to his knees. Against explicit instructions from the principal, he'd worn shorts today because the weather was hot and the ceremony was long and in theory the gown would cover his legs. Now his pale, thin calves were bare in the sunlight above orange socks and sneakers.

A minute later, the principal's finger was jabbing four inches from his face.

JEFF HOBBS

"You're a mess, Owen. This is a disgrace. An absolute disgrace."

Owen shook his head: of course this had happened to him. "Sir, I can't really be blamed that someone screwed up my gown size and it's two feet short."

"That's it, Owen. You're out. You didn't listen and you're not graduating."

Owen pulled in a deep breath in the face of another needless confrontation with an adult—hopefully the last one in the context of high school. "I know this is ridiculous," he said. "But it really isn't my fault. I guess I could have checked the gown in advance—but does anyone really do that?"

The principal seemed to consider this and then abruptly concluded, "Okay, you're back in. You can graduate."

The class had agonizingly arranged seats so that friend groups could sit together, and they'd rehearsed the entry for hours, but somehow the rows ended up five seats off and most groups were fragmented. Families were scattered across the field and western bleachers. The sun was very bright gleaming off the brass instruments of the band playing.

"Everyone here wants to achieve success. But how does any person define success? It's unlikely that there will be a clean, shining moment in your life where you can stand there and say, 'I did it, I'm successful.' Success is a vague, ever-evolving concept, and it's different for all of us . . ."

The class president's remarks were well wrought and stirring in a way, though their gravity was lessened—as the gravity of graduation remarks always are—by the protracted time spent sitting and waiting in the heat, wearing silly gowns and hats. Later, the principal began walking among the student section, repeatedly affirming that this was not a school but a family, calling students out by name and sometimes mangling the pronunciations. Oddly, he bade Owen to stand up so that he could present the boy—at whom an hour earlier he had been bellowing at point-blank range while rescinding, then unrescinding, his diploma—as "Beverly's own future Oscar winner." It was all predictably ridiculous, as most of their time in school had been in some benign way. Yet these hours held meaning, too, at least inasmuch as four years' worth of eight-plus–hour days was converging on this field, under this sky, with these people. Owen felt the meaning far more weightily than he'd anticipated.

After two hours that felt like many more, the diplomas had been dispersed, caps had been tossed high, and high school graduation passed on into group and family photos on the football field, then early dinners hosted in various homes across this small subsection of a gigantic city, and from there into parties and late nights filled with embraces, remembrances, people taking the last opportunity to voice romantic crushes long held secret, exchanging proclamations of "It's over!" and "We did it!" After so many classroom moments during which people had yearned for minutes to pass more quickly, they stretched this time out.

Owen went to two of the parties, where he mostly wedged himself in corners with his friends. Bennett took a moment to speak on the phone with one of his half sisters from his biological father's gene pool. He wasn't sure if he would ever actually meet his father, or wanted to. But the half sister was about to start her freshman year at a private high school in San Francisco, and she'd asked him for general advice. Bennett told her, "High school is kind of bullshit, but there's the bullshit that matters and the bullshit that doesn't. I'm very happy to help you sort through the bullshit."

"It's strange," Owen said later in the night, when certain kids had just about lost their minds and it was clearly time to leave. "Whatever these little spheres of influence we've built up in the last four years, the little things we've done that mattered to us but don't matter at all outside of the empire that is Beverly High, theater or awards or whatever—they're just gone now. They ceased to exist at noon today. We spent, like, a decade building them. Now they're irrelevant, absolutely meaningless."

"Yeah," Bennett replied. "We came, we saw, we conquered—in Beverly Hills, where it means nothing. Now do it again, somewhere else, where hopefully it means a little more."

Ceremony

Each ending, from awards dinners to senior nights to graduations, was intended to prompt reflection, yet so many endings were occurring in such concentration that ultimately little time was left to reflect upon what any of them truly meant, aside from serving as a running reminder of the vague, aspirational metrics of American life: *win things, collect paper, make memories, leave a mark.* According to statistics, they'd each lived almost a quarter of the time allotted, though never promised, to their own individual versions of that life. Nearly all of that fraction had had school at its center; to this point, there'd been little question regarding how and where most days would begin and end, or what generally would transpire in between. Novelty, when it had arisen, had done so in the form of the antics engendered by placing a large number of people in a limited amount of space and asking them to figure out who they were, who they wanted to be.

The moment between reaching for the diploma and bringing the rolled-up sheet of paper back to one's chest lasted only two or three seconds. Nothing ostensibly changed in its duration. A student of a place became a former student of a place. The moment was a symbol, as was the document, and it belied the certainty that most of the challenges that had existed before its transference would still remain after, that certain trajectories, no matter the direction, had been set long ago—generations ago in some cases, predicated on the movement of people and culture and language, the concentration of wealth, the tides of commerce, the dreadful durability of racism and classism, the many different forms of human knowledge and the weight these forms carried in different places.

What changed—maybe all that changed—was that when gripping that roll of paper, and as it later hung framed on the wall of a no longer inhabited bedroom or else yellowed in some bottom desk drawer, they might expect to be taken more seriously than before. Their original thoughts might hold more perceived value than they once had—just a little bit more than they once had. Maybe—*maybe*—they gained some incrementally greater capacity to influence the world around them, and perhaps more important to be influenced by the world around them. This capacity was indeed earned. Right now, it was celebrated. Soon enough, it would be all but forgotten amid the more pressing concerns of living day to day.

Not much regard seemed to be given to those clusters of young people, walking away from their schools in the afternoons, clothes and backpacks slung low, holding up traffic at crosswalks, laughing at their own jokes, flirting, shuffling, snarfing processed food, not appearing in any urgent rush to get anywhere or accomplish anything of note. Every neighborhood had them, race and attire varying from place to place, but the idle pace and wanton manner fairly constant. A few people fought loudly about what it was they were learning and where and how and from whom and at what cost. Most people didn't give them much thought at all and simply steered clear of the schoolkids—even as most people had been them, some version of them, once.

Carlos, Tio, Byron, Luis

The mezzanine and balcony of the University of Southern California's towering auditorium were packed and raucous with parents, siblings, aunts and uncles and cousins. Small children waved shimmering pom-poms over the railings.

The Ánimo Pat Brown seniors in their light blue robes occupied most of the orchestra section, with space around them reserved for teachers. Heavy maroon drapes with gold trim formed the backdrop for the stage, where the principal welcomed and congratulated everyone, first in Spanish and then in English. A high-achieving student read a letter she'd composed as inspiration for the underclassmen. Another read a letter of gratitude to families. The last directed her remarks to the graduating class before her. All spoke of the achievement of a high school diploma as something valuable, nearly impossible, certainly sacred. The keynote speaker was the current poet laureate of Los Angeles, a Latino man in his fifties. He spoke of being homeless as a young adult and spending many nights sleeping in one of the alcoves footing the Los Angeles Public Library, a building in which he now gave speeches to hundreds of people. His grand words and upthrusted arms roused all present, but particularly the families peering down for whom a child's high school graduation had never been a given, and now—in this isolated moment, anyway—was life defining.

The seniors received their diplomas alphabetically, their school pictures and college choices lighting up a projector screen at stage right. Byron was among the first to walk. Though his photograph showed a boy grinning brightly, the young man walking across the stage wore only a tight, jaded smile. His college was listed as Santa Monica College, but in reality he hadn't committed and wasn't planning to go. Tio walked a few minutes later. After taking the diploma, on his way to the far side of the stage, he curiously stopped and made an abrupt jabbing motion with his arm, slanted upward toward the balcony. The awkward gesture was interpreted as a salute to the class, maybe, or an acknowledgment of someone watching from up there, or just Tio making an ass of himself.

Regardless, it prompted a short surge of applause. Luis lumbered along, his gown way too small for him, a cardboard-cutout pink unicorn dangling from his cap for reasons no one could discern as he mugged for the crowd. Carlos was in one of the last rows. When announced, he walked dutifully, his posture bent slightly forward, a bashful smile on his face as the applause reached a new register befitting his celebrity in this space, among these people, seven or eight hundred people who spanned four generations, seven or eight hundred people living their lives alongside nearly a million others in South Los Angeles, seven or eight hundred people now connected eternally to Ánimo Pat Brown Charter High School.

Each student clutching his or her leather-bound certificate knew objectively that the grandiose remarks and the many tear-streaked faces and the overall volume of the auditorium did not equate with the rather ubiquitous achievement of passing successfully through high school. They knew that a lot of their time spent as APB students amounted to nonsense, and that nonsense would comprise much of their lasting memories. They knew that this ceremony guaranteed them absolutely nothing in any of the days after. But, shit, the ceremony was actually happening, commemorating an experience that maybe hadn't always unfolded as they wished it had, or in the way that they retold it afterward, or with the gravitas being ascribed to it tonight—but it had all occurred on the small plot of land by the Blue Line tracks, and that was worth a few lofty words, and tears, and the full-throated shrieks pouring down on them.

They lingered on the lawn outside the auditorium after, carrying crude signs that siblings had crafted expressing pride, making faces of exaggerated astonishment, finding teachers they might never see again to say thank you.

Carlos's brother was there, recently home from Yale for the summer. Jose remained off to the side, chatting graciously with teachers who approached to ask him about Ivy League life. Carlos was quickly overwhelmed by all the people wanting to shake his hand and offer one last sentiment wishing him well and assuring him that he would continue his ascent from here, that he had no ceiling anymore. A classmate who'd gone to middle school with him pulled him aside to say that he remembered seeing Carlos in the eighth-grade yearbook labeled *Most likely to be successful* and wondering, *Who the fuck is this guy?* "I guess everyone knows who the fuck you are now," he declared.

Carlos shrugged and replied, "I don't know about all that, but thanks."

As soon as a window presented itself, Carlos slipped away with his family. They found a nondescript pizza counter right off campus—just the word *Pizza* and a phone number on a strip mall window—and they celebrated his graduation there. His mother noted casually that when Jose returned to New Haven in the fall, Carlos would be on the plane with him. Unvoiced was the fact that their parents had never seen the Yale campus, and possibly never would. Also unvoiced was their tremendous, shared relief at having found an apartment with two days to spare before eviction, on a street near Washington Park where the marathoners had trained. The rent was $300 more than the home he'd grown up in. The layout was cramped and the complex was shoddy. Since they'd moved in, he was hearing gunshots on a nightly basis rather than monthly. But they could afford it since they wouldn't be responsible for Carlos's daily needs much longer.

"What was that arm thing you did?" Luis asked Tio as the grass in front of the auditorium was finally clearing. "On the stage—that weird thing you did that made no sense."

"Oh, that?" Tio shrugged as if there'd been no real meaning to it. "I don't know, just messing around. I felt like I should do something cool, but I fucked it up."

"Stupid you didn't come up with something beforehand."

Tio had in fact come up with the gesture beforehand, alone at the skate park. The motion was directed toward his father and was intended somehow to say, *Fuck you, thank you, I love you,* simultaneously. Tio returned to the skate park that evening, as quickly as he could. He didn't attempt anything difficult. He mostly just coasted around the perimeter, pivoting left and right. Most of the skaters there were kids, maybe in fourth or fifth grade, not able to do much besides hurl themselves over a ramp and then sprawl facedown on the concrete. Tio caught himself laughing at one particularly paltry attempt at a trick, then approached the kid and explained that he was getting too far ahead of himself: he had to work first on the smaller ramps, perfect the lame tricks that would impress no one, silently endure all the horrible names people would call him, and then one day, which would begin unremarkably, he'd hit a big jump almost by accident. "After that day," Tio said, "you'll keep fucking up a bunch more times, it'll hurt, but you'll eventually get good." The kid nodded vacantly, not listening to the advice he hadn't sought from this skate punk he didn't know. He went straight back to the punishment of the big ramp, while Tio meandered the twenty blocks home to Juniper Street.

The following weekend, Tio, Luis, and Byron worked again for Victor's parents at the Santa Anita racetrack carnival, for Memorial Day. After a cool, wet winter, the dry and throbbing heat had reclaimed the atmosphere. Summer jobs had yet to start, so they were all glad for the money. They each managed different game booths set along a dusty row. Tio sat by his booth wearing sunglasses, lightheartedly jeering at kids as they failed again and again to land a ball in a shallow, slanted bin. He finally started telling them, "This game's rigged, fool. It's never going to stay in. Do the rings instead." A teenaged girl kept coming around, a little bit flirty, and Tio indulged her friendliness despite his girlfriend's scowling at him from a few booths down. "Why is she pissed at me now?" he asked Luis at some point.

"Because you look like you're having the time of your life with that girl," Luis replied, "like you've never been happier."

"I'm wearing sunglasses—how can you tell if I'm happy or not?"

"Dude. We see you welcoming that girl."

"My job is to get people to do the game. She keeps coming to do the game. I'm doing good at my job."

"Tio, damn . . ."

The San Gabriel Mountains loomed a mile north. At this point, after roughly a dozen weekends working here, they'd all memorized the unmoving contours. The topography's massive beauty had ceased to amaze, had become just another physical aspect of home, like the downtown skyline, like the sunsets, like the auto-body shops along Manchester Boulevard. The day wore on and grew boring. Many such summer days promised boredom, quickened only by their capacity to insult one another and rehash crass stories, as well as the less vocal and more weighty process by which each anticipated the imminent phase of life that would look so very different from the just-completed one. For now, they slumped in lawn chairs amid carnival games. Though the scenery seemed to demand some manner of sublime contemplation, they inexorably thought about food.

"Where's Carlos at?" Luis asked.

"He's at some kind of UCLA camp for fancy brilliant people," Byron answered.

"Of course he is. While we sit around here in the hot dirt." Luis spent some time scuffing his foot around that dirt with a contemplative expression that rarely appeared on his face. "You know, it's possible we'll just never see that dude again. Because, you know, *Yale*."

"I don't think he's the kind of person to ghost us like that," Byron said softly.

There followed a reflective, strangely somber quietude that Luis shattered by blurting, "Yo, remember when I stapled Byron's hand? He told me to do it, and I fucking did it?"

Tio said, "I remember. It was, like, two weeks ago and you haven't stopped talking about it since."

"That was the greatest thing that happened in high school, to be honest."

Byron flexed his still slightly swollen hand, shaking his head. "We're so stupid."

"Is anyone else starving?" Tio asked.

"I could eat," Byron concurred.

"Is the burger stand still open?"

"It should be," Luis said. "I'll go check it out."

Luis set off on his reconnaissance, while Tio and Byron remained sitting in the waning heat.

"I could definitely eat," Byron repeated. Those four words he'd said hundreds of times during high school.

And Tio had said these hundreds of times as well: "Yeah, bro. Yeah."

Epilogue

I am unironically happy to be back in school.

—Jon

Jon

Star, moon, and planet aligned, and across a narrow band of the country slanted southeast to northwest, the sun's light winked out for a time. Jon stood within that swath, alongside a few dozen gasping others, in Bush's Pasture Park in Salem, Oregon. They used thick, dark lenses or boxy helmetlike contraptions they'd made according to Internet instructions to see the light without damage to their corneas. As the eclipse reached its full phenomenon status, Jon splayed his fingers and watched the narrowing crescent's beams break through them onto the asphalt. He waved his arms and made the beams dance before the light vanished entirely. He experienced exactly what he'd road-tripped here searching for: a small bit of wonder that was right now connecting him to others craning their necks in South Carolina, Missouri, Idaho. For thousands of years, eclipse events had astounded and terrified humans with apocalyptic portents, the sun's constancy being perhaps the most taken-for-granted facet of existence. Now everyone beyond toddlerhood not associated with a cult knew exactly what was transpiring and why; it was just a brief shadow, but one that framed life's smallness in a way worth witnessing.

Until the early summer, Jon had been certain that he wouldn't need to buy a winter coat because he wasn't going to Chicago. The computations of likely aid and loan options and all the repercussions of piecing together the roughly $80,000 per year they were faced with made for ghastly outputs—especially when UCLA, where he'd also been admitted, was such a strong school. The dream to leave home that he had maintained for so long, that had alternately brought him guilt and inspiration, would be bested by math. Dreams were nearly always bested by math. And Jon had come to healthy terms with that equation; he knew that a person whose worst college option was UCLA was factually a fortunate person. He was a bright guy and he was going to college. He was okay.

Then they received the actual aid package, which was unexpectedly generous, along with an Odyssey Scholarship, part of the university's $100 million endowment to "dismantle obstacles to education and careers for talented, hardworking students in financial need." Suddenly, if he and his parents squinted their eyes just right, the math worked—well, not really, but he would find a campus job and his father was performing well and his mother would begin working again with Jon gone. With regards to whatever the shortfall turned out to be, they all fell upon the words his mother had always repeated, words of which he'd been generally skeptical until recently, "We will find a way."

Owen

The eclipse was the central theme of the Kenyon College president's convocation address, given to the 460 newly admitted residents of this hilltop idyll listening from their chairs. The speech employed the eclipse as a metaphor to rhapsodize about the importance of rigorous scientific inquiry, of listening to different perspectives, of exploring subjects that were unfamiliar and seeking answers to heady questions, the balance of community and support with challenge and discomfort—pretty much every societal tenet college presumed to signify. The president ended with a reflection on the Bonnie Tyler song "Total Eclipse of the Heart" and its opening lines regarding the loneliness, tiredness, nervousness, and terror that touched all people now and again. Owen himself was feeling somewhat lonely, tired, nervous, and terrified.

His freshman class in college was about the same size as his senior class in high school. The Kenyon kids regarded the convocation assembly with the same odd combination of solemnity and amusement with which the Beverly Hills kids had regarded graduation. They were as eager for the pageantry to be over so that they could continue attending to their actual lives: furnishing rooms and syncing entertainment systems with Wi-Fi networks and selecting classes and becoming acquainted with roommates and hallmates and figuring out where to eat and which parties would give them entrée. As they milled around campus during the orientation days accomplishing all this—some casually, some frantically—labels were already being applied between people: boarding-school kid, Deep South kid, European kid, athlete kid, weed kid, sandals kid, neurotic kid, shy kid, etc. Owen, unavoidably, was LA kid. Later, once Facebook pages had been clandestinely tilled, he would no doubt become more specifically Beverly Hills kid.

He was here at a certain level of internal crisis after he'd spent much of the summer dwelling on death. Partly, this spiral was the result of a terribly conceived mushroom experience—his first and only, in his backyard with a friend, another regretful box checked— as well a mutually agreed-upon but excruciatingly vague decision to "see how things go" with his girlfriend, and the prospect of living so far from the secure bower of his family. Beyond these situational factors unique to his own existence, his ruminations on death's joint abstraction and certainty—which were at turns frightening, depressing, and comical—tended to center upon what they always did: notions of self-worth, or a lack thereof. The last time he'd been to Kenyon, during the Plato discussion, he'd felt buoyantly liberated from the allegorical cave. Now, he was feeling very much locked within it, as if leaving home had tightened the limitations of his own mind rather than expanded them. The disconcertingly avid attempts of fellow freshmen to identify the essence of one another—*If you were a vegetable, what kind would you be?*—failed to dispel his circular angst. Though the campus was absolutely stunning, Owen spent many of his first hours and days in college brooding in his dorm room, watching YouTube videos made by meditation gurus or lying on the floor listening to the Kendrick Lamar song "Love" repeatedly. He wished that he were home, with Bennett and his friends, somewhere doing not very much at all, together.

Neither of his parents had come with him to campus: his mother because of her health and his father because of a severe aviophobia. The crying and embraces and affirmations that everything was going to be "great"—the goodbye ritual that was occurring millions of times over on thousands of campuses right now—had taken place in his mother's bedroom before he left for the airport to make his own way. He was holding on to the moment tightly during these early, uncentered days: his mother's frail but firm hand enclosing his as she sat up in bed, his father's distraught but reassuring eyes, the joint chorale of their crying, the infinite small moments that had led to this parting and were contained in it. Once he left home, the moments suddenly felt irretrievable.

And yet he was fascinated by the fact that no one around him yet knew who his father was, or that his mother was mostly bedridden, or that he'd grown up in a mansion in Westwood. He would be permitted to create the impressions he would make on others with no base of knowledge grown from eighteen years living in the same community and subject to school gossip. And he did feel some excitement at the prospect of taking courses that were not assigned to him by decree, so he spent many hours scrolling through the catalog, no longer obliged to focus on prereqs and the progression of APs and the optics of college admissions. The freedom to take classes that actually seemed interesting was an empowering if fleeting reprieve from ennui, as was the grandness of course names like Playwriting and Dramatic Theory, Classical Pragmatism, Identity in American Society.

Soon enough the schedule of tests and papers would become tiresome and mundane, the patronizing tics of certain professors exasperating. New acquaintances would start to annoy each other due to proximity and clashing habits and hygiene; the campus that had seemed so vast and open would begin to feel cloistered; the days pitched initially as holding limitless intellectual potential would fall into formulaic repetition. The rhythms of young human life were as unavoidable in college as they'd been in high school, and within them he would have to locate and claim some kind of existential space. On its face, the prospect was intimidating, even hopeless.

But he thought back four years to the similar predicament he'd experienced at the outset of high school. He'd overcome it then, for the most part.

Tio

The chancellor of UC Riverside, at Tio's convocation in late September, spoke not of eclipses but of the first day of kinder-garten: excitement, nerves, schedules, books, a few friends and many strangers and much unknown. He equated those feelings and details with their first day of college, but with two key differences.

First, they were no longer given books—they had to buy them. Second, they were no longer in school to learn the content of those books, but rather to learn how to write those books.

On one level, the words were part and parcel of yet another speech, and Tio wondered how many speeches an average American person must listen to during the first two decades of life. On another, the words rang quite true, carrying echoes of *ánimo*, his particular high school's ethos. On still another, the words were somewhat deflating, a reminder that they were back at the beginning once more, conquerors of nothing, continuing to flail their way through the many rounds of the orbed labyrinth that comprised their education.

Yet the day was smogless and pretty, the campus lawns wide and clean and thoroughly watered, the freshmen around him listening intently, for the most part, nodding with the hopeful gravity the speaker aimed to elicit. Tio felt proud to be one of them, the pride itself braided with his awe at how many of them there actually were. Five thousand freshmen were gathered here, five thousand different pathways, five thousand ambitions, five thousand unique stories converging on this lawn. The magnitude was difficult to process, and suddenly that stretch of time in the spring of his senior year, when the mechanics and stigmas of college admissions had made matriculation at UCR feel like such a defining failure, seemed distant and childish. Now he joined with a steady succession of whoops amid the call-and-response segments that concluded convocation, all with a keen abandon for whatever this whole huge apparatus—college—was going to do to them.

The campus was gigantic, though not attractive in the classical collegiate sense. No turrets wrapped the roofs, no tall cathedral with ornate stained-glass windows rose from the central quad. The Bell Tower, the primary landmark, was an uninspired postmodern block. The campus had been built out through the latter half of the twentieth century with a mandate for efficiency that catered to population growth and demographic shifts but rarely to aesthetics; in places it seemed designed simply to blend into the drab office parks and desert that surrounded it. He was already familiar with the school because of his sister, had seen many of its spaces before, had never been impressed. But having a student ID card hanging from a lanyard around his neck that unlocked most of the doors drastically altered the perspective. His high school had been comprised of six hundred people of the same skin color in three hallways on half an acre of land. He now shared space with over twenty thousand classmates using dozens of buildings on a thousand acres of land, in one of the most ethnically and economically diverse schools in the country. He was quickly, deeply attuned to the hugeness and import.

His first act as a student there was to wait in a long, snaking line to explore possibly transferring from the college of agricultural sciences to the college of engineering. Many dozens of others had the same fancy. At first, the majority of students leaving the registration desk ahead appeared pleased with the outcome. Then, after about twenty minutes, they began passing by Tio's place in line with taut, dejected faces while crumpling the forms in their hands. Word seeped back that mechanical engineering, chemical engineering, and structural engineering were all full. When Tio reached the desk, rather than put forward a preference, he simply asked, "Is there any space anywhere in engineering?"

"Material engineering has a few slots left."

Tio didn't entirely know what material engineering was. But since he didn't have time to find out, he signed the transfer document and, in so doing, blindly hoped to be stepping somehow toward that dream born years ago when, as a boy, he watched his father fix their neighborhood's broken and discarded machines.

Later, returning to the sprawling concrete dorm buildings, he smelled a totally alien yet alluring aroma. Through an open doorway a few rooms down from his, a freshman was cooking on an electric hot plate: chickpeas sautéed with a bunch of vegetables Tio didn't recognize.

"That smells dope," Tio commented. His new neighbor invited him in and shared his food, which he'd begun cooking in a fit of homesickness. "Tastes dope, too," Tio added. After eating, he revealed that he'd never met a Persian person before, nor had he ever tasted saffron, the scent that had drawn him.

Carlos

At any age and in any endeavor, a blank page was unnerving. Whether it appeared in the form of a white computer screen with a narrow vertical line blinking in the top left corner, or a composition sheet, or typewriter paper rolled manually beneath the platen, whether the task was a school paper, a thank-you note, a PowerPoint presentation, the emotional weight was the same: here was an emptiness that required filling with defined thought. The emptiness Carlos faced in the first week of November demanded eight hundred words that would become his first column in the *Yale Daily News*.

Mexico: my place of birth, but somewhere I never really considered home. Perhaps justifiably so, as I only spent the first six months of my life there.

In some ways, the task recalled his college essays in that he needed to encompass his own experience in order to illuminate some greater understanding of people and places and the currents running through them, with strict word-count limitations. The stakes were at once lower and higher: lower because he was already in college, one of the most revered in the world, and whatever musings he ultimately published would have no numerical impact on his future; higher because some substantial portion of his five thousand undergraduate classmates, people with whom he actually interacted day to day, would read this in their morning newspaper, and they would judge him for it. Steadily and late into the night, working in the suite he shared with three other freshmen, in a Gothic building named after the Vanderbilt family, he fleshed out the piece. He wrote that while he was growing up as an American, his parents had been disappointed in his apparent apathy toward Mexican culture even while that culture absolutely surrounded him in his neighborhood. Only after coming to Yale—where one had to look hard for evidence of any Latino presence at all—had he begun to value that heritage to the point of hanging a Mexican flag above his desk, where the Virgen de Guadalupe his mother had given him bookended works by Carlos Fuentes, and in front of that display he roared the national anthem before soccer games. He didn't take risks in the piece, neither rhetorically nor thematically. He didn't aim to provoke or offend anyone. He didn't mention that he was undocumented or poor. His goal was simply to remind his new peers, using details plucked from his new life, of the odd and universal component of existence by which people could only seem to value the essence of where they came from after they'd left. The idea had been trod by many thinkers before him; he tried to lace it with a certain Mexican authenticity and the humanity of his own homesickness.

Carlos's introduction to Yale had been, of all things, easy—aside from the fact that his mother, who had wept miserably upon driving Jose to the airport before his first year, seemed to treat Carlos's departure as a casual event. His roommates were diverse in interests and extraction and all quite gracious. The suite he lived in was spacious by his standards, though room size was a staple of the complaints made by incoming freshmen. While he was a first-generation college student, he was not the first in his family to attend college—he was not even the first in his family to attend Yale—and so his brother had guided him through the intricacies of class registration and social groupings with a fluency that even the boarding school legacy kids lacked. The university offered many layers of help in the transition, both official and unofficial, to those wishing to take advantage, and Carlos had never been prideful when it came to receiving help. And so he'd had a relatively uneventful time shifting from his small, young charter school in South LA to the cavernous, centuries-old hallways of Yale, from McDonald's in Luis's car on Firestone Boulevard to gourmet meals at heavy oak tables with the children of United States senators, from classes with devoted, earnest high school teachers who would never forget him to lectures with renowned, sometimes pompous scholars who would never learn his name.

The first real shock occurred in his intro physics and math classes, in which he learned within weeks that these subjects held no inherent joy when, instead of Tio and Luis and their incessant commentary, he was surrounded by deeply serious, competitive students intent on silent mastery of the material; if the entire engineering track was this severe, he wasn't certain that he could survive it with his sanity intact. The second shock fell with a cold that gripped him for weeks in the early fall, with a mercilessness unknown on the West Coast (the virus also depleted almost all of his living stipend via over-the-counter lozenges and syrups). The third shock came with the federal government's approval of his DACA application in October, thirteen months after he'd submitted it.

He'd harbored a latent aspiration coming into college to develop his writing skills further in some way, but he'd never intended to become a regular columnist for the publication students read loyally every day. He certainly hadn't been inclined to put himself forward as a primary Latino voice on campus. But he'd been recruited through a friend of a friend who contributed to the paper, and being as he was one of four undocumented Yale students—he and his brother comprising half of that particular demographic—he couldn't fault the editor in chief for pressuring him, not discreetly, to cover that beat.

"I know some things that don't involve Mexico," he said meekly in an editorial meeting, after his first piece seemed to spur some thoughtful conversation and he was encouraged to press the topic further. "I know a lot about food, for example. And politics, not just immigration politics."

"A lot of people know a lot about food and politics. No one knows what it's like being illegal—no one here, anyway."

Carlos didn't mention that his recent DACA acceptance meant that he wasn't illegal anymore—that for one year, he would be recognized as a functioning member of the United States (after that year, he would have to reapply). Instead, he did as instructed, and as he began producing the work and meeting his deadlines, he located within himself an eloquent and rational anger, one long kept dormant by his lifetime plight of voicelessness, that found its ideal form in the editorial arena—a skill he'd learned and honed tirelessly in his childhood journals but had only gained society's permission to employ at Yale. In "Waking Up from the American Dream," he informed readers that "liking" a Facebook post did not qualify as "support" for immigrants and others under threat by the rhetoric coming from the White House and nationalist groups. In "The DACA Motif," he wrote about how very thin the layer of rights granted him by DACA actually was, after he'd worked and waited so long just to procure it. In "Spring Break Haven," he described what it was like to remain on the mostly deserted campus for a full two-week break, because he could not afford to travel home; he detailed long, circuitous walks around the campus during which he admired the intricacy of the architecture, the small, loving stonework tucked beneath eaves and windowsills, while subsisting on canned food from the dollar store a few blocks off campus. In "Yale's Invisible Price Tags," he listed the many ways that he and others were hindered by costs that most did not consider: winter clothes, notebooks for classes that prohibited laptops, and above all textbooks (in the piece, he chastised professors who assigned textbooks—often written by themselves—in which only one chapter was relevant to the class).

Much of his work came to involve money and rights, and what it looked like and felt like to be so limited in both in an environment where most people seemed to have tapped an inexhaustible supply (and where the university itself had an endowment of over $27 billion, which was paying his tuition). And while he did manage to publish pieces outside this sphere (an uncharacteristically vitriolic and profane screed directed at Boston and Harvard was a predictable crowd-pleaser for his readership), the rapidly dawning truth was that Carlos did know a lot about Mexico, he did know a lot about living in poverty, and he did know a lot about being an illegal immigrant. With a first-semester class load that included a lit class called US-Mexico Borderlands and an art history class called Mexican Art Renaissance, he was actively learning more. He came to believe that he owed his new community a parcel of his knowledge, because—at least according to convocation rhetoric—it was what they'd all come here to gain: a different perspective, even if at times certain sects were inflamed by precisely this commodity.

His readership was composed of very intelligent young people, filled with conviction, generally liberal, accustomed throughout their schooling not only to being right but to being praised for how right they were. In the meantime, he was writing as a Yale student with full financial aid, the beneficiary of vast volumes of attention and financing from myriad people and organizations, and yet he persistently stated in firmly worded print that he was not at all satisfied with the system as it currently stood. Such declarations were uncomfortable. He didn't receive much backlash, but when he did, it came fiercely—and, in keeping with the craven arrangements of social media, often anonymously. He was called narrow-minded, dumb, racist, a beaner, socialist. More than anything, he was called ungrateful.

Carlos was grateful—exhaustingly so. But he was also empowered. Growing up, the most constant complaint expressed by both himself and his friends—equivalent in frequency if not gravitas to complaints about Yale's room sizes—had to do with being unheard and unknown and uncounted. Here at Yale, he felt wonderful being heard, and known, and counted. He did not much concern himself with whoever might be pissed off about it.

Bennett, Jon, Harrison

Bennett never contacted his biological father, even after all those hours staring wonderingly at the man's social media feeds. He'd ultimately decided that his father was just some guy coded into his DNA without any connection to his life. The man presumably didn't possess some lockbox filled with wisdom that he itched to pass down. He would probably prefer to be left alone—and in the meantime, Bennett was quite occupied taking up residence at Fifth Avenue and Tenth Street, a corner in the very center of Manhattan above which few people in the world could afford to live. The building had once been a hotel frequented by Mark Twain and now was a dorm inhabited by a group of aspiring student filmmakers. His new classmates were all united in the ambition to explore and conquer New York City: meet the most interesting people, find the most authentic dive bars, call friends from home with the wildest late-night stories. They were also all in direct and edgy competition with one another for esteem and internships, encapsulated by the "compliment sandwich" that was a staple of all college creative workshops: a moderate praising of some innocuous detail, followed by a meaty dismantling of the work as a whole, concluding with another shallow commendation. The predictability of such constructions made him wonder if his mother's skepticism regarding film school was indeed valid. Between classes like Looking Back on Growing Up and Storytelling Strategies, he wandered the streets of various neighborhoods and marveled at the human interface gifted by the act of walking, which in Los Angeles was relegated to a few short pedestrian-friendly districts. On any given block, he might pass a person weeping on the phone, or performing a show tune for no one, or ditching school, and then he'd turn right or left and the next block would unfold with its many small enchantments, each stretch a stanza of a song he wanted to memorize. He quickly subscribed to an unsourced quote, *Los Angeles is a shitty heaven, and New York is a fun hell.* He used his go-to phone apps to meet girls from Barnard and NYU. He played much Super Mario Kart in his room. And he found that investing earnest effort into schoolwork that he actually cared about was, in fact, very rewarding.

Though he was in constant touch with Owen at Kenyon, and Owen's forthcoming visit to the city would no doubt place them immediately back into the easy banter and kinship that had sustained them in Los Angeles, the fact was that Owen was living on a small campus in an isolated rural village—an actual *village*—while Bennett had moved from the second-largest city in the country to the largest. Their respective continuums from Beverly Hills High School had diverged quickly and drastically. A particularly odd night found one of Bennett's text girlfriends bringing eight of her friends to his dorm room at midnight without warning, all of them strangers in various levels of drunkenness, and one kept challenging him to video game contests with his jacket at stake (she never won). His first instinct the following morning was to tell the story to Owen, which he did, and they laughed. But the laughter sounded just a little bit hollow—maybe due to the not great cell phone coverage in central Ohio, more likely related to the lack of parallels between Bennett's world and Owen's. Even if the lack held no consequence within the lasting nature of their friendship, it was strange to process the slight effort of realignment required each time they connected, a wholly new demand that shaded the humor, the anxieties, the love, the basic act of storytelling.

This realignment shaded everything, for a time. Jon had arrived in Chicago at the very end of September, the shake of the plane as its wheels contacted asphalt at O'Hare completing an aspiration entertained basically since he'd defied that childhood piano teacher in sixth grade. That he was already missing his parents to a degree that his sixth-grade self would have never conceived made the landing somewhat complicated. The University of Chicago itself was somewhat complicated, with its acreage of grand stone buildings housing a rarefied education in the middle of the South Side of Chicago, one of the most impoverished and violent urban neighborhoods in the country. The library had almost twelve million books; the campus had the third-largest private police force in the world.

Harrison came from Purdue during Jon's second weekend on campus. His quiet, humble manner remained constant, but his muscles had swelled considerably after another summer of heavy weights and plyometrics and repeat sprints up into the Hollywood Hills. Realistically, due to the strict allotment of space and money in Division I college football, he had little chance of ever seeing the sideline of a Purdue football game. But he continued to work obsessively toward the idea on the grassy flats of western Indiana. He had no pressing reason to visit Jon; the two hadn't been particularly close in high school. But the campuses were an hour apart by train, the strain of schoolwork hadn't fully settled yet, and both were still enwrapped in the novelty of being far from home such that they were compelled to share it with someone who knew what home felt like.

The two of them made a circuit around the city by subway, visited Grant Park and Willis Tower, and used phone apps to find the best cheap food. They talked about high school in brief, fond snippets of shared history. But for the most part, they talked about college and their rooms and the new people with whom they divvied up space, comparing experiences that were in the very earliest stages of unfolding. They were reporting information, but really they were seeking comfort and commiseration as each acclimated to an unfamiliar place and strove to wedge the shape of new experiences into the not-quite-aligning hole of long-held expectations, like toddlers with their classic wooden toys. As toddlers learned, the pieces all eventually fit with some jiggering. That seemed to be what much of life amounted to, then, now, and moving forward: fitting experiences into expectations, with some jiggering.

Luis, Byron, Carlos, Tio

As Carlos had done at Yale, Luis dropped physics at UCSB. For four years of high school, the boys had largely condemned the humanities as a refuge for flighty nitwits. They'd all hewed to the conviction that true intelligence was most usefully applied to science and math. A few college courses had left Luis not just humbled by the difficulty but also stunned by the possibilities in other, heretofore unconsidered areas of intellectual and professional life. Both Carlos and Luis independently switched their tracks to political science. Their reasoning was pragmatic. Luis felt like his brashness, wit, ability to talk as fast as he thought, and general lack of shame might make him a decent lawyer someday (he'd gone to court by himself in June prepared to contest his March traffic citation, only to learn that the officer who'd written it had never logged it into the system, out of either carelessness or a forgiving impulse). Carlos, having realized his aptitude as a columnist, was suddenly keen to join the political sphere—and he found it entirely remarkable that he could drastically alter the vector of his life through a ten-minute stop at the registrar's office.

At the same time, Byron still struggled with carving any viable pathway at all. He extended his summer internship with the Los Angeles Metropolitan Transportation Authority into a job in place of college. He was essentially a dispatcher: a human relay point between those who identified problems and those who fixed them, all somewhat reviled by people who actually used the trains and buses. And while the paychecks meant that he could suddenly afford things that had been unavailable to him before, like decent food and electronic accessories, he was neither content nor fulfilled nor self-sufficient as he lived at home with his parents, continued to negotiate shaky accords between his German shepherd and his father's Doberman, and incrementally saved small fractions of his monthly salary that might see him into college, in some form, sometime.

The Facebook feeds of all his friends contained successions of pronouncements regarding classes taken, parties attended, swell times had, all footed with the names of their four-year college campuses. Byron sat alone late at night, weary from his day of inputting information, scrolling through these bright images, and he still didn't quite understand why he wasn't doing what those kids were doing right now—he couldn't triangulate the source of his precise failure. Aside from being late with some forms, investing less than stellar effort in some essays, and displaying social clumsiness in a few interviews, he'd been a fairly dedicated student. He assumed that a lot of teenagers in a lot of places had been late, or lazy, or awkward at times, and that most of them were now in college. Some unidentifiable unfairness had occurred during his progression, he was convinced. At the nadir of such spirals, he would submissively decide that he was wrong, that the adages of self-determination in America were truthful and that he alone had failed. But then he would read the ongoing news stories detailing how UC Irvine had rescinded almost five hundred freshman admissions during the summer of 2017 based on technicalities, because eight hundred more students had accepted admission than their statisticians had predicted, and Byron figured that self-determination was not as powerful a force as he'd always been told. He continued trudging through his days and living vicariously through the illusions of social media until whatever dodgy entity it was that governed their outcomes—administrators, money, blind luck—might work in his favor, or not.

"I'm all good," he would say to his high school friends whenever they spoke on the phone, conversations that occurred less frequently as months passed. "Work's all good, the neighborhood's all good, I'm all good . . ."

Such plaintive assurances made across wide distances masked all of their various struggles, such as the way Tio's uplifting entry into college waned quickly into a morass. He was the only member of his high school class to go to Riverside, and the lack of even one familiar face among all the thousands of passing faces unnerved him. During his initial days on campus, the numbers had felt empowering. Soon enough, they seemed to render him an obscurity. He'd hoped to establish a Caballeros con Cultura chapter at Riverside, but he found that what had required three conversations with faculty and a few days of organizing in high school was intimidatingly laborious in college with its layers of bureaucracy and forms. Classes and labs and skateboarding between them consumed most of his days anyway: metal alloys and the way nickel and titanium were incorporated into bioengineering, the nanostructures of elements, the limitations of biofuels. All were fascinating, but the long-term effort of discerning which to dedicate his life to felt almost arbitrary. He had thought the whole effort might end—had thought that he would actually die—after accidentally inhaling the fumes of a pH 10 buffer solution in the lab and feeling his entire body itch while his lungs contracted. A few deep breaths of outdoor air had remedied the symptoms, but the startlingly macabre aspect was thinking how small of a loss he would have been.

Joining the Phi Kappa Sigma fraternity helped somewhat. What helped more was calling home; even innocuous, five-minute conversations with sisters and parents seemed to nourish a part of himself that he had previously not recognized, or maybe one he'd willfully ignored after his sophomore year in high school had pressed him to grow up faster than he deserved. It was a part of himself that he, like most young men, didn't reference often, the vulnerable sector of his consciousness that relied on love to endure.

During one of these calls in the late fall, his father happened to answer, and Tio spontaneously told the man that he was proud of him.

"What do you mean?" His father seemed sincerely confused by the statement.

"I'm proud of you. You raised a family. You have two kids in college. You got through a lot of hard things that a lot of other people don't get through."

Tio didn't expect him to reflect the sentiment back, and his father didn't. He just stammered for a moment before blurting, "Here's your mom," and passing the phone off. But perhaps the sentiment was present in the brief, preceding silence. Tio chose to believe that it was, and that silence was where such sentiments between fathers and sons usually resided.

Owen, Jon, Bennett, Harrison, Jonah, Carlos, Tio, Luis, Byron

Living, day to day: Sociology 110 from 12 to 12:50 on Tuesdays and Thursdays, Introduction to Intracellular, Molecular, and Developmental Biology from 1:30 to 2:20 on Mondays and Wednesdays, Literature of Imperialism from 9 to 11:30 on Fridays. An intramural basketball game followed by a study group followed by a professor's office hours followed by a frat event, call home at some point to check in, catch up on reading that can't be avoided any longer, text back and forth a dozen times with a new friend or girlfriend about not much in particular. Do some laundry. Eat something. Sleep. Such immediacies amassed, filled the hours, and dimly seemed to resemble progress. Progress toward what, they tended not to have time to ask themselves. Adulthood, maybe. Degrees. Jobs, careers, stability. Fulfillment, hopefully. The routine obligations of the present kindly helped mask whatever was to come, its taut and unnerving mystery. Routine obligations had always aided them that way in high school. They did now. Most likely, they always would.

Owen found enjoyment and belonging in an improv troupe called Fools on the Hill. He was skilled at grabbing whatever someone had just said and hitting them in the face with it, and he parlayed his growing campus renown into a central role in *The Rocky Horror Picture Show* (which found him nearly nude for most of the production) while choosing to major in drama, which itself was really just a conduit into philosophy, gender, race, politics, family structures—drama was the essence of all his interests, such that he didn't have to confront the minor terror of committing himself to just one. He also found that the warped authoritarianism of adults was not limited to high school administrators: a professor who was pretentious even in the context of a small liberal arts college (he often wore a beret over his long romance-novel hair) accused Owen of "slander" in a lancing email sent to the dean of students; he sent the email after Owen, in an aside on his campus radio show (which was listened to by maybe eight people, he believed), facetiously thanked this professor for failing him and for being generally an ass. Jon continued overextending himself not only with a double major in music and computer science and playing piano (now on a dorm room–friendly melodica, for which he'd paid thirty dollars) late into the night, but also with his job at the new Media Arts Center, involvement with multiple student organizations and music ensembles, an educational policy research assistant position, and serving as a dorm RA. He tried to call his parents every week but typically managed to do so every other week. And he went to a lot of parties—probably more than he should, definitely more than he ever thought he would. Bennett found that his new classmates and teachers, despite some typical posturing, were thoroughly devoted to supporting one another creatively as he sought to make a student film containing that nearly impossible balance of intelligence and humor—an aspiration he somewhat achieved with a short feature about a technologically advanced alien puppet beaming to earth and finding himself powerless against his eight-year-old human captor. Film school did in fact feel like a perfect incubator for ideas and craft (even if it was indeed part of an exceedingly expensive, multinational corporation). He also began seriously dating a girl, and that felt perfect, too. Jonah spent his freshman year living at home with his mother and siblings, entering the premed track and finding it just as mind-wreckingly stressful as it was said to be—the stress still quelled by weekend movie nights. Harrison exercised heavily in the early morning and late evening, and during the hours in between he slogged back and forth across Purdue's featureless, frigid campus to various physics and humanities courses, performed fraternity duties while remaining a teetotaler, and constantly begged the football coaches for a chance—just a chance—to play football (halfway through sophomore year, he would be denied after three semesters of hazy promises, and he began thinking about transferring elsewhere). Carlos continued writing about his complicated Yale experience, focusing on the sliver of marginalized people he represented but also widening his ideological orbit; sophomore year, he began reporting for the *Broad Recognition*, Yale's premier feminist publication. He concluded that while some classmates he met at Yale were oblivious or uninformed or misinformed regarding issues he cared about, only a very small few were actual assholes, and most were seeking and expansive. As at home in South LA, the objective was to commune with the seekers and avoid the assholes. Tio, the lone member of the APB group who was carrying on in a scientific field, carried on, feeling beaten down often, feeling small, yet with his mind subsisting on those invisible, powerful moments in which he mastered a previously mystifying concept, newly connected synapses igniting in his brain. Luis, having left at home the car that had designated him central to the movements of all his friends from APB, used a one-speed bicycle to move back and forth across the beachside bluffs on which the UCSB campus perched, and his large bulk balanced unsteadily on the narrow frame became a familiar silhouette as he called fond insults to pretty much everyone. Byron did matriculate at Cal State Northridge a year and three months after graduating high school, where, by the screwy interplay of space and access, he had to major in art—even though he'd never taken an art class before and couldn't draw a circle. But he was a student at a four-year college. Experience had reduced his goals—once stated, in his disastrous Cornell interview, as building an Iron Man suit—solely to that.

Day to day, they all remained themselves, every bit themselves. But they were no longer themselves together, and they felt it even in its subtle and gradual unfolding: the fading away. From Riverside to

New Haven, from Gambier to New York City, the phone calls and Facebook DMs and text messages grew not only less frequent but less substantial; the Snapchat feeds of new and proximate friends began to hold more relevance than those of friends from high school; promises to reunite at home during holidays were casually forgotten as the definition of home itself changed. Lives that had shared the same canvas, even the same intricate brushstrokes, began to feel distant, then strange, then hardly known. They were all familiar with this aspect of life; it wasn't new or novel or even something to be mourned. It was part of the passage. Tio in particular, who had lived his whole pre-Riverside life on the same street, had known dozens of kids with whom he'd spent nearly all his free time, absolute fixtures of his childhood, until their families had moved elsewhere—even a few blocks away—and then were gone, the adjacency of their lives ruptured with the image of a loaded car turning a corner. It had happened to them all. It had happened when middle school friends had gone to a different high school, or not gone to high school at all, or had gone to the same school but migrated into different cliques. It had happened when allegiances had turned from families and school toward drugs or gangs or both. It had happened in divorce or when parents changed jobs. It had happened when political moments exposed irreconcilable views. It had happened over girls. It happened when people grew up, and when people changed. It happened because it was the nature of being a person, and everything they did—every single thing, in school or at home, with others or alone, conscious or unconscious, meaningful or nonsensical, *every single thing*—was geared toward discovering what exactly it meant to be a person. The meaning would always elude them, because elusiveness was in fact its very heart.

They all returned home now and again. Winter breaks and summers saw them there, though less dependably as their chosen fields presented opportunities on campus or elsewhere. For those close enough, the draw was as old and simple as a decent meal. When they were home—or really what had once been home and was now becoming the place they were from—they would gravitate toward school. Maybe they would stop by to knock on an admired teacher's door during passing period, say what's up, ask how things were, express gratitude in some way. Maybe they would knock and learn that that teacher had moved on, and someone new occupied that desk. Maybe they would seek advice from a counselor who had given it caringly before. Maybe they would even speak in front of a classroom and offer some form of stock encouragement and inspiration, without even realizing that they had become the orator whose audience was yawning and waiting for the speech to end so they could go eat. Maybe they would notice how young the students looked, and how comically exhausted beneath their backpacks. They would invariably feel mature and sophisticated— they would feel *adult*—in comparison.

Or maybe they would just pass by the building on the way to somewhere else, by happenstance, because the city was huge but the neighborhoods were small, and they'd notice the front door and the people walking in and out of it, the kids loitering or playing ball games in front or urgently organizing some papers that were overdue for some class, as they had done themselves every day for a number of years, days and years that in the happening had seemed both vital and oppressive, and now in fleeting retrospect seemed faint and so very brief. Their gaze would linger on that door and those kids, the building that was simply there, as they passed by.

Many Yale classmates with political interests gravitated toward Washington, DC, but Carlos spent the summer between freshman and sophomore year working in the Los Angeles mayor's office. The landmark building rose tall above Grand Park, peering down over the concerts and food festivals regularly held on the lawn, and over the Frank Gehry–designed Disney Concert Hall, and over the courthouse that Luis once called "the belly of the beast" for an undocumented person such as Carlos (just before their mock trial team had been summarily manhandled there). Carlos did his share of coffee runs and answering phones along with other interns, who collectively admired that he "didn't give off an Ivy League vibe," which he took as high praise.

His primary role was in the Office of Public Engagement with a focus on South LA communities. In the arid heat of a particularly stifling LA summer, he attended town halls and church groups and community meetings that often took place in schools. His reason for being in any of these places was to gather input as to how the city government could better address community concerns—not an easy or comfortable task in areas where the pervasive feeling was systemic neglect. Carlos was intrinsically capable of maintaining a reasonable tenor while presenting himself as someone who truly desired to help, and whose education rendered him actually able to help. He also came off as a decent human being. He stayed at the small apartment his parents had found following their eviction. He talked with them about his summer work—identifying public assets, grappling with gentrification, theorizing on job creation—in a deeply felt way that he could never use with them when talking about school: his parents knew the communities intimately; of calculus and philosophy, they knew nothing. Though he didn't see many people from high school, mainly because he was busy, the connection with his parents instilled him with confidence that this was what he should be doing—not just the specific internship, but the whole configuration of his summer: living at home, empathizing with people where they lived, striking the closest balance he could between the place he'd come from and the place he now inhabited.

He returned to the latter place in September to begin his sophomore year, and he found himself sharing a shuttle van between the Hartford airport and the Yale campus with three students who he could immediately tell were first-generation freshmen by their too thin projections of poise failing to hide the apprehension beneath. They rode as well with a handful of more prototypical Yalies with their brand-name luggage and blithe chatter about trips to Europe and grueling Wall Street internships. Carlos engaged casually with both groups. Though ahead of him lay another year of school holidays spent alone in his dorm room closely tracking each dollar and cent spent, he also looked forward to late-night video game sessions with roommates and long walks beneath the famously bright autumnal leaves and pickup soccer games on the quads and greater autonomy in his writing. That he had come across a firm understanding of where he wanted to direct his life, as well as the means by which to do it, was reason enough to feel self-assured. Until very recently, direction in life had been defined only by a single nebulous word, or ideal, or destiny, or gateway, or whatever it was supposed to be: *college*. Now, a great many potential pathways veined the terrain ahead, just as his airport shuttle pivoted from the interstate onto the latticework of ramps surrounding his new city, and the campus's many striking spires came into view.

Acknowledgments

Above all, thank you to the boys—all men at this point—who gave up so much of their time on behalf of this project during a year in which they possessed so very little of that commodity. I am so grateful for your kindness, patience, trust, and in particular your insights and self-reflection regarding that weird, vital, uncertain passage in life. Tio, Carlos, Luis, Byron, Owen, Jon, Bennett, Harrison, Jonah. The dozens of hours sitting around tables with you while you talked and listened to one another with sensitivity, vulnerability, and also much shared laughter not only turned into these pages but also, I think, made me a more expansive father.

Thank you equally to Noah, Ryan, Ivan, Victor and John. With great regret, the dictates of editing, length, and balance in this kind of work precluded your own powerful stories from the pages, but they informed the pages deeply. I'm so glad you shared them, and I'm so sorry they couldn't appear here.

Thank you to all the families who permitted their sons to put themselves forward. You allowed me into your homes and lives with a lot of trust, and to believe in my positive intentions required a lot of courage. I really admire you all for the young men you've raised.

At Ánimo Pat Brown Charter High School, thank you to Mr. Reed, Ms. Brown, Mr. Snyder, Mr. Sandoval, Ms. Reyes, Ms. Jian, and Mr. Pickering. At Beverly Hills High School, thank you to

Ms. Goler, Ms. Tedford, Ms. Kim, Ms. Weiss, Mr. Van Rossum, Mr. Carey, and Mr. Mead. You all gave over your classrooms and time and support because you believed that these students were worthwhile, admirable people. I agree, and I also feel the same about all of you.

David Black, you nurtured this entire, very long process as I struggled to figure out and articulate exactly what it all meant and why it hopefully mattered. I don't think many agents would have had that kind of faith or been willing to devote that kind of time. You always ask the sharpest, hardest, most helpful questions. And you always answer your wife's calls over mine or anyone else's. I'm grateful to know you.

Colin Harrison, I was pretty nervous sitting down with you in a strange diner in the California desert, trying to present the idea of telling the stories of a bunch of random high school kids in Los Angeles. You talked through it, with your particular wit and intuition and roving curiosity, for nearly four hours. Over the ensuing years, you continued to talk through it for many hours more, with kindness not just toward me but toward the boys and their families. Thank you.

Also at Scribner, Kate Lloyd is just a wondrous professional, human being, and friend. Sarah Goldberg, Jaya Miceli, Kathleen Rizzo, Kyle Kabel, Ashley Gilliam, Brian Belfiglio, Roz Lippel, Nan Graham: I think I'm specifically aware of a small fraction of what you all do on behalf of your authors, but I know it's a titanic effort and you undertake it with grace and care, and I'm so glad to be among this group.

Adam and Aubrey Siegel, Matt and Staci Eddy, Marty and Bellinda Scott: it's really a privilege to be part of your families as we try to bring up all these kids and help each other with some work along the way. Michelle Weiner and Kim Stenton, you're always so supportive and kind on the work front and, more importantly, the family front. Martin and Sugar Goldstein, thank you, as ever, for everything.

Lucy and Whit: on a lot of school days off and summer days, instead of pools and parks and whatnot, you were obliged to sit for hours in school classrooms and strangers' living rooms while your dad talked to people about their lives. You attended to your books and puzzles and crayons with patience and good humor (most of the time). Maybe you'll read this book someday and smile at those memories. More likely, you'll roll your eyes. Regardless, I love you both, and I really admire you both.

Rebecca, always and forever.

About the Author

Jeff Hobbs is the author of *The Short and Tragic Life of Robert Peace*, which won the Los Angeles Times Book Prize, and *The Tourists*. He lives in Los Angeles with his wife and two children.